BLOOD ON THE HILLS

The Canadian Army in the Korean War

BLOOD ON THE HILLS

The Canadian Army
in the Korean War

DAVID J. BERCUSON

UNIVERSITY OF TORONTO PRESS
Toronto Buffalo London

© University of Toronto Press Incorporated 1999
Toronto Buffalo London

Printed in Canada

ISBN 0-8020-0980-8

Printed on acid-free paper

Canadian Cataloguing in Publication Data

Bercuson, David Jay, 1945–
Blood on the hills : the Canadian Army in the Korean War

Includes bibliographical references and index.
ISBN 0-8020-0980-8

1. Canada. Canadian Army – History – Korean War, 1950–1953.
2. Korean War, 1950–1953 – Canada.   I. Title.

DS919.2.B47 1999   951.904′242   C99-930968-4

University of Toronto Press acknowledges the financial assistance to its publishing
program of the Canada Council for the Arts and the Ontario Arts Council.

This book has been published with the help of a grant from the Humanities and
Social Sciences Federation of Canada, using funds provided by the
Social Sciences and Humanities Research Council of Canada.

University of Toronto Press acknowledges the financial support for
its publishing activities of the Government of Canada through
the Book Publishing Industry Development Program (BPIDP).

Canadä

To Barrie

In ways uncountable and
for reasons immeasurable

There is blood on the hills of Korea
'Tis the blood of the brave and the true
Where the 25th Brigade battled together
Under the banner of the Red White and Blue
As they marched over the fields of Korea
To the hills where the enemy lay
They remembered the Brigadier's order:
These hills must be taken today
Forward they marched into battle
With faces unsmiling and stern
They knew as they charged the hillside
There were some who would never return
Some thought of their wives and mothers
Some thought of their sweethearts so fair
And some as they plodded and stumbled
were reverentially whispering a prayer
There is blood on the hills of Korea
It's the gift of the freedom they love
May their names live in glory forever
and their souls rest in Heaven above

– Pte Patrick William O'Connor,
stretcher bearer,
2nd Battalion, Royal Canadian Regiment,
killed in action 30 May 1951

Contents

Illustrations follow 76 and 172. Maps appear on xvii–xix.

Preface

The Korean War was a series of firsts for Canada. It was the first military action in which Canada took part under the auspices of the United Nations. It was the first war in which Canadian soldiers fought under U.S. corps and army command. It was the first time the Canadian government knowingly sent ground troops to a land war in Asia. And it was the first Canadian war that elicited little interest from the folks back home. As Canadian soldiers bled and died in the hills of Korea, their fellow citizens at home experienced no rationing, no victory bond drives, no wage-and-price controls, and no exhortations from politicians, entertainers, business, and labour leaders to pull together for an all-out struggle. But then, the Korean War was not an all-out struggle; victory was not the ultimate objective, the surrender of the enemy was not the aim. The ultimate aim, settled on by Washington and the UN Command at the end of 1950, was to drive the Communists back across the 38th parallel and keep them there while trying to reach a cease-fire at a negotiating table. That is the main reason why Korea was a first, and different.

The shooting war for Canada's soldiers began in February 1951; the first tentative truce talks began only five months later in Kaesong, near the 38th parallel. After fits and starts, negotiations shifted to nearby Panmunjom in the late autumn of 1951 and continued to the end of the war. When that happened, Canada's soldiers in Korea were entrenched on, and a bit north of, the 38th parallel in a defensive position dubbed the Jamestown Line.

When Washington came to the final determination that U.S., indeed Western, interests could not be served by a prolonged land war in Asia, possibly involving the USSR, the Jamestown Line and other UN Command defensive lines on the 38th parallel became the far border of 'civilized' Western society. This was to be the mid-twentieth-century equivalent of the North West frontier of India in the mid-nineteenth. It was the place where the passes of the 'free world' were to be guarded against the wild tribes of Asian Communism by a new 'thin red line.' Thus the Canadians who defended the Jamestown Line in November 1951, and through the rest of the war, had much in common with those red-coated soldiers who guarded the far flung reaches of the British Empire in the late nineteenth century. From the autumn of 1950 Korea was to be a war with political limits and political objectives that the military were bound to serve. Those limited political objectives had a profound impact on each and every rifleman in each and every line rifle company fighting under UN Command.

This book is about the Canadian army in Korea. Canada had a small naval presence in Korean waters throughout the war; Canadian transport aircraft and crews helped maintain the air bridge to Korea while Canadian fighter pilots flew U.S. air force Sabre jets and shot down a number of Communist aircraft. But this book is not about those efforts because it is intended to provide an analysis of the Canadian army's performance, not a full account of Canada's participation in Korea. In analysing the performance of the army, I concentrate on the infantry because this was an infantry war supported by artillery, armour, and air power. My aim is to determine how ready the army was to fight in Korea and what efforts it made during the course of the war to remedy its deficiencies.

Korea was the first post–Second World War 'come as you are' war, in which an enemy attacked without warning, using devastating local fire-power and threatening to achieve its objectives almost before a real defence could be mounted. The UN's non-Communist members, Canada among them, were forced to defend South Korea with standing forces – with the aircraft, ships, army formations, weapons, training, officers, and soldiers immediately available to them. They took what they had from the shelf and used it. They could not begin a slow build-up to war as the British had done with their Dreadnought-building program of the early twentieth century, or as the United States had done with its army starting in 1940.

In July 1947, Canada's minister of national defence, Brooke Claxton, had set three goals for the post-war armed forces: to be ready to defend Canada against external aggression, to assist the civil power in maintaining order, and to assume 'any undertakings which by our own voluntary act we may assume in cooperation with friendly nations.' As events would prove, neither Canada nor the Canadian army met that third challenge well in the Korean War. Canada's soldiers went to the peninsula poorly armed and equipped, inadequately trained for the type of war they were about to fight, unprepared for their encounter with Korea and Koreans, and ready to do battle based on their experiences fighting the *Wehrmacht.* Canada made a political commitment to make a military contribution to a war for which its army was not ready.

Although the Korean war, with its limited political objectives, set the pattern for virtually all the other wars in the second half of the twentieth century, no one knew that at the time, of course. Initially experts saw it as a virtual throwback to the First World War, with its static lines of opposing armies facing each other over a no man's land, struggling for years for mere metres of advantage. They thought that Korea had nothing to teach them in a world where armoured vehicles and ground attack aircraft had made trench warfare obsolete. That was bad thinking, and the post-Korea Canadian army suffered for it, though not nearly as much as the U.S. military did.

More than 25,000 Canadians served in Korea in less than thirty-six months, and more than five hundred never returned. That alone makes Canada's effort in the Korean War a story worth telling. It is also a story worth telling because those Canadians who fought in Korea were ill-served by their government, by their coalition partners, and by much of their own high command. They were sent to Korea improperly armed, under-trained, and ill-prepared. They helped hold the line of freedom against Communist aggression, but they were never properly recognized for their sacrifice. It took the government of Canada more than four decades to issue a dedicated Korea service medal to the veterans of that war; it has taken the people of Canada half a century to acknowledge properly what those veterans did.

It is an unfortunate truism that the true trial of nationhood often comes in the midst of the organized brutality that war is. Canadians have become justly proud that Canadian men and women in uniform patrol the streets and roads of killing fields such as Bosnia, helping the victims of war put their lives back together in peace and security. Almost no one in Canada today knows, however, that that process of serving the cause of international peace and security began in the bloody hills of Korea so long ago. I present this book to help remedy that oversight.

David J. Bercuson
Rockyview, Alberta

Acknowledgments

I had much help in writing this book. My research assistants were especially enterprising in ferreting out sources: Peter Archambault, Michael Bernards, Christopher Cook, Bruce McIntyre, Jim Sterrett, and Boris Stipernitz. Jamara Sherwin helped proofread the text and prepared the index. Brent Watson was generous with his time and in sharing research material that he had gathered for his PhD dissertation. Lynn Bullock helped me gather photos from the PPCLI Museum in Calgary. I also want to thank John Parry for his diligent work on the manuscript – the second he has copy-edited for me.

Major (ret'd) William Henry Pope shared translations of articles that he had written for the Royal 22nd Regiment's Regimental Journal, *La Citadelle,* and reports done at the close of the Korean War. Col. (ret'd) Jack English gave me photocopies of pages from the James Van Fleet Papers. Col. (ret'd) Charles Simonds allowed me to examine the papers of his father, General G.G. Simonds. Jeffrey Grey arranged for me to acquire the official history of the Australian part in the Korean War and sent me information on Australian sources. Sir Anthony Farrar-Hockley met me in Colorado Springs to allow me to interview him on British sources. Maj.-Gen. (ret'd) M.P. Bogert filled in a questionnaire and sat for an interview conducted by Jim Sterrett. Field Marshal Sir James Cassels allowed me to interview him. Andrea Hawkes processed the Canadian army casualty list for Korea, putting it into a form that I could more easily use.

I am grateful to all those members of the Korea Veterans Association (KVA) of Canada who sat for interviews at their August 1996 meeting in Calgary or who filled out questionnaires. Thanks also to Hub Gray for allowing me to use his detailed research report on the Battle of Kap'yong and to Jack English, Jack Granatstein, W.H. Pope, and Robert Peacock (whose memoir of his time as a platoon commander in Korea – *Kim-chi Asahi and Rum* – is the best I have read of the genre) for reading and commenting on the manuscript.

I am grateful to the Social Sciences and Humanities Research Council and to the University of Calgary for grants in aid of the research for this book.

Thank you, Barrie, for your love, your support, and your friendship. I owe you more than words ever can say.

Inevitably, there will be mistakes in this book. Battles are particularly difficult to reconstruct. I alone am responsible for the errors.

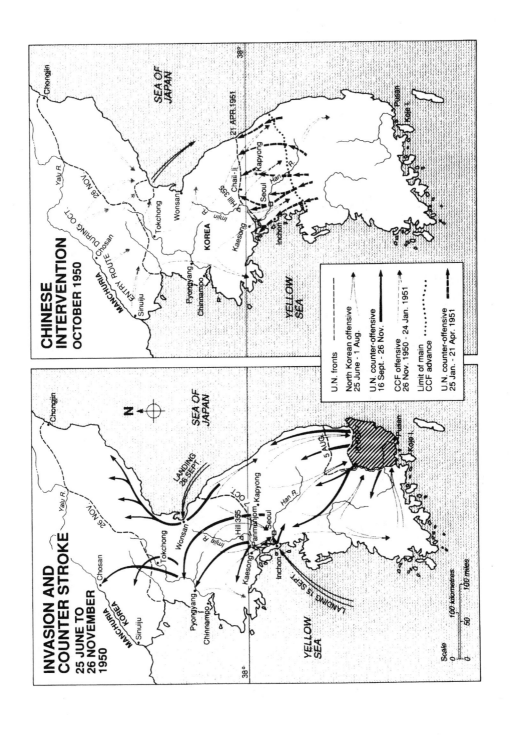

INVASION AND COUNTER STROKE

25 JUNE TO 26 NOVEMBER 1950

MANCHURIA
Sinuiju
Chosan
Tokchong
KOREA
Chongjin
Yalu R.
26 NOV
Wonsan
SEA OF JAPAN
N
Pyongyang
Chinnampo
Imjin R.
Hill 355
Panmunjom
Kaesong
Kapyong
Han R.
OCT
LANDING 28 SEPT.
5 AUG
Seoul
Inchon
LANDING 15 SEPT.
YELLOW SEA
Pusan
Koje I.
38°

Scale
0   50   100 kilometres
0   100 miles

CHINESE INTERVENTION

OCTOBER 1950

MANCHURIA
Sinuiju
Chosan
ENTRY ROUTE DURING OCT.
Yalu R.
26 NOV
Chongjin
SEA OF JAPAN
Tokchong
Wonsan
Pyongyang
Chinnampo
KOREA
Imjin R.
Hill 355
Chail-ji
Kapyong
Han R.
Seoul
Kaesong
Inchon
21 APR.1951
YELLOW SEA
Pusan
Koje I.
38°

U.N. fronts

North Korean offensive
25 June - 1 Aug.

U.N. counter-offensive
16 Sept. - 26 Nov.

CCF offensive
26 Nov. 1950 - 24 Jan. 1951

Limit of main
CCF advance

U.N. counter-offensive
25 Jan. - 21 Apr. 1951

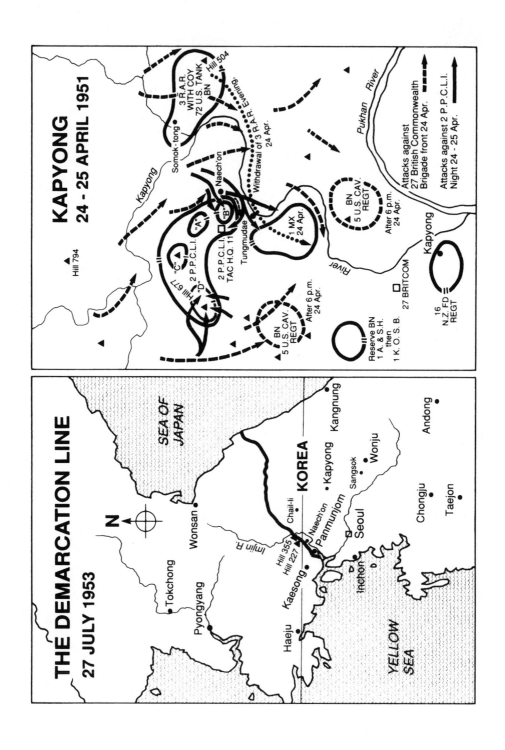

KAPYONG 24 - 25 APRIL 1951

Hill 794

Somok-tong

3 R.A.R. WITH COY 72 U.S. TANK BN

Hill 504

Kapyong

Naech'on

"A"

"B"

2 P.P.C.L.I. TAC H.Q.

"C"

2 P.P.C.L.I.

"D"

Hill 677

Tungmudae

Withdrawal of 3 R.A.R. Evening 24 Apr.

Pukhan River

MX 24 Apr.

BN 5 U.S. CAV. REGT

After 6 p.m. 24 Apr.

River

BN 5 U.S. CAV. REGT

After 6 p.m. 24 Apr.

Reserve BN 1 A. & S.H. then 1 K.O.S.B.

27 BRITCOM

16 N.Z. FD REGT

Kapyong

Attacks against 27 British Commonwealth Brigade front 24 Apr.

Attacks against 2 P.P.C.L.I. Night 24 - 25 Apr.

THE DEMARCATION LINE 27 JULY 1953

SEA OF JAPAN

N

KOREA

Wonsan

Tokchong

Pyongyang

Imjin R.

Chail-li

Hill 355

Hill 227

Kaesong

Naech'on

Panmunjom

Kapyong

Kangnung

Sangsok

Wonju

Seoul

Chongju

Taejon

Andong

Inch'on

Haeju

YELLOW SEA

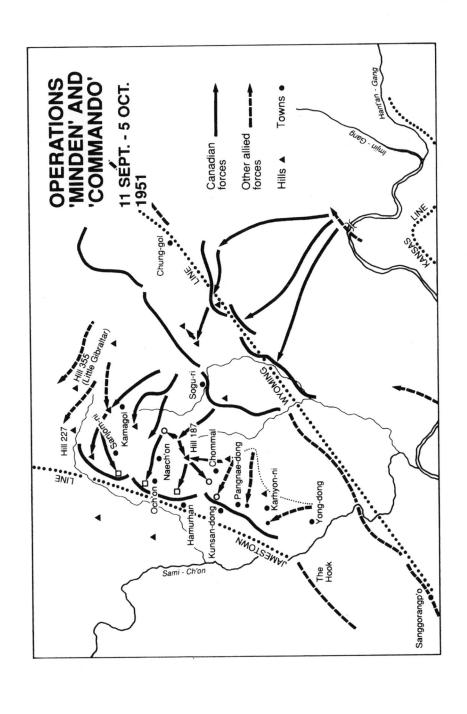

OPERATIONS 'MINDEN' AND 'COMMANDO'

11 SEPT. - 5 OCT. 1951

Canadian forces

Other allied forces

Hills ▲   Towns ●

Hant'an - Gang

Imjin - Gang

KANSAS LINE

Chung-gol

LINE

WYOMING

Hill 355 (Little Gibraltar)

Hill 227

Sangjom-ni

Sogu-ri

Kamagol

Hill 187

Naech'on

Chommal

Pangnae-dong

Karhyon-ni

Yong-dong

LINE

Och'on

Hamurhan

Kunsan-dong

JAMESTOWN

Sami - Ch'on

The Hook

Sanggorangp'o

BLOOD ON THE HILLS

The Canadian Army in the Korean War

The Forgotten War

Lindsay, Ontario, 22 November 1951. Ontario Tory Premier Leslie Frost was ecstatic as the results of the day's provincial election poured in to his committee rooms. 'It sure looks like victory,' he told the swelling crowd early in the evening. It was more than just victory, it was a triumph. The people of Ontario had plumped for the Progressive Conservatives for the third election in a row. As the night passed and the liquor flowed in victorious Tory committee rooms across the province, the triumph turned into a crushing defeat for the opposition; Frost was going to have the largest majority in the history of Ontario.[1]

By late November 1951, Canadians had outlived the misery of the Great Depression and the agony of the Second World War to settle into a somewhat boring but certainly prosperous post-war life. The suburbs of cities such as Montreal, Toronto, and Vancouver resounded to the sounds of hammers and saws as street after street of new, split-level homes drew the growing middle class to suburbia. The 1951 census figures, released in late November, showed that Canada was a nation of 14 million people: 4.6 million in Ontario, 4 million in Quebec, and 1.2 million in British Columbia. More people were on their way. The liners SS *Argentina* and SS *Vulcania* docked in Halifax towards the end of November bringing some fourteen hundred immigrants, most from Italy and Greece.[2]

As the voters of Ontario went to the polls, most other Canadians struggled through the year's first real cold snap. As usual the Prai-

ries led the way into winter, with temperatures plunging to −25°C
in Brandon, Manitoba. And, just as usual, British Columbians were
mostly spared winter's icy grip; New Westminster basked in +10°C
sunshine. In Toronto, the Western Interprovincial Football League
champion Regina Roughriders prepared to meet the eastern Big
Four champion Ottawa Rough Riders in the Grey Cup. Toronto's
venerable Royal York Hotel, just across Front Street from Union
Station, steeled itself for a week of drinking and carousing as fans
from across Canada poured in.

The National Hockey League (NHL) race was tight; the Detroit
Red Wings led the Toronto Maple Leafs by seven points, the Montreal Canadiens by ten. The Habs' Maurice 'Rocket' Richard
topped the league in scoring with eleven goals and six assists, but
the Wings' Gordie Howe had started a torrid goal-a-game pace. A
few Canadians in border cities such as Windsor and Vancouver
spent part of their evenings peering at small, flickering, black-and-
white screens, watching images sent north by U.S. border television stations, but radio was still the standard fare of home entertainment for most. Canadian Broadcasting Corporation (CBC)
president A. Davidson Dunton had some bad news for women lis-
teners. Dunton told the House of Commons Radio Committee
that the CBC would soon reduce its soap opera content, even
though 'a great many Canadians, particularly women, like soap
operas.'[3]

Halfway across the world, on a rugged, snow-covered ridge in
Korea, a handful of Canadians had matters other than the NHL
scoring race, soap operas, and Christmas shopping on their minds.
They were the infantrymen of the 2nd Battalion, Royal Vingt-
deuxième Regiment (2R22eR), or the Van Doos. On this night of
Tory election victory in Ontario, or Christmas shopping in Montreal or Winnipeg, this cold and somewhat bedraggled group of
Canadian soldiers had only one real thought in mind – how best to
hold the rocky ridge that they were sitting on when the Chinese
across the valley came at them, to kill them and to take the ridge
away.

The ridge was a kilometre-long saddle connecting two hills

marked on the map as Point 355, to the east of and higher than the Canadians, and Point 227, to their west. Point 355 (more commonly referred to as Hill 355) had been dubbed 'Little Gibraltar' by the U.S. soldiers who held it. It looked like the Rock of Gibraltar, though smaller, and was the dominant feature in a sea of hills overlooking the frozen rice paddies and the bottom land of the small Sami-Ch'on Creek. The Sami-Ch'on flowed out of the hills to the west of the Canadian positions and south to the Imjin River 15 km away.

Hidden in the hills to the north and west of the Van Doos were the bunkers, caves, ammunition dumps, artillery positions, and communications trenches of the 64th Army of the so-called Chinese People's Volunteers – in reality, the soldiers of the People's Liberation Army of the People's Republic of China. They had crossed the Yalu River en masse into Korea, and into the Korean War, almost exactly a year earlier, when UN forces dominated by the U.S. Army and Marines, under the command of Gen. Douglas MacArthur, had pushed across the 38th-parallel pre-war border between North and South Korea and driven north towards the Yalu River, which formed the Korean border with Manchuria.[4]

The Van Doos who held the ridge between Little Gibraltar and Hill 227 made up about one-fifth of the Canadian army presence in the Korean War. They and two other infantry battalions drawn from the Princess Patricia's Canadian Light Infantry (PPCLI) and the Royal Canadian Regiment (RCR) had come to Korea with the 25th Canadian Infantry Brigade Group, attached to 1st Commonwealth Division. Technically the Canadian army in Korea fought under overall United Nations Command but in fact the Americans ran the show. Higher formations (with the exception of the Republic of Korea army) – corps and army – were all American. The Commonwealth Division was under command of I U.S. Corps, which was part of Eighth U.S. Army. On the night of 22 November 1951, the division held about 15 km of front between two U.S. army divisions.[5] In their sector that front was known as the Jamestown Line. It would eventually become the post–Korean War demarcation line between the two Koreas.

The UN forces had established the Jamestown Line after a series of offensives, beginning the previous summer, in which they had driven the Chinese back across the 38th parallel. Those attacks had been mounted after the defeat of China's last major offensive of the war, launched towards Seoul in mid-April 1951. The main UN objective had been to recover as much as possible of pre-invasion South Korea. That object had become even more urgent when armistice talks between the Communists (Chinese and North Koreans) and the South Koreans and UN began on 10 July 1951 in the ancient Korean capital of Kaesong.

Each time the UN forces established a new front, or extended an existing one to the east or the west, the new line received a name; first, it was the 'Kansas' Line, then the 'Wyoming' Line, and finally, the 'Jamestown' Line. And each time that happened, UN forces dug new bunkers, slit trenches, firing pits, weapons bays, and communications trenches facing the enemy, which lurked across 'no man's land.'

There was no continuous line of trenches across the width of Korea as there had been on the Western Front in the First World War. The steep hills, terraced slopes, and boggy valley bottoms jammed with rice paddies did not allow this. Instead, the soldiers encircled hilltop positions with communications trenches dug behind minefields and rolls of concertina wire. They then dug firing trenches forward, at right angles to the communications trenches, facing the enemy to the north. These defended positions were usually held by an infantry company or two. The valleys in between them were mined, wired, and patrolled at night. Tanks, mortars, heavy machine-guns, and both field and medium artillery zeroed in on pre-selected targets in those valleys – paths, water crossings, defiles – to kill any enemy soldier who tried to sneak through after dark.

That part of Korea occupied by the 1st Commonwealth Division in the autumn of 1951 was not unlike Quebec's Laurentian Mountains or Gatineau Hills. The slopes were steep, but the hilltops were not especially high. At 355 m, Little Gibraltar was the highest for many kilometres. There were fewer trees and more exposed slopes than in Canada, however, especially where months of artillery, mortar, and rocket fire had stripped the hills bare. The bottom land was all heavily cultivated; irrigated with human excrement, the paddies stank like cesspools until they froze over in the hard Korean winter.

By the third week of November, that hard Korean winter was moving in on these hills with a vengeance. Temperatures dipped below freezing after nightfall, and a mix of rain in the day and snow flurries at night made road maintenance virtually impossible. It was hard slogging to keep food and ammunition coming forward and casualties moving to the rear. The Korean Service Corps (KSC) personnel, who humped the hills with large A-frame packs piled high with supplies for the UN forces, kept the supply lines open but were incapable of bringing in heavy munitions such as 25-pounder shells. Helicopters were used when possible but could hardly ever land near the forwardmost positions.

The Jamestown Line lay where it did largely because of political, not military considerations. It was as far north as the U.S. Joint Chiefs of Staff were prepared to push once the peace talks had started at Kaesong (they were interrupted for several weeks, then resumed in Panmunjon). UN Commander General James Van Fleet thought this a bad decision. He believed that the Chinese were licked and that the UN ought to push on for a final all-out battle with them.[6] A new UN offensive would have put tremendous pressure on the Communists, who might have shortened the talks and saved tens of thousands of lives on all sides. But Van Fleet was restrained by his superiors. So the men on the line – the Americans, the Commonwealth Division, the Republic of Korea Army (ROKA), and all the other UN troops from countries such as Belgium, France, Holland, and Turkey – were stuck where they were. They would defend the ground they stood on while the diplomats negotiated a few tens of kilometres to the west. To mark that inviolate patch of negotiating territory, four barrage balloons floated in the sky during the day and a huge searchlight cast its beam straight up each night. Along the Jamestown Line, that light mocked the soldiers as they stood tense watch night after night and listened for Chinese troops creeping close in the dark.

All through November 1951 Chinese burp-gunners and grenadiers had assaulted the hilltop positions held by the 1st Commonwealth Division. Their attacks had been preceded by massive barrages from self-propelled and towed artillery, Soviet-designed Katyusha rockets, and medium and heavy mortar fire. Because the Chinese had few hand-held radios and no sound-powered telephones, they coordinated their night attacks with bugles, whistles, gongs, and just plain shouting of instructions. When the gongs banged and the bugles and whistles blew in the dark, the men on the Jamestown Line steeled themselves for the Chinese infantry that always followed.

On Friday, 2 November, just after dark, bugle-blowing Chinese infantry attacked Able ('A') and Charlie ('C') Companies of the RCR atop Hill 157. Two nights later, the Chinese hit two companies of the PPCLI; one was spending its very first night in the lines. As the days grew shorter and the nights colder, the hill fights intensified. In the first weeks of November, the fighting centred on the 28th British Commonwealth Infantry Brigade (BCIB), which held the front to the right of the Canadians. Nameless hills changed hands night after night as the Chinese attacked and the British counter-attacked. Often the Chinese would take a hilltop after nightfall, only to lose it – or give it back – before dawn.[7] No one was really interested in holding captured territory after these raids; the raids were designed to unnerve, to reconnoitre, to capture prisoners, to kill, but never to hold. In late November the 28th Brigade was relieved by the 7th Infantry Regiment of the 3rd U.S. Infantry Division, while the General Officer Commanding (GOC) the Commonwealth Division, British Maj.-Gen. A.J.H. Cassels, shifted his position and repositioned his brigades to shorten his front.[8] All three Canadian battalions came into the line with all four of their rifle companies; the RCR was on the left, the PPCLI in the centre, and the R22eR on the right.

Under the command of Lt.-Col. Jacques Dextraze, who had commanded the Fusiliers Mont Royal in the Second World War, the Van Doo rifle companies set out for their new positions in the pre-dawn dark of 22 November. When they got up to the ridge, they organized and prepared their defences. At about 1530, Chinese shells began to scream in from across the valley. The men took cover as the shells exploded on the hillsides around them.

Soon the whoosh of incoming heavy-calibre rocket fire added to the din. Most of the Chinese fire was concentrated on Dog ('D') Company and/or fell on the American positions on Hill 355. The shelling began to take its toll. Pte D. Isabelle of 'C' Company was blown to bits when a shell exploded in his slit trench. Others were wounded by flying shards of hot, razor-sharp steel. Dirt, rocks, and pieces of smashed bunker beam rained down on the men as they huddled in their shelters. The barbed wire in front of the firing trenches and weapons pits was shredded. Telephone lines were cut. The defensive minefields on the forward slopes of the ridge were pulverized.

Each man did what he could to keep his sanity under the intense barrage, trying not to think of the very real possibility that in the next split second he might be maimed or wiped from the face of the earth. As Sgt Jean Paille of the PPCLI told Bill Boss: 'The Communists are using much more artillery now and sometimes it gets hard to just sit and take it. My fellows are good, fairly new, and sometime they get jittery during the shelling, and if the Chinese come in and attack, they get excited during the grenade throwing.'[9] All too often, that is just what the Chinese did when the fire lifted. Bugles and gongs would sound, whistles would blow, and hundreds of Chinese infantrymen would attack, yelling, throwing grenades, firing their burp guns, and killing as many Canadians as they could.

Night fell, and the cold penetrated into the very bones of the Canadian infantrymen. It started to snow heavily, the first real downfall of the winter.[10] Surely the Chinese would come now. But the shelling slackened towards morning, and the Chinese did not come. Soon the sun struggled through the low cloud to warm the hillsides and melt the fresh snow. Weary soldiers struggled to down a bit of breakfast and repair damage to wire, bunkers, and telephone lines. In mid-morning a lone Chinese scout was captured near the pioneer platoon wire; minutes later shell explosions began to blossom once again, this time on the left flank of 'D' Company. Again the shelling forced the men to ground. In the early afternoon, an artillery observation plane reported at least a company of Chinese infantry advancing from the northwest, about a kilometre away. Canadian and New Zealand field guns to the rear opened up, plastering the paddy land in the low valley to the front of 'D' Company.

At 1620, Chinese rocket and shell fire began to rain down on Hill 355; less than ten minutes later, at least two companies of Chinese infantry hit the wire in front of 'D' Company. All along the line the Canadians feverishly threw grenades, worked the bolts of their Lee-Enfield rifles, and fired magazine after magazine of Bren-gun and belt after belt of Browning machine-gun ammunition as the Chinese tried to swarm over the wire. One badly shot-up soldier, Cpl Earl Istead of 12 platoon, grabbed a Bren from a fallen comrade and kept up a steady fire at the Chinese from close in, jamming new magazines into the gun and killing a score of Chinese trying to cross or crawl under the Canadian wire.'[11]

Back at battalion HQ, about 2 km to the rear of 'D' Company, the crackling radio told the story of the unfolding battle. Dextraze listened grimly: 'E,' 'F,' and 'G' Companies of the 7th Infantry on 355 were being engaged by an entire Chinese battalion; hundreds of Chinese infantrymen were swarming over the slopes of Hill 227. The Van Doo platoon commanded by Lieut. R. MacDuff was almost overrun, one section had broken, but MacDuff had rallied his men and led the section back into position. American soldiers from 355 were beginning to come through the Van Doo lines; the Americans had abandoned Hill 355 to the Chinese.[12]

Dextraze was worried; his right flank was open. The Chinese in the U.S.-dug trenches and bunkers on Hill 355 could look right into his battalion's positions. But the Chinese were not up there to sightsee; any minute now, they would charge down the ridge from the right and swarm up the slope in front of the Van Doos' positions. Then, lots of Canadians would die. Grimly Dextraze reached for the radio set. He was about to remind his outnumbered, outgunned, outflanked men that they were Van Doos, that Van Doos held their positions, no matter what, and that he would accept nothing less.

The Chinese attack on Little Gibraltar and the ridge connecting it to Hill 227 on the night of 23–4 November 1951 was only a minor skirmish compared with other battles for the control of Korea. It pales next to the massive clashes of armies that marked the Second World War just a few years earlier. Yet the thirteen Van Doos who were about to be killed that night[13] would be just as dead as any of their regimental forebears who had lost their lives wresting Italy from the Axis in 1943 and 1944 or helping to liberate Holland in the closing weeks of the war.

What was different was that by the late autumn of 1951, when Canada's soldiers had been in the front lines in Korea for less than a year, most Canadians did not know, or care much about, what was happening to their soldiers half a world away. That had not been true of the Second World War, when the stakes had seemed so much higher. This time, while the Van Doos and other Canadians lay dying in Korea, the folks at home were too busy celebrating election victories, or doing Christmas shopping, or following the NHL race to pay much attention. The Korean War had become a 'forgotten' war even as Canadian soldiers were dying in it.

ONE

Canada's Post-War Army

The Hague, the Netherlands, 21 May 1945. It was a beautiful day for a parade, warm and sunny, and the capital of the Netherlands was decked out in its finest. Canadian and Dutch flags and the Union Jack hung from windows and balconies; red, white, and blue bunting festooned street lamps and road signs. The sidewalks and roads were swept and clean, and the red brick of the houses contrasted starkly with freshly painted trim. The immaculately washed windows sparkled in the afternoon sun.

Today was the day on which the Dutch would thank the Canadians for their part in the liberation of Holland. All the major units of First Canadian Army were present at The Hague to represent their comrades, living and dead, and to accept the adulation of the crowds. The parade began on time and rolled through the afternoon with military precision. On the reviewing stand, Gen. H.D.G. Crerar, the only man in Canadian history to command a Canadian army in the field, stood and saluted the passing soldiers in front of him. Behind him were standing Dutch dignitaries in morning coats and Canadian officers in sharply pressed uniforms. A pair of military policemen (MPs) on motorcycles moved slowly in front of the reviewing stand, leading the way for the first of five brass bands and the sixteen pipe bands of the Canadian highland regiments. The crowds cheered wildly for the army that had played so great a part in the battles for Holland, first in the autumn of 1944, then in the spring of 1945. They cheered also in memory of those thousands of Canadians lying in the new Commonwealth war cemeteries at Bergen Op Zoom, Groesbeek, and a dozen other locations from the Normandy beaches to the Rhineland.

By the end of the war, Canada, then a nation of but eleven million people, had sent one out of every ten of its sons and daughters into the armed forces in the struggle against the Axis. The active army, consisting only of those who had volunteered for overseas service, had swelled from less than 4,200 regular officers and other ranks on the outbreak of war to just under 500,000 at its peak size in March 1944. When Germany surrendered on 7 May 1945, First Canadian Army consisted of an army headquarters, two corps, two armoured divisions, two independent armoured brigades, and three infantry divisions. The Canadian army had participated in the liberation of Sicily and Italy, fighting in some of the most horrendous battles of that campaign. It had stormed one of the five Normandy beaches on 6 June 1944 and protected the Allied left flank thereafter, until the victory. It had fought and won the Battle of the Scheldt Estuary, one of the keys to victory in Europe. The Canadians deserved the accolades of the Dutch, and others, for their part in the Allied victory, but they paid a high price for the honour. First Canadian Army suffered 75,596 casualties during the war; 22,917 of its soldiers were dead.

Then the Canadian army virtually melted away; within twenty-four months it was almost all gone. Although a small contingent took part in the Allied occupation of Germany until the spring of 1946, headquarters of the army, corps, and most of the divisions and brigades quickly disbanded. The citizen army went home to begin life anew. Some officers stayed, reduced in rank to fit the small size of the post-war army, but most left. Canada had no discernible enemies and no reason to keep an army of any significant size. During the war the army General Staff dreamed of a post-war force of at least six divisions and four independent armoured brigades, with two divisions and one brigade on active service, but that was not to be. The government had far better post-war projects for the $162 million per year that such an army would cost.[1]

The Liberal government of William Lyon Mackenzie King (in power since 1935) began to make clear just what those better

projects were in its 1944 throne speech and in legislation that followed over the next eighteen months. Canada was to build the
foundations of a welfare state; only the amount of money available
and the degree of provincial cooperation would set the limits of
the new cradle-to-grave state. The military may not have grasped
the significance of the new political direction as the fighting in
Europe reached a climax following D-Day, but it began to learn
quickly enough once the Nazis surrendered.

In his diary, King himself established the basic direction that
would govern Canadian defence policy after the war. His aim was
to 'get back to the old Liberal principles of economy, reduction of
taxation, anti-militarism, etc.'[2] The massive war-time Canadian
armed forces would be reduced, drastically. The new army would
be much larger than the 4,000-man skeleton Permanent Force of
pre-war days, but it would still have only a very limited fighting
capability. Douglas Abbott, Canada's first post-war minister of
national defence, presided over the first of the reductions – to an
army establishment of some 25,000 men, only 7,000 of whom were
to be in the combat arms. The remainder were to consist of headquarters and administrative personnel and soldiers training the
militia.

The policy was based on the assumption that if Canada fought
another war it would mobilize in the way it had in 1914 and in
1939, meaning that the militia would form the core of the army.
Abbott explained this to the cabinet in mid-November 1946:
'It should be borne in mind that the Reserve Army (the former
Non-Permanent Active Militia) formed the essential framework of
the traditional Canadian defence scheme. It was based upon the
assumption of a citizen Army whose fighting would be done
abroad to keep the war away from Canada.'[3]

Abbott left his post at the Department of National Defence
(DND) shortly thereafter. The man whom King then selected to
guide the forces in this era of major constraint was Brooke Claxton. Claxton had first entered the cabinet in 1944 at National
Health and Welfare, guiding the introduction of the Family Allow-
ances program in 1945. He moved to DND in December 1946 and
set about to make the required reductions in some logical fashion.
He believed that a rational and achievable post-war defence policy

had to be put into place, not so much to determine what reductions would be made, or how, but to provide the armed forces with some guidance as to their reduced post-war role.

King believed strongly that Canada had to 'decide whether we were going in for increased military expenditures or to seek to carry out our programme of social legislation.'[4] That meant that the prime determinant of Canadian defence policy, guiding the degree of military preparation that the nation might achieve, was not going to be some abstract military necessity, such as the U.S. desire for extensive continental defence measures, or even the growing but still potential threat from the USSR. Defence policy would flow from the proportion of the national budget that was to be allocated to DND. In other words, the size of the defence budget would decide the scale and scope of the role that would be defined for the armed forces.

It was easy for Claxton to determine the basic outline of that role. All of Canada's important ties – cultural, political, historical, and economic – dictated that it would join the Cold War on the 'Western' side. If the Cold War turned hot, Canadians would again fight beside Britain and the United States. But fight with what? Where? And how soon after the conflict began? These questions had to be answered before a realistic role could be determined for the forces.

Claxton's initial stab at defining a post-war defence policy came in early January 1947 in a short memorandum to King. Claxton declared that, even though there was little chance of war in the next decade, North America still had to take active measures to defend itself because of advances in weapons technology. Self-interest and good relations with the United States dictated that Canada cooperate with the Americans on defence, but Canada had to do as much as possible to defend its own soil, on its own, especially in the north. If it did not, the Americans would take up the slack.

How was Canada to accomplish the somewhat contradictory objectives of keeping the United States satisfied while making deep cuts in the defence budget? In Claxton's view, it could never do so by adopting an expensive defence based on 'static ... Maginot Line' thinking. Post-war Canada could not afford and would not tolerate the large standing forces that such a policy would require. So Claxton outlined a strategy reminiscent of that adopted prior to the two world wars – the professional military would develop facilities and techniques to train sufficient reserve forces to allow Canada to create a viable expeditionary force when necessary. Unlike the periods prior to the two world wars, however, the military would need to keep current with the latest defence technology, especially that developed in conjunction with 'our principal allies.'[5]

The role of Canada's small peacetime army was thus to defend Canada, train the reserves, and prepare for possible mobilization – someday. It would need training, doctrine, and equipment that were up-to-date, second to none, and sufficiently advanced to enable the army to fight beside Canada's allies with little or no adjustment. In practice this implied that the army would have to set high educational and proficiency standards for officers and other ranks in the regular force and the reserves. It would have to conduct intensive, up-to-date training in accordance with the latest doctrines of ground warfare. It absolutely required first-class, modern equipment so that its soldiers could be trained to first class standards following the latest doctrine. A shortcoming in any of these areas would mean that the army would not be trained or equipped to fight a modern war when the time came.

The assumption underlying Claxton's thinking was that the next war was going to be very much like the last.[6] There would be a period of up to a year after the commencement of hostilities before a Canadian expeditionary force would need to take the field. Claxton foresaw no possibility that Canadian troops would be used abroad in anything other than a full-scale war: '*Any* operations outside Canada would be similar, although not identical to the operations of the Canadian forces in the first and second World Wars.'[7] If war of any sort were unlikely, then Canada did not really need much of an army – and not much of a navy or air force either, for that matter.

The budget-cutting continued after Claxton took up his new position at DND. In fiscal year 1947/8 DND spent about $195.4 million out of a total federal budget of $2.2 billion, or just 8.9 per cent of that budget and 1.7 per cent of the gross national product (GNP).[8] The army achieved its new targets by reducing cadet services, severely cutting militia training, and capping active force recruitment when it reached 75 per cent of establishment.[9]

The government's abrupt turn away from heavy defence spending is reflected in the amount it devoted to defence and mutual aid in the years immediately following the Second World War. Wartime defence spending had peaked in the 1943 fiscal year at just over $4.2 billion. By then it was obvious to just about everyone in higher Allied military circles that victory was just a matter of time. Since it would have been ruinous to peacetime recovery to continue all-out defence spending until the last shot was fired, Ottawa began to cut back orders for aircraft, ships, and other munitions in the budget adopted in early 1944, chopping about $200 million from defence and mutual aid. Another $1 billion was removed in the 1945 budget. Once the fighting in Europe and the Pacific actually ended, however, the real slashing began. From just under $3 billion in 1945 the defence budget fell almost 90 per cent to just less than $400 million in 1946, then again to $196 million in 1947. When Cold War tensions increased in late 1947 and early 1948, the government added back about $70 million for 1948. Canada's adherence to the North Atlantic Treaty when it was signed in the summer of 1949 (Canada had been part of the secret preparatory discussions since the start of 1948) brought another $90 million or so in 1949 and $400 million more for 1950. Thus, at the outbreak of the war in Korea, the defence and mutual aid portion of the national budget was about three times larger than it had been at its nadir in 1947.

It was a rare immediate-post-war year when the army even approached its authorized strength. Pay was low, housing was bad, and opportunities were few. In western Canada, where costs of living were somewhat higher than in the rest of the country, those in the lower ranks were forced to seek part-time jobs to support themselves. One DND study showed that 60 per cent of service personnel in western Canada used their holiday time for outside work. The average weekly wage for servicemen stood at $35.48 at the end of 1948, about 11 per cent less than that for comparable civilian

work. Some service personnel owed medical bills as large as a full
year's pay.[10]

The cuts reduced the army to a pitiful state. In 1948 the combat
arms included only two armoured regiments – Lord Strathcona's
Horse and the Royal Canadian Dragoons. Each consisted of a
headquarters and a single squadron (the normal Second World
War establishment for an armoured regiment was a headquarters,
a reconnaissance troop, and three squadrons of nineteen tanks
each).[11] There was just one operational field-artillery regiment.
The regular infantry regiments – the PPCLI, the RCR, and the
R22eR – fielded but a single battalion each. As late as the summer
of 1950, those battalions were each about one hundred men under
strength. The Royal Canadian Signals Corps and the Royal Canadian Electrical and Mechanical Engineers (RCEME) were also
chronically under strength. In addition, the army had little transport capacity, no modern anti-aircraft or anti-armour capability,
and no first-line, post-war-design tanks.[12]

In the autumn of 1947 Lt.-Gen. Charles G. Foulkes, Chief of the
General Staff, told the Cabinet Defence Committee that the combat arms could muster only up to 45 per cent below authorized
strength. This condition was partly the result of insufficient intake
and partly the result of increased administrative duties and reserve
training. It would be 'difficult if not impossible to provide troops
for operational purposes,' he added.[13] The shortage of personnel
forced the military to lower basic educational requirements for
recruits in the spring of 1948. Henceforth applicants who had fin-
ished only grades 9 or 10 would be considered if they met the
other physical and psychological standards.[14]

Conditions of service in the armed forces improved somewhat
starting in late 1948, when additional cash was injected into the
defence budget because of increasing Cold War tensions in
Europe.[15] Given the government's preoccupation with air defence,
it was not surprising that the Royal Canadian Air Force (RCAF) was
the chief beneficiary. In 1948/9, for example, the army's share of
the DND budget was 37.7 per cent, the RCAF's 32.3 per cent;
the next year the RCAF was alloted 38.8 per cent, and the army
33.1 per cent.[16]

The army did see some of the benefit, however. On army bases across Canada work started on demolishing the temporary clapboard buildings thrown up during the war and replacing them with comfortable quarters for both single and married personnel. There was even a modest pay raise late in 1948, which attracted recruits of a somewhat higher calibre; the junior-matriculation (grade 11/12) requirement was restored. The marginal increase in volunteers did not lead to a larger army. More soldiers meant higher costs; the army put a new freeze on recruiting in February 1950. That cap then led to a drop in numbers because of normal 'wastage' – soldiers leaving (or thrown out) for a variety of reasons. When the Korean War broke out, the strength of the army's active force stood at 20,369 in all ranks, far below the 26,000-person establishment.[17]

An old army quip goes, 'There are no bad soldiers, there are only bad officers,' and there is much truth to it. Although it is the non-commissioned officers (NCOs) who administer the army on a daily basis and who see to the execution of orders issued by the officers, it is the commissioned officers who give an army its direction. A highly trained, proficient, and talented officer corps does not in itself guarantee success in battle, but it is an essential element for success. In the Second World War the majority of officers who accompanied Canada's soldiers to Europe were not competent to lead those men in battle. Most of them were weeded out in the training and evaluation that took place in the United Kingdom before the Canadian army went into action. Many of those who assumed command in their place were also sifted out when they failed to show the requisite traits of courage, leadership, and imagination under fire. The Canadian army in northwest Europe began consistently to receive highly competent commanders only in the autumn of 1944.

No matter what size the post-war Canadian army would eventually be, it would have to have officers who were well-trained, educated, and capable of leading troops in modern war. In 1947 there was much discussion in the Chiefs of Staff Committee and the Cabinet Defence Committee about the best route to take to ensure a steady supply of trained and talented officers. There were arguments over curricula, over whether each service should have its own cadet college, over how the military college system was to be organized. Lt.-Gen Charles Foulkes's idea – that a baccalaureate, whether gained from a service college or from a civilian university – be the minimum educational requirement for army officers was not adopted. Indeed, it would not be accepted until 1997!

Foulkes believed that 'the increasing requirements of the Army for highly trained technical personnel due to the increasing complexity of modern warfare made a university degree or equivalent essential for all officers if the Army was to be competitively efficient.'[18] He wanted officers who would serve in technical branches, such as the RCEME, to be commissioned through the Canadian Officers' Training Corps (COTC), which had been operating in one form or another since 1912. The COTC combined civilian university education with military training in the summer. Cadets from high schools and soldiers seeking commissioning from the ranks could attend one or another of the service colleges – Royal Military College (RMC) in Kingston, Ontario, or Royal Roads in Victoria, British Columbia.[19] While RMC was a four-year, tri-service academy in the post-war period, Royal Roads offered only the first two years of the tri-service curriculum beginning in 1948. Those who chose to complete a four-year military education could then attend RMC for the last two years or go to a civilian institution.

RMC reopened in 1948, while the mandate of Royal Roads was broadened to include the education of first- and second-year officer cadets from the army and air force. The National Defence College, also in Kingston, opened in 1948. It was an advanced-study institute for persons, both civilian and military, involved with the making of defence and security policy.[20] Throughout this period Canadian and U.S. army officers crossed the border to serve as exchange officers with the other country's military and to attend each other's staff colleges and service schools.[21] This program was part of a larger attempt to move the Canadian military closer to the U.S. forces as continental defence became the top Canadian defence priority.

One of the Canadian army's most important tasks in this period was to train a first-line reserve that could augment the small regular force in the event of mobilization. The army's goal was to be able to expand within twelve months from its 26,000 establishment to a force of two infantry divisions with headquarters, ancillary troops, and reinforcements for three months of fighting – about 115,000 men.[22] The army never came close to that goal prior to 1950. In fact, the government could not quite make up its mind about the size and type of reserve force that it wanted. At one point a number of militia infantry regiments were ordered to convert to anti-aircraft.[23] At another, year-round and summer training was cut back drastically, only to be restored when more money became available. The size of the militia was reduced or expanded according to political, rather than military, requirements.[24]

There were two main factors hindering the post-war army's ability to keep current with modern tactical and technological developments; deep budget cuts and the ongoing struggle to get access to U.S.-pattern equipment. One of the major determinants in the development of an army's doctrine – its basic method of fighting wars – is its equipment. Doctrine and equipment exist in a symbiotic relationship, with each influencing the other and both determining how sections, platoons, companies, battalions, and divisions approach battle. Adopting this rifle, rather than that one, will, for example, invariably influence section assault tactics, because a rifle's size, weight, range, rate of fire, calibre, and muzzle velocity will all help determine what a section can do and what it cannot.

Throughout this period the *Canadian Army Journal*, published quarterly by the Directorate of Military Training under the authority of the Chief of the General Staff, was the premier means (outside of training, of course) by which Canadian army doctrine was distributed through the ranks. First published in April 1947, it printed articles on military history, foreign affairs, news of the militia, and strategy and tactics. Articles such as 'Anti-Tank: Land Defence against AFVs'[25] and 'Hitting the Airheads: Use of Airborne Infantry'[26] were supposed to keep Canada's soldiers current with the latest tactical or technical developments. In its first two years of publication, however, only 24 out of 140 articles dealt with tactics, strategy, or modern weapons systems. The Canadian army was being starved of doctrine.

One major reason for this deficiency was that the army was supposed to be in transformation from the use of British- to U.S.-pattern equipment.[27] The changeover was more easily advocated than carried out, however, because U.S.-pattern equipment was very difficult to obtain. Part of the problem was lack of money, but U.S. arms-sales policy was a major obstacle. The Canadian-U.S. defence-production agreement initiated by the Hyde Park Declaration of 20 April 1941 expired at the end of the war. It then became very hard for Canada to purchase U.S. military equipment or even to pay for it when it was available.[28]

In the autumn of 1948, for example, the army gave up trying to purchase new U.S.-built tanks when the Pentagon informed it that the United States 'would not be in a position to supply them for some time to come.'[29] That meant no refurbished and up-gunned Second World War U.S. Shermans for the Canadian army, let alone the newer M-48 Patton tanks about to come into operation. When Canada's soldiers joined battle in Korea in the spring of 1951, they carried some U.S. equipment with them, all acquired after their arrival on the peninsula. Canadians fought in Korea mostly with Second World War British-pattern equipment; in the case of the infantry's most basic weapon, the rifle, they carried the bolt-action Lee-Enfield .303 Mk IV.

The heart of the Canadian army in the period between VE Day and the outbreak of war in Korea was a formation known as the Mobile Striking Force (MSF). Although Ottawa sometimes referred to the MSF as an airborne brigade, it was never really that. It was rather a jury-rigged agglomeration of three infantry battalions trained in airborne operations. On paper, these battalions were to be ready at any time to be air-dropped into the Canadian north in the event that Soviet airborne troops tried to seize a northern airfield to be used as an airhead for a larger Soviet invasion. The MSF's task in such a situation would be to mask off the Soviet incursion, prepare an airfield into which reinforcements (read 'American') could be flown, and then await the arrival of reinforcements that would presumably eliminate the enemy air-head.[30]

Princess Patricia's Canadian Light Infantry (PPCLI) was the first of the infantry regiments to begin airborne training in early 1948.[31] But the MSF concept was doomed from the start because the RCAF did not have enough transport aircraft, of the right type, to drop by air more than a token force of men at any given time.[32] The bulk of its transports were Dakotas (Douglas C-47s), which were too small for the intended task.[33] The problem first showed up during a combined Canadian–American air–ground exercise conducted along the Alaska Highway in early August 1949. Dubbed Exercise Eagle, it was designed specifically to test the MSF idea. After it was over, *Canadian Aviation* magazine called the Canadian effort 'inadequate,'[34] while Southam Press's military correspondent Ross Munro wrote: 'The unvarnished fact is that as yet Canada hasn't got a combined army–R.C.A.F. striking force that could do the counter-attack task properly.'[35]

The armed forces made some effort to improve matters after that, specifically by purchasing thirty-five U.S.-built Fairchild C-119 'Flying Boxcar' assault transports. But thirty-five was not nearly enough. Exercise Sweetbriar, mounted in early 1950, produced results not much better than those of Exercise Eagle.[36] After the USSR tested its first nuclear weapon in 1949, the notion that it might try to seize an airfield in northern Canada grew even more remote. Although the MSF hung on as a concept until the early 1950s, it never proved itself out.

The Canadian army was not ready for even the mildest sort of international emergency in the summer of 1950. Despite Canadian lip-service paid to the notion of collective security under the auspices of either the United Nations or the North Atlantic Treaty Organization (NATO), Canada had no troops to send into a conflict at any level of intensity. The army's operational formations had been reduced to a bare minimum, and even then they could not recruit to authorized strength. The army's anti-tank guns, mortars, small arms, tanks, field artillery, radios, and signals equipment were all hold-overs from the Second World War. So was the army's doctrine. These deficiencies were related partly to budget and partly to repeated failures to acquire new U.S.-pattern equipment. But then, what did it matter? As far as the government was concerned, war was as likely as a visit from Martians, and if it did come, there would be plenty of time to prepare an expeditionary force to fight overseas beside Canada's allies.

Suddenly, war came. It began at about 0400 on 25 June 1950 when some 135,000 soldiers of the North Korea Peoples' Army (NKPA) struck across the 38th parallel dividing the Democratic Peoples' Republic of Korea in the north from the Republic of Korea in the south. The attack was a complete surprise. The NKPA was larger than the Republic of Korea (ROK) army. It also was better equipped, better trained, and contained a far larger number of veterans, men who had served with the Soviet Red Army in the Second World War or with the Communist forces in the Chinese civil war.

Led by a brigade of Soviet-supplied T-34 tanks, a force of seven assault divisions quickly overwhelmed most of the ROK defenders and struck for the South Korean capital of Seoul. The ROK Capital Division put up a stiff battle, but it was outgunned and outnumbered and soon outflanked. Within three days the Communists entered the outskirts of Seoul, sending panicked refugees fleeing across the Han River bridges just south of the city. On 28 June, some of those refugees were killed when ROK forces blew the bridges prematurely; the destruction of the bridges trapped much of the ROK army north of the river. Within hours the flag of North Korea was flying over the capital, and South Korean President Syngman Rhee was fleeing for his life.

Korea had a long history of being victimized by wars launched by more powerful neighbours long before the Second World War. The Japanese occupation of Korea, which stemmed from Japan's victory over China in the Sino–Japanese war of 1894–5, had been particularly harsh. That occupation ended with Japan's formal surrender to UN forces on 2 September 1945 aboard the USS *Missouri* in Tokyo Bay. But even then Korea was not yet free. When the USSR had entered the war against Japan in early August 1945, its forces had quickly occupied Manchuria and driven down the Korean peninsula to the 38th parallel. U.S. forces then occupied the rest of Korea, according to a prior agreement with the USSR to the effect that Japanese forces north of the 38th parallel would surrender to the Soviets, and those to the south, to the Americans.

The Korean peninsula was supposed to be reunified after elections, but that never happened. When the issue of Korean reunification was turned over to the United Nations in the autumn of 1947, the UN responded by establishing the United Nations Temporary Commission on Korea (UNTCOK), charged with organizing free elections throughout the peninsula. By then, however, the Cold War between the USSR and the Western allies had set in, and the Soviets refused to allow UNTCOK even to visit the north. At that point there were some nine million people living in North Korea and about twenty-one million in the south. UNTCOK therefore went ahead with elections in the south in May 1948, and the United States began a complete withdrawal of its occupation forces from the country. The assembly of the new Republic of Korea then elected long-time nationalist Syngman Rhee to be president. The Soviets responded by announcing the establishment of the Democratic People's Republic of Korea in September 1948, with long-time Communist Kim Il-sung at its head.

It was Kim Il-sung who hatched the idea for a 'reunification' of the peninsula by force and who proposed it directly to Soviet leader Joseph Stalin in the spring of 1949. When Mao Zedong's armies entered Beijing to proclaim the People's Republic of China (PRC) in October 1949, Kim appealed to him too for support. China's backing would be important in any such escapade, but Stalin's was crucial, because the USSR was an atomic power and far superior in weapons technology to the PRC. At first Stalin was unenthusiastic. He had other, more important goals in eastern and central Europe, and he was not willing to risk a war with the West. But he changed his mind in the spring of 1950, after it started to appear that the United States would not fight to defend the south. With Mao and the new Communist regime in Beijing watching closely for signs of Soviet hesitancy – hence weakness – Stalin gave his approval to the invasion and committed Soviet arms and 'advisers,' primarily to protect his position 'as the pontiff of world Communist revolution.'[37]

With Stalin's blessing, the Soviets opened the floodgates of supplies. They provided the North Korean forces with tanks and aircraft, giving them fire-power far superior to the ROK forces. They sent observers and instructors. At a later stage, they even sent combat pilots. Kim had the force that he needed to annex the south and take Syngman Rhee prisoner. After a short period of intensive training in the use of the T-34 tanks and in tank-infantry cooperation, his army struck. U.S. intelligence completely missed all signs of the impending offensive; the attack was a shocking surprise in Seoul, in Tokyo, where the U.S. Far East Command was located, in Washington, DC; and at UN headquarters in New York.

When the United States had withdrawn its troops from South Korea in 1948, it had inadvertently signalled that it was not willing to commit lives to defending the independence of the new republic. That error was compounded a year and a half later when U.S. Secretary of State Dean Acheson, speaking at the National Press Club in Washington in January 1950, appeared pointedly to leave Korea off a list of Asian nations that the United States considered part of its defence perimeter in Asia. In fact, the United States had made no such determination; the Communists erred badly in assuming so.

As soon as news of the North Korean invasion reached the United States, President Harry S. Truman quickly concluded that his country had to respond with force. He saw the situation in Korea as somewhat analogous to central Europe in the late 1930s, when the West's weak responses to Hitler's expansionism had led directly to global war. Truman immediately decided to raise the matter with the UN Security Council, which met in New York on the afternoon of 25 June.[38]

The permanent Soviet delegate to the UN was boycotting UN meetings. It was the Soviet Union's way of protesting the UN's failure to seat a representative from the Communist government in Beijing in the General Assembly and Security Council in place of the delegate from Chiang Kai-shek's regime on Taiwan. That absence was fortunate; it allowed the United States and its allies to shepherd a resolution through the Security Council accusing

North Korea of mounting an 'armed attack upon the Republic of Korea.' The council demanded an immediate cease-fire and withdrawal of Communist forces to the 38th parallel.[39] There was no diplomatic response from the Communists. Instead, their attack continued to roll forward; U.S. Gen. Douglas MacArthur, commander, Far East Command, told the Joint Chiefs of Staff in the Pentagon that ROK forces were on the verge of 'a complete collapse.'[40]

Truman could not wait; he ordered MacArthur to use the air and naval forces at his disposal to aid the Republic of Korea south of the 38th parallel. He issued a public announcement to that effect three hours before the Security Council met again to consider further action. This time the council voted to call on member states to 'furnish such assistance to the Republic of Korea as may be necessary to repel the armed attack.'[41] MacArthur's air and naval forces were not enough, and the ROK army could not stop the NKPA's T-34s. The NKPA's advance towards the southern port of Pusan continued as defence line after defence line was overwhelmed. On 29 June 1950, MacArthur was told to send U.S. ground forces to Korea to maintain communications and guard Pusan. The next day, he was ordered to commit U.S. ground forces to battle.[42]

Canada's response to the outbreak of war in Korea was confused and hesitant. On 26 June Secretary of State for External Affairs Lester Pearson informed the House of Commons that Canada supported the UN Security Council's resolution of the previous day, but he also told members of the press in an off-the-record briefing that he doubted that the United States or the United Nations would send troops to Korea.[43] Claxton thought that the north's forceful annexation of the south was just a matter of time.[44] It was clear, however, that Canada had an obligation to make some positive response to the UN's request for assistance,[45] and thus Prime Minister Louis St Laurent announced on 30 June 1950 that Canada would send three destroyers to far eastern waters. They were not actually being committed to Korea just yet, but they could be made available at some future point. St Laurent was careful to explain that if Canadian forces got involved in the fighting in

Korea, such an act would not constitute 'participation in war against any state. It would be our part in collective police action under the control and authority of the United Nations for the purpose of restoring peace.'[46]

The United States was far from ready to send powerful, well-trained, well-equipped ground forces to the Korean front. The closest U.S. ground troops were occupation forces based in Japan. They were green, poorly equipped for combat, not tough enough mentally or physically for the rigours and horrors of war. When a task group of these troops, hurriedly flown to Korea, met the North Koreans on the Suwon–Osan highway south of Seoul on 5 July, they were annihilated. By then the ROK forces had lost some 75,000 men. U.S. aircraft based in Japan bombed and rocketed NKPA spearheads and tried to disrupt NKPA supply trains but succeeded only in slowing the Communist advance.

On the day U.S. ground forces first clashed with the NKPA, the Canadian cabinet met to consider what further action to take. Claxton thought there was little realistic chance for 'an early and decisive' UN success. Pearson reported that UN Secretary General Trygve Lie had under consideration a U.S. proposal setting up a Unified Command and designating MacArthur as its commander. That would place the United States in overall charge of the military effort to aid South Korea – a natural arrangement, since the great bulk of the land, sea, and air forces required for that task were going to be American. Claxton thought that the government could at least announce that the three destroyers sailing that day (HMCS *Athabaskan, Cayuga,* and *Sioux*) would be made available to the UN, but St Laurent disagreed, so the government did nothing.[47] A Communist war of aggression was about to produce a quick and stunning victory for the Kremlin, and the United States and the United Nations had made their positions on Korea crystal clear, but Canada was waffling. Why?

St Laurent, Pearson, Claxton, and most of the Canadian policy-making community were North Atlantic men. Their chief concerns in 1950 were the same as those that had guided Canadian foreign policy since its very beginnings – the North Atlantic basin that tied Canada to Britain, Europe, and the United States. Canadians did not know Asia or Asians and, for the most part, did not like what they knew. Immigration exclusion had been practised against Chinese, Japanese, and East Asians. Poll taxes and high prices for immigration permits had put additional burdens on those Asians who had immigrated. Canada's limited military involvement with Asia had been short and painful. It had taken place in 1941, when two largely untrained Canadian battalions had been sent to help garrison Hong Kong prior to the outbreak of war in the Pacific. They and the other defenders were quickly overwhelmed in the ensuing Japanese attack. Out of 1,975 Canadian soldiers in Hong Kong, 290 were killed and 483 wounded. Another 287 died in unspeakable conditions in prisoner-of-war (POW) and slave-labour camps in Hong Kong and Japan.

It was therefore wholly consistent with the upbringing, experience, and background of most Canadian policy-makers in 1950 that they might think of Canadian involvement in Korea as an unwise adventure that would detract from Canada's main concern – namely, Europe. Lester Pearson seemed to be one of the very few who agreed with Truman, Dean Acheson, and other American leaders that the Korean conflict was NATO's first true test, even if it was taking place half a world away.[48] When Brooke Claxton examined this issue from the perspective of cold military logic, for example, he concluded that Canada should avoid entanglement in Korea. But as his long-time friend E.J. Tarr pointed out, Korea was one of those circumstances 'in which cold logic [could not be] the controlling factor.'[49]

On 7 July the UN Security Council recommended 'that all members providing military forces and other assistance ... make such forces and other assistance available to a Unified Command under the United States.'[50] As anticipated, Douglas MacArthur was to head the Unified Command. In effect, the UN had named the United States as the leader and chief organizer of an international military force provided voluntarily by UN members, fighting under the UN flag, to stop North Korean aggression. Canada's tepid reaction came five days later, when the cabinet decided to place the three Canadian destroyers under MacArthur's command.

Trygve Lie's answer to Canada's token move came in a rather

forceful message sent to Ottawa on 14 July and released to the
press at the same time. In it, he asked Canada to consider sending
ground forces: 'I have been informed that the Government of the
United States ... is now prepared to engage in direct consultation
with your Government with regard to [your contribution] for the
attainment of the objectives set forth in the Security Council resolution [of 7 July]. In this connection, I have been advised that
there is an urgent need for additional effective assistance. I should
be grateful, therefore, if your Government would examine its
capacity to provide an increased volume of combat forces, particularly ground forces.'[51] This was an invitation to a 'come as you are'
party, and Canada was naked. Canada had no capacity to respond
in the affirmative; the army was not ready to embark on a foreign
campaign without a full mobilization and a year to prepare.

It took official Ottawa four days even to begin to respond to
Lie's message. Claxton was in Newfoundland discussing continental defence with U.S. military officials. St Laurent was fishing.
When one reporter tracked the prime minister down by telephone
to sound him out, St Laurent was greatly annoyed at the intrusion:
'I wish reporters wouldn't bother me when I'm on holidays,' he
complained before he hung up.[52] St Laurent was out of touch with
public sentiment, if the editorials in Canadian newspapers were
any judge. A storm of editorial opinion protested the government's obvious failure to move quickly to commit ground troops to
the fighting.[53]

The Canadian Chiefs of Staff Committee (COSC) met on 18
July 1950 to prepare a recommendation for its political masters. Its
statement regarding a possible contribution of ground forces to
the Korean War was short and to the point: 'No despatch of Canadian ground forces is recommended.' Canada did not have
enough soldiers. The only force ready for action of any sort was the
Mobile Striking Force (MSF), and it was also the only force available for the defence of Canada. All army formations were under
strength, and no units could be sent for up to half a year, even if
augmented by first-line reserves. Foulkes was beginning to believe
that Canada might be able to recruit a force specially enlisted for
service in Korea, but no action was taken on his suggestion.

Instead, the chiefs recommended that Canada offer a squadron of North Star transports to help with the airlift of troops and materiel from the United States to Japan.[54]

The cabinet met the next day. St Laurent was angry that news of Lie's appeal for ground troops had been circulated in the press before it arrived in Ottawa. That set the tone for the rest of the meeting. Claxton relayed the concerns of the COSC and the Cabinet Defence Committee that 'Canada was not in a position to contribute ground forces in Korea' because the only standing force available was the MSF. Pearson did not challenge the COSC's evaluation of Canadian military preparedness, but he did warn the cabinet that the United States was putting considerable pressure on other countries to contribute troops, 'mainly for psychological reasons.' But Claxton won out for the moment, and St Laurent issued a statement to the press noting all of Canada's current defence commitments, including the destroyer force sent to Korea. He then made an offer to send an RCAF transport squadron[55] and concluded: 'Well gentlemen, I hope to be out fishing again the day after tomorrow.'[56]

Brooke Claxton felt especially strongly that Canada should not send ground troops to Korea. He believed that the United States was 'getting [Canada] into something to which there is really no end.'[57] He also worried that the Communist attack in Korea would divert American and British attention and military resources from Europe – the main area of danger – to Southeast Asia. If that happened, Claxton feared, the USSR would 'extend this process, perhaps to the extent of producing other incidents where [the Soviets] could exploit the apparent military weakness of the other Western Powers.'[58] Foulkes agreed with him.[59]

Official Washington was upset by Ottawa's apparently studied indifference to the plight of South Korea and the possibility of a quick Communist victory. The U.S. Defense and State departments were in a virtual frenzy as the Communists seemed to draw closer to outright victory. Ottawa, in contrast, seemed to adopt an 'ostentatious calm' as *Maclean's* Ottawa editor, Blair Fraser, put it.[60] Canada, however, was not alone in its reluctance to commit ground forces to the defence of South Korea, because Australia, New

Zealand, and even Britain had also allowed their military forces to
deteriorate in both size and quality since 1945. None the less,
those three Commonwealth countries were far quicker than
Ottawa to grasp the meaning of a virtual collapse of South Korean
and U.S. forces. That awareness no doubt arose out of their proximity to Southeast Asia and their interests in maintaining a strong
Western presence in the region. On 26 July all three countries
announced the dispatch of ground forces to Korea.[61]

Those statements almost coincided with a specific and private
request from U.S. Secretary of State Dean Acheson to Pearson for
Canada to do the same. In a somewhat macabre twist of events,
Pearson informed cabinet members of Acheson's request on 27
July while all were aboard William Lyon Mackenzie King's funeral
train enroute to Toronto from Ottawa; King had died five days earlier. Pearson urged his colleagues to comply with the U.S. request;
he believed that Canada had committed itself too closely to NATO,
to the UN, and to the whole notion of collective security to duck
this responsibility. He thought that the government should recom-
mend to Parliament that a special brigade group be recruited for
service in Korea – the suggestion first mooted by Foulkes. In Pearson's words, 'Canada had every interest in strengthening the U.S.
position as leader in the struggle against Communism.' He could
not overcome Claxton's reluctance and St Laurent's ambivalence,
however, so the ministers decided to postpone the decision for a
few days more.[62]

The cabinet assembled again on 2 August and met for three
straight days. Pearson reported on discussions that he had had in
Washington with Acheson, Lie, and representatives of the United
Kingdom. They had strengthened his view that it would be wrong
for Canada to stay out of the Korea fighting. He told St Laurent:
'Personally I would have great difficulty in reconciling [such a
decision] with my views on the menace which faces us, on the
expression of that menace in Korea, and the necessity of defeating
it there by United Nations action.'[63] Pearson suggested that Canada raise a mixed brigade of volunteers, which it could then associ-
ate 'with other forces made available to the United Nations by
countries other than the United States.' He was eager that the

Canadians be joined in some way with the other Commonwealth contingents in Korea. He believed that Canada would thereby send a clear message to the international community that from now on 'we fight only as a result of U.N. decisions, and with other U.N. members.'[64]

Here perhaps was the germ that would later grow into the United Nations Emergency Force (UNEF), helping to end the fighting between Egypt, Israel, and the Anglo–French forces in 1956 – and win Pearson a Nobel Peace Prize. Here also was the curious notion that Canadians would in future be obligated to fight and die only for the UN. Pearson seemed to have momentarily forgotten the North Atlantic Treaty that Canada had signed just a year earlier, and that bound Canada to fight under NATO command if a NATO member were attacked. Still, Pearson was correct about what the Korean War meant in the global confrontation between Soviet Communism and the Western democratic powers and correct too in believing that Canada could not sit out the war if the Americans insisted that Canadian troops were needed. He was far wiser than Claxton in knowing this.

With Pearson leading the way, Claxton came aboard. The British were making inquiries about possible Canadian participation in a Commonwealth Division in Korea, the minister of national defence told his colleagues. Canada could set up a 'special service force ... which would not be specifically tied down to Korea but designed to serve the purposes of the North Atlantic Treaty or of the United Nations.' The army just might attract enough men for that force 'if it was indicated that recruiting was definitely for service in Korea or elsewhere.' He predicted that it would take about six months to raise and train this special force. Then St Laurent came around; he and the nation really had little choice under the circumstances. Thus was born the Canadian Army Special Force (CASF).[65]

On the evening of Monday, 7 August 1950, the prime minister went on national radio to address the nation. He told Canadians that the UN action in Korea was not war but a 'police action intended to prevent war by discouraging aggression.' He evoked the experience of the late 1930s, when the democracies had failed

to put up a strong front to Hitler and had thereafter paid the price
in the worst war in history. 'That must not be allowed to happen
again,' he declared. The United States had been fighting in Korea
almost from the start, and other nations were now building up
their forces 'with the greatest urgency.' Canada too had made commitments of naval and air transport forces but had stopped short
of offering ground troops because no ready force existed for that
purpose. Nevertheless, since Canada had to do something more to
help stop Communist aggression, the government had decided to
authorize 'the recruitment of an additional army brigade' to be
known as the Canadian Army Special Force. It would be 'specially
trained and equipped ... for use in carrying out Canada's obliga-
tions under the United Nations Charter or the North Atlantic Pact.
Naturally this brigade [would], subject to the approval of Parliament, be available for service in Korea.'[66]

When recruitment centres opened across the nation the next
morning, hundreds of men were already lined up; many more
came the next day, when recruiting for Korea was actually supposed to start. Each had his reasons for wanting to go to Korea;
each had to be prodded, poked, questioned, probed by army doctors and medical personnel to see if he was suitable. Since the army
had neither the manpower nor the time to do the job properly, five
years of neglect were about to take their toll.

TWO

The Special Force

Vancouver, Monday, 7 August 1950. John Meredith Rockingham sat behind his desk in the offices of the Pacific Stage Lines bus company and listened as the executive of the Amalgamated Transit Union presented their case. It had been a busy day at the bus company, and even though it was now well into the supper hour, Rockingham just knew that these union men had lost no ardour for their cause. Rockingham – Rocky to his friends – was superintendent of Pacific Stage, responsible for labour relations.

Would the company allow its drivers to take an hour off for lunch each day? The union executive demanded an answer.

Rockingham leaned over his desk: 'Do you think I can close the system down for an hour each day while the men all have lunch?'

'Well, why not hire extra men to cover the lunch breaks,' they replied.

The conversation dragged on. It went nowhere. Pacific Stage could not operate with built-in lunch breaks. Besides, there was a shift system in place, determined by seniority, with layovers after each trip, just as the union had demanded. That left lots of time for meals. What more did the union want?[1] Rockingham was hungry and bored. Every now and then his gaze drifted to the front fold of the *Vancouver Sun*, sitting on a side table. Lurid headlines announced the latest news from the Korean War. The news was not good.

By 7 August, North Korean forces were pushing from the northwest and the southwest against the U.S. and ROK armies holding

the Pusan Perimeter. The 1st Provisional U.S. Marine Brigade,
rushed to Korea from Hawaii, was moving into the main line of
resistance along the Naktong River, north of Taegu, to stiffen the
defences. But at midnight on 5 August, thousands of North Koreans from the 16th Regiment, 4th Division of the North Korea People's Army (NKPA), had waded across the Naktong and surprised
the 24th U.S. Division. They had driven several kilometres into the
perimeter. When they stopped to consolidate, they could see the
town of Miryang just up the road; it was the key to the northwest
sector of the UN defences.[2] A decorated soldier in the Second
World War, Rockingham could appreciate how desperate was the
battle raging half a world away.

The phone rang. The union men stopped talking as Rockingham answered with some obvious irritation; he had left instructions that they were not to be disturbed. The voice on the other
end asked him to wait on the line for Lt.-Gen. Charles Foulkes calling from army headquarters in Ottawa. Rockingham waited quietly, anticipating the question that Foulkes would ask him. Foulkes
got on the line. He told Rockingham that in a few hours the government was going to announce the creation of a special formation, a brigade group, for service in Korea. To save time, it was
going to make a special effort to attract men with previous military
experience, especially Second World War veterans. There was no
other choice. Some active army men (i.e., regulars) would be
assigned to the new brigade, but the integrity of the existing home-
defence battalions had to be preserved. Would Rockingham consider commanding the brigade? He would have to organize it,
train it, and lead it in the field. He would get all the help that he
needed and could hand-pick as many of his staff as he wanted,
even battalion commanders.

Rockingham listened intently, then gave Foulkes a guarded
answer. With the union representatives sitting right across the desk
from him, he had to be careful. He told Foulkes that he wanted
twenty-four hours to decide and that he would talk to his wife and
his boss before then. He put the phone down, turned to the union
representatives, and told them that their proposal was unaccept-
able. They threatened to go over his head to the president of the

company. He told them to go ahead. He already knew what his answer to Foulkes was going to be; lunch-hour breaks for bus drivers were soon going to be the farthest thing from his mind.

Handsome, rock-jawed, solidly built, John Meredith Rockingham looked every inch a soldier, even in his business suit. At six feet, four inches, he towered over most other men. But it was his strong personality, his decisiveness, his attention to detail, and his ability to carry through under very difficult circumstances that had made him one of Canada's most successful wartime brigade commanders. Born in Australia in 1911, Rockingham had come to Canada in 1930 and, despite the Depression, had soon landed a job with BC Electric, cutting brush along the company's power lines. His great energy, his leadership abilities, and his willingness to put in long hours brought him quick promotion, first to foreman of a labour gang, then to superintendent of his department.[3]

Like many men of his age, Rocky had joined the militia in the hope of adding a few extra dollars a year to his take-home pay. The militia had been a hollow organization for most of the 1930s; there had been too little money from Ottawa to sustain realistic training, and almost nothing in the way of new equipment, training manuals, or even uniforms. Still, Rocky had stuck it out; by the time war broke out, he had earned a commission as a reserve lieutenant in the 1st Battalion – the Canadian Scottish – a highland militia regiment headquartered in Victoria.

The Canadian Scottish had gone overseas as a machine-gun regiment in August 1941, and Rockingham had gone with it. Within a year he had been promoted to major and transferred to the Royal Hamilton Light Infantry (RHLI) of the 4th Brigade, 2nd Canadian Infantry Division. The RHLI had been devastated at Dieppe on 19 August 1942, and capable officers were badly needed to help rebuild the battalion before the looming invasion of France. Rockingham had excelled as a company commander, particularly as a trainer of infantry. He had left nothing to chance, overseeing the smallest detail of training and not hesitating to correct his subalterns and his NCOs if he disagreed with the instructions that they were giving the men. He had tolerated paperwork well enough, but he had been determined to lead his company from the front when the time came. The men had developed a deep respect for, and trust in, the tall man with the Aussie twang, and Rockingham had soon taken command as battalion commanding officer (CO).

Prior to D-Day, Rocky had been temporarily detached from the RHLI to attend the British Army Staff Course at Camberley. When he had resumed command after the invasion, his battalion had been in the thick of the fight to break out of the small strip of coast where the Germans had bottled up the Allies. Rockingham's first battle as CO of the RHLI had been the bloody Operation Spring of 25 July 1944; the RHLI had been the only attacking unit in the entire corps to gain and hold its intended objective – the small village of Verrières atop the ridge of the same name.

Counterattacked by German armour in the late afternoon, Rockingham had directed a spirited and imaginative defence that lasted through the night. That battle, and the skirmishing that followed over the next three days, had cost the RHLI 200 casualties, 53 of them fatal. Undaunted, the proud battalion held out and recovered all its dead. When the history of that day was written more than a decade and a half later, official army historian C.P. Stacey wrote: 'The R.H.L.I. may well remember Verrières.'[4] Rocky had been awarded the Distinguished Service Order (DSO) for his talented command of the RHLI in that battle. By then, the men's faith in their CO was unwavering. 'From what I saw of Rockingham,' one later remembered, 'he feared neither man nor devil but I believe he put a lot of trust in God, because the rest of us did.'[5]

Normandy was a weeding-out phase for the Canadian army. The three Canadian divisions and one independent armoured brigade that had fought there had been essentially untried, except for that one disastrous day at Dieppe. After battle had been joined, there were many changes among officers from division level on down. In that highly fluid command situation, Rockingham had emerged as one of the best, which was why he had been promoted yet again, in August, to command the 9th Canadian Infantry Brigade of the 3rd Division. His three-year rise from lieutenant to brigade commander had been positively meteoric for a militia officer, even in wartime.

Rockingham had then led the 9th Brigade through some of the

bloodiest fighting of the war – to clear the Channel ports, in the Battle of the Scheldt Estuary, and in the Battle of the Rhineland. His brigade had been one of the first Canadian units to cross the Rhine (which earned him a bar to his DSO). When the fighting in Europe had ended, he had volunteered to command a brigade in the Pacific, but the Japanese had surrendered before the Canadian Army Pacific Force could be organized.

Rockingham had stayed in the militia after the war, command- ing the reserve 15th Brigade on arctic exercises, while he resumed his career with BC Electric. Given his outstanding record as a commander, and the fact that he was still a militia officer, he was a natural choice to lead the Korean contingent. As he later remem- bered: 'The reason for my selection rather than one of the regular Brigadiers was that it was hoped that there would be many ex-sol- diers and civilians in the force, and it was thought a "civilian sol- dier" could handle a situation of this sort better.'[6] Rockingham's wife supported his decision to go to Korea, and so did his boss, who guaranteed that his position would be waiting for him when he returned. Claxton made the announcement in Ottawa on the morning of 9 August. The final edition of that day's *Vancouver Sun* trumpeted: 'B.C. Brigadier Heads Canada's Korea Force: "Rocky" Rockingham Called to Ottawa.'[7]

Rockingham's Canadian Army Special Force (CASF) was to exist side by side with the active, or regular professional, army. The order-in-council establishing the CASF declared that it was 'part of the Canadian Army Active Force and therefore personnel enrolled [in it] are members of the Active Force to all intents and pur- poses.' None the less, Special Force recruits signed up only for the Special Force, and only for eighteen months. Since they were vol- unteers only for the Special Force, however, they could be sent any- where the government decided to send that force – to Korea or to Europe for NATO service. If the government decided to integrate the CASF into the active army, the men who had volunteered for the Special Force would have to volunteer all over again.[8] That condition did not apply to regulars who were transferred to the Special Force to fill in the brigade-group establishment. Despite their 'stand alone' status, Special Force soldiers were accorded the same veterans' benefits as active army soldiers.[9]

When Foulkes had mooted the idea of raising a special force for Korea, he had envisioned it as a brigade, later as a brigade group. So had Pearson. No evidence has yet come to light as to why this type of formation was chosen, but it is not hard to discern. An infantry-brigade group would normally consist of the usual complement of an infantry brigade (three infantry battalions, one heavy machine-gun/mortar battalion, and brigade headquarters) augmented by supporting units. These might include an organic field-artillery regiment, an armoured squadron, engineer and signals squadrons, or formations of other essential support services such as medical, transport, and ordnance units. A brigade group would in effect be self-contained and, unlike a brigade, might more easily be organized to fight as a single, recognizable Canadian unit. It had been consistent government policy since the Boer War that Canadian soldiers, sailors, or airmen fight in distinctly Canadian formations so this nation's contributions could be easily recognized, no matter how small they were compared to the overall Allied effort.

The Special Force brigade group authorized by order-in-council on 7 August was initially to consist of three infantry battalions, one regiment of artillery, a field ambulance, an infantry workshop, a transport company, and two field-repair detachments, with an authorized strength of 4,960 all ranks and a reinforcement group of 2,105.[10] In the next few months, more formations were added, including an anti-tank squadron from the 12th Canadian Armoured Regiment (Lord Strathcona's Horse [Royal Canadians]). The infantry battalions and the line rifle companies were to be the cutting edge of the formation.

Given the haste with which the Special Force was to be raised, trained, and dispatched, there never seems to have been any question but that the basic structure of its infantry battalions would mirror that of Canadian infantry battalions in the last half of the Second World War. That arrangement, adopted in the autumn of 1942, gave each battalion an establishment of thirty-eight officers and 812 other ranks (ORs) organized into four infantry companies, each consisting of a company HQ and three platoons. A platoon was commanded by a lieutenant and contained three sections of ten men. Each section was commanded by a corporal. There was also a support company equipped with battalion-level arms, such as anti-tank guns and three-inch mortars, a carrier platoon, a pioneer platoon including snipers, and a headquarters company that handled signals, administration, and supply.

The ten-man section was the foundation of a Canadian infantry battalion – eight riflemen, a Bren gunner, and the Bren gunner's assistant, who also carried a rifle. The Bren gun was a Czech-designed light machine-gun weighing 10 kg that fired 500 rounds per minute when set fully automatic. It was fed by a top-inserted banana magazine containing thirty rounds and fired from a bipod or from the hip. Standard section-attack doctrine called for the Bren gunner, with his assistant and up to three riflemen, to pin the enemy down with fire (to 'fix' him in military parlance), while the other six men outflanked the enemy, cut him off, and neutralized him in one way or another. It was not until late 1951 that Canadian infantry battalions in Korea were assigned a second Bren per section to augment their fire-power in the face of increasing Chinese use of automatic weapons in the attack.[11]

Toronto, Tuesday, 8 August 1950. As Major R.G. Liddel drove through the gates of No. 6 Personnel Depot in Rosedale this hot morning, he was surprised to see some five hundred men lolling on the lawn in front of the main recruiting office. The setting was Chorley Park, the château-style former viceregal residence closed by Premier Mitchell Hepburn in the 1930s and used as a military hospital in the Second World War. Liddel had not heard the prime minister's speech the previous night; he was unaware that a call for volunteers for Korea had been issued. Technically, recruiting was not to begin for another day in any case, but across the country hundreds of men showed up at recruiting depots on Monday morning, and the army was not ready to receive them.

The normal recruiting process in the summer of 1950 was not much different from that followed for most of the Second World War. When a man came to the recruiting office, he was interviewed, then examined for both physical and mental competence. There were forms to fill out, X-rays to be taken, chests to be thumped, throats to be peered into, knees to be knocked, and tests to be administered before a volunteer was pronounced fit to serve in His Majesty's Canadian army. Only then was a volunteer attested or 'sworn in.' So, although Liddel and his staff got to work immediately, only one man was formally enlisted by the end of the day.

Claxton was appalled. The Toronto newspapers had reported hundreds of men stepping forward. Where were they? How long was this going to take? He would later write: 'The facilities we had in Toronto were quite inadequate to handle the flood of recruits.'[12] That was not so, but Claxton intervened anyway. On Tuesday, he flew to Toronto in the back seat of a prototype CF-100 and was whisked to the personnel depot by a police escort. For two hours he and his entourage haunted the halls and rooms of the depot, trying to discover what was going wrong. Nothing was, but Claxton was not placated. Ottawa had hesitated and delayed for weeks. Now the Americans and the South Koreans were barely holding the line along the Naktong, and Canada was under pressure to make up for lost time. Claxton wanted to report that large numbers of men had already been taken in, even though that was just not so.

Claxton's solution was to order the recruitment process reversed; men would take their oath of attestation *before* the testing. That was not all. He also decided that the selection procedure was too elaborate in the present emergency. He instructed Foulkes to speed things up; Foulkes quickly complied.[13] Although the army had enrolled only 169 men in July, it eventually took in 7,116 in August and 4,146 in September.[14] Almost half were Second World War veterans.[15] The only shortages were in specific, specialized trades and French-speaking volunteers. This last difficulty prompted the Van Doos to lower the bar, take in officer volunteers with a less-than-adequate understanding of French, and group them together.[16]

Claxton's intervention, born of haste, produced a very mixed result. On the one hand, the army grew by about 50 per cent in less than two months and was quickly able to begin structuring and training the brigade group for Korea much quicker than it might have. On the other hand, many men were taken in who were soon found to be 'medically unfit for the rigors of the Korean campaign or who ... had, and concealed, a criminal background.'[17] The 'lack of proper screening' affected both training and morale; the army was forced to spend almost as much time weeding undesirable men out of the Special Force as it did training them. This constant departure of unwanted men and arrival of replacements affected morale; by mid-October, absenteeism skyrocketed. Unauthorized absence became 'something of a way of life,' in the words of one officer,[18] with more than seven hundred men from the original contingent either deserted or listed as 'absent without leave' (AWL).[19] The AWL rate eventually declined, but as late as February 1951 the adjutant-general, Maj.-Gen. W.H.S. Macklin, reported that the number of men discharged from the Special Force was still 'substantially greater' than in the rest of the army.[20] By the end of March 1951, more than 25 per cent of the original contingent was gone; the comparable replacement figure for the entire Canadian army for the first seven months of the Second World War had been 12 per cent.[21]

Claxton spearheaded the raising of the Special Force, as he recorded in his memoirs: 'I insisted that I be told of every proposed development and at every stage exercise a close personal supervision.'[22] It was thus not surprising that he was personally blamed for many of the manpower and morale difficulties that later befell the force. Lt.-Col. Jim Stone, Commanding Officer 2PPCLI, later remarked: 'They were recruiting anybody who could breathe or walk. Brooke Claxton pushed the enlistment along because he was a politician at heart and didn't give a damn about what else was happening.'[23] That was partly true, but only partly. The five previous years of cutbacks, underfunding, neglect, and failure to modernize the forces was not Claxton's fault alone, but that of the entire nation. Given the sudden emergency in Korea, Claxton had little choice but to take special steps to ensure that Canada's army might make some useful contribution to the fight.

For two months the flow of recruits remained strong; Foulkes recommended that an additional number of men be taken in over

and above the 7,000 to 8,000 first envisaged, to provide for reinforcements. That would mean a new total of just under 10,000
officers and men.[24] At first the army planned a reinforcement system consisting of a Reinforcement Group, to hold, administer, and
train reinforcements, and a Reinforcement Stream, composed of
those men training in Canada and those in transit to Korea.[25] But
this scheme soon gave way to the formation of a 25th Reinforcement Group, made up of newly established 3rd battalions of the
active infantry regiments.[26]

The Special Force's reinforcement system was another legacy of
the army's unpreparedness for a 'come as you are' war. It was supposed to work this way: the initial Special Force infantry battalions
('Special Force' was soon dropped in favour of 25th Canadian
Infantry Brigade Group,' or '25 CIBG') were to be set up as
2nd battalions of the active army's three infantry regiments – i.e.,
2nd Battalion, Royal Canadian Regiment (2RCR); 2nd Battalion,
Princess Patricia's Canadian Light Infantry (2PPCLI); and 2nd Battalion, Royal 22e Regiment (2R22eR). The same scheme was followed for the other combat arms. Men surplus to the 2nd
battalions' requirements were to be formed up into 3rd battalions,
which would be used to reinforce the 2nds. Regular-force personnel were not allowed to volunteer for Korea, since it was thought
that many would do so if given the chance and that that would
leave the active army short of trained personnel.[27]

When the 1st Canadian Infantry Division had been sent overseas to fight Hitler in late 1939, the Department of Militia and
Defence had activated the 1st battalions of the three Permanent
Force infantry regiments as well as the 1st battalions of six militia-
infantry regiments. Although the division's core was professional,
its majority were part-time soldiers from across the country and
from a wide range of social and economic backgrounds. That held
substantially true for the composition of most of the army divisions, air-force squadrons, and naval escort groups formed thereafter. The whole nation was at war, and hundreds of thousands of its
young men (and several tens of thousands of women also) volunteered for the three services.

Circumstances were very different in the summer of 1950, and so too was the composition of the new brigade group. No doubt some of the men who volunteered did so out of a sense of patriotism, or a desire to fight Communism, but most who went did not. They went for the adventure of it, or because they had failed to see action in the Second World War, or because they were just dissatisfied with their lives. Kenneth John Blampied was then twenty-three years old. Born into a Catholic family of six children in Verdun, Quebec, Blampied was single and held a job as a freelance photographer for a local newspaper when he volunteered for service in Korea. He had volunteered and trained with the Canadian infantry in 1945, hoping to see action in the Pacific theatre, but the atomic bombing of Japan abruptly ended the war: 'When the call went out for WWII veterans, especially those from infantry,' he later recalled, 'I knew this was my last chance.'[28] Given a choice between the Van Doos and the RCR, he chose the latter and was sent to the Wolsely Barracks at London, Ontario, for his initial training.

Harry Repay, twenty-eight, was born in a small Saskatchewan farming community. As soon as he turned eighteen, he had joined the South Saskatchewan Regiment, staying in the infantry until demobilized in 1946. He then went into the mines, where he found life boring and monotonous. He jumped at the chance to go to Korea and went to Winnipeg to enlist with the PPCLI. He was sent to the Currie Barracks in Calgary, for training.[29]

Ross Wilkes, twenty-three, was born in Walkerville, Ontario. He had joined the Canadian Technical Training Corps in 1944. His goal was overseas service with the Royal Canadian Electrical and Mechanical Engineers (RCEME), but he never made it. When the call went out for volunteers for Korea, Wilkes was unemployed; someone asked him to volunteer for the RCEME. It was just the opportunity for which he had been waiting: 'I wanted a chance to fight for freedom, seeing I had missed out in the last war.'[30]

Robert Molesworth, twenty, had been born in Middlesex, England. He had arrived in Canada with his family in 1937, settling in Montreal. In 1946 he had joined the Black Watch (Royal Highland Regiment of Canada), a militia unit with a long and proud record of service in two world wars. When the conflict in Korea broke out, he was a clerk-salesman with few career hopes. He decided to join the army. Many of his friends signed up, and he did not want to be left behind: 'It was the thing to do back then ... A call to arms meant a sense of duty to my new country of Canada.'[31]

Most of the men who crowded No. 6 in Toronto, and the other personnel depots across Canada in that summer of 1950, did not say then, and for the most part do not claim now, that they were going to Korea for God, King, and country or to save the world from Communism.[32]

The motives were mixed, but were those volunteers so different from those who had gone to soldier since the dawn of time? The Canadians who went overseas in the first years of the Second World War also had a variety of reasons. That war had broken out in the dying years of the Great Depression; many young men entered the military for the steady pay, three square meals a day, and warm barracks that it provided. Others were employed, but at boring, unchallenging jobs, with no prospects and little pay. Still others joined because their pals did, or because the militia regiments with which they had spent a weekday night and occasional weekends and summer camps, had been activated. Few volunteered specifically or solely because Naziism was a great evil or because Hitler had invaded Poland.

The Canadian public has always perceived the veterans of Korea differently from those of the two world wars. It has lionized the latter, rightly, as participants in two great crusades – people who volunteered in the hundreds of thousands to destroy the evils of German militarism in the 1914–1918 war and the scourge of racism and fascism in the 1939–1945 war. In those crusades, hardly anyone in Canada did not have a friend, relative, father, brother, or sister in uniform. When Canada's soldiers went off to war, everyone knew that they were going to France or Italy or Belgium or Holland, and everyone knew that they would not return until the job was done.

It was all different with the volunteers for Korea. Few of them were from the middle-class mainstream of Canadian society. Canada's middle-class males, including the vast majority of the 1.1 million who had served in the Second World War, were caught up with more mundane matters in the early 1950s. They had started families in the late 1940s and were going to work each day to keep moms and kids in groceries and shelter (few moms worked in those days). Others were completing the education that their veterans' benefits had paid for and were settling in to decent jobs. Still others were starting post-war businesses selling cars, or washing machines, or radios, or even television sets. Not many of them were willing to answer the call to go to Korea, especially if they had survived years crossing the deadly Atlantic in a corvette, or flown umpteen missions over Germany, or slogged through the flooded polder land of Holland and Belgium. They had done their bit for democracy; now it was time for home, job, and family. Someone else could fight the Reds in Korea.

The volunteers for Korea distanced themselves from the great majority of Canadians, no doubt inadvertently, when they enlisted. In a nation with an all-volunteer military, there is always a gap between the military and society in peacetime. People who join the military are always thought to be somewhat different from everyone else. This was especially true in 1950, because the volunteers were not only joining the military, they were doing so to fight a small war in a far-off place that had no apparent connection to Canada or to the vast majority of its citizens. Great masses of Canadians did not go to Korea, did not know anyone who did, and did not follow the progress of the war. When some veterans of Korea later returned to Canada, they discovered that some of their friends had hardly been aware of their absence. They just seemed to disappear for a year or so, then come back with tails of Chail-li, or Kap'yong, or Hill 355 – places about which no one in Canada knew or cared. When this isolation from society was added to by tales of rampant absenteeism and ill-disciplined behaviour, particularly in the first contingents, an impression grew among many Canadians that the men who had gone to Korea were misfits, mercenaries, and malingerers who could not fit into normal, peacetime society.

In fact, however, the Korea volunteers, for whatever reason they joined, turned out to be the first breed of Canada's post-war military. They set the pattern for all who have followed. The advent of nuclear weapons made all-out war between East and West so poten-

tially catastrophic, even by the early 1950s, as to be virtually
unthinkable. In the United States and Britain, conscription was
quickly increased as Cold War tensions mounted. NATO built mass
armies and air forces in West Germany, the Low Countries, and
France to fight a defensive war against potential Soviet and Warsaw
Pact invaders on the plains of northern Europe. Canada's soldiers,
sent to Germany to form part of the NATO Integrated Force in the
autumn of 1951, were to be part of that defence.

The Canadian army that fought in Korea, that was stationed in
Europe through the Cold War, or that sent peacekeepers on UN
missions from the 1950s to the 1990s was close in mission, mentality, and attitude to the British army's 'thin red line' that guarded
the far outposts of the nineteenth-century British Empire. It was
nothing like the mass Canadian armies of the two world wars. In
Korea and afterwards, Canada's soldiers abroad were almost always
professional and always sent wherever their government believed
that they were needed to shore up the outer defences of Western
democracy, usually with little fanfare at home. Like the volunteers
for Korea, they were a breed apart from Canadian society. They
formed a self-selected, professional, all-volunteer military, staffed
by men and increasing numbers of women who chose their voca-
tion because they wanted a military life. While other Canadians
enjoyed the advantages of living in a peaceful, prosperous nation,
far from danger, Canada's soldiers went into harm's way primarily
because they were soldiers carrying out the duties assigned to
them by their government, not because they had any particular
ideological objectives to achieve. Given that the chief responsibility
of Canada's soldiers, sailors, and airpersons has always been to protect their nation and its interests, it matters little what additional
individual motives prompted them to join in the first place.

Ottawa, Thursday, 9 August 1950. Rockingham stepped off the
Trans Canada Airlines North Star at Ottawa's Uplands Airport and
was whisked by staff car to National Defence headquarters. The
three clapboard buildings on Cartier Square were little changed
since they were thrown up early in the Second World War, except
that the Canadian red ensign now flew in front of the main

entrance, rather than a Union Jack, and covered walkways connected the buildings. Rockingham's first major job was to select the officers with whom he would work at brigade HQ and those who would command the battalions, regiments, and squadrons that would make up the brigade group. He conferred with Charles Foulkes to reconfirm that he would have the final word on who was to be put into what command or staff position, and he began to read the personnel records of all those former officers who had volunteered for service.

The next day, Rockingham got down to work with the Command and Staff Selection Committee reviewing the lists of volunteers and going through the records of serving officers of the active army who would be considered to fill positions not taken up by Special Force volunteers. In keeping with the army's policy that no active force personnel were to be allowed to volunteer for service in Korea, officer cadets attending RMC were instructed to continue their studies and graduate before putting in for service in Korea.[33]

Rockingham and the government wanted the brigade commanded primarily by war-veteran volunteers. Given that Canada had fielded some fifteen infantry and armoured brigades in Europe in the Second World War, that might not have seemed too difficult a task. But it was. Few experienced world war commanders came forward from civilian life. In the end, some two-thirds of the officers filling staff positions at brigade headquarters, or taking command of field formations, were assigned from the active army.

The process worked this way: with the help and advice of the selection committee, Rockingham first chose officers from among those who had volunteered. He was then given lists of active-force officers from which he selected men to fill the remaining posts.[34] The procedure was unusual because Rockingham hand-picked virtually every senior officer in the brigade.[35] It did ensure, however, that the brigade would have a very high level of competence among the field-grade officers of the first contingent because Rockingham himself had been a successful brigadier and knew what it took to make a good battalion CO.

The fate of an infantry brigade will be determined mostly by the quality of the officers who command its battalions. Although the brigade commander is in overall command, it is the battalions and their companies, platoons, and sections that actually do the fighting. When the fighting starts, the brigade commander will largely be a bystander while the battalion COs manage the battle. The battalion COs also bear chief responsibility for training their battalions and for preparing them for action. Battalion morale will be directly affected by how the CO administers justice; by his relationship with his regimental sergeant major (RSM), who is the unit's highest ranking NCO, and by the example that he sets (or does not set) at all times. If a battalion CO, through word and deed, gives his soldiers the impression that he is honest, trustworthy, skilled at the art of war, and, above all, mindful of their welfare, he has an excellent chance of becoming a good field commander.

Rockingham was fortunate in having two decorated and experienced Second World War battalion commanders volunteering for service in Korea. Articulate, intelligent, and tough, Jacques Dextraze, thirty-one, was thin (almost wiry), with round shoulders, and had jet-black hair and a neatly trimmed moustache. He had enlisted in the Fusiliers Mont-Royal (FMR) as a private in 1939. He saw action after the Normandy landings, throughout the campaign in northwest Europe. By the end of the war he was CO of the 1st Battalion of the FMR, holding the DSO and bar. His leadership style was highly charismatic. He believed in maintaining close contact with his company commanders when the bullets were flying, and, if necessary, intervening personally in their direction of the battle. To do that he needed excellent communications, something that he stressed in training and in the field.

In the summer of 1950 Dextraze was woodlands manager for the Singer Sewing Machine Company, responsible for selecting the wood to be used in the manufacture of the company's product. When the call went out for volunteers, several wartime colleagues urged him to sign up so that the French-speaking regiment to be raised would have an experienced leader. He volunteered, on condition that he have a free hand to select his company commanders and staff officers. He was an easy choice to command 2R22eR.[36]

From the west came Jim Stone, the oldest at forty-one. Almost bald, with a thick brush moustache, and thick, muscular arms, Stone was as tough physically as he was mentally. Born in England, he had migrated to Canada in 1927, living as a farmer and forest ranger in Alberta's Peace River country. At the outbreak of war in 1939, Stone enlisted as a private in the Loyal Edmonton Regiment, one of the first militia battalions to be activated. He and the regiment first saw action in Sicily in the summer of 1943. Stone was soon elevated to company commander, then battalion CO. He too received a DSO by the end of the war. Stone knew how to command a battalion in heavily wooded hill country – he had done so in Italy – and his experience was going to be invaluable. Rockingham selected him to lead 2PPCLI.[37]

No volunteer officer proved suitable to command the 2RCR, so Rockingham selected a man then serving with the Directorate of Military Operations and Plans at army headquarters in Ottawa. Robert A. Keane, thirty-six, was from Fort William, Ontario. Broad-shouldered and with thinning hair, he was rarely seen without a cigar between his fingers. He had commanded the Lake Superior Regiment, an armoured-car regiment serving with the 4th Canadian Armoured Division, from August 1944 until the end of the war. Like Rockingham and the other battalion COs, Keane had been awarded the DSO, for 'gallantry and leadership' of his regiment.[38] Although he had not had much experience in command of infantry, his leadership skills had been tried and proven during the Battle of the Scheldt Estuary and the assault into the Breskins Pocket.

Dextraze, Keane, and Stone had almost as much leeway in the selection of their battalion staff officers and company and platoon commanders as Rockingham had had in picking his staff and battalion COs. Dextraze had insisted on the freedom, apparently over the objections of the adjutant-general. As Dextraze would later put it: 'All majors would be selected from captains who had wartime experience. Captains would be selected from senior lieutenants who had wartime experience, and the subalterns (lieutenants) could be green as grass.'[39] Whereas Rockingham had little choice but to choose active-force officers to fill brigade-level positions, most of the platoon and company commanders in the three infantry battalions were returning war veterans.[40] As with the commissioned ranks, NCOs – from section leaders (corporals) to company sergeants major (CSMs) – were selected from volunteers with previous military experience or from the active forces. In the case of 2PPCLI, for example, the first twenty-six men chosen to begin training as section leaders (each rifle company had nine sections, hence thirty-six for the battalion) were all Second World War veterans.[41]

The initial training regimen for the Special Force was slapped together hurriedly. It had two basic objectives – first, to teach only the essentials, and as quickly as possible;[42] second, to avoid another disaster such as took place at Hong Kong in 1941 when two untrained Canadian battalions had been sent to help defend Hong Kong and had been decimated in the Japanese attack following the outbreak of the Pacific war. There was a fine line to be walked in the late summer and autumn of 1950. Just what does 'combat ready' mean? How much training would be necessary before the brigade would be truly ready for combat? There was debate about this issue in army circles and discussion of establishing some sort of checklist to determine when the brigade could be pronounced ready to go to Korea. In the end, the army left it up to Rockingham to decide.[43] That was entirely appropriate, because once the brigade was able to concentrate in one location Rockingham was to have far greater responsibility for training the formation than was usual for a brigade commander.[44]

Normally an infantry battalion trains and prepares for war in a measured, orderly way designed to teach soldiers the basics, such as discipline, weaponry, and fieldcraft, as well as tactics. Officers and non-commissioned members learn together because they will fight together. Training begins at the most basic individual level, then proceeds to add the skills required to fight in sections, platoons, and companies, and then as an entire battalion. During the process, each commander, from the corporals commanding sections to the lieutenants commanding platoons, to the captains and majors commanding companies, learns how to work with his NCOs (the section leader, of course, *was* an NCO), and they with him. The relationship is crucial because even though officers decide basic unit tactics, they rely heavily on the NCOs once the fighting begins. It was standard doctrine for the platoon commander, a lieutenant, to take up a position in the centre of his platoon's assault line with his sections, ordinarily led by corporals, on either side of him. The company commander should be as far forward as possible and within line of sight of his platoons to know what is going on and to be able to direct artillery fire to support them when necessary.

The normal method of training infantry and other combat arms formations was set aside in the haste to get the Special Force prepared for Korea. To speed up training it was decided that officers would be split off from the other ranks to concentrate on getting their command structures and procedures into place without having to bother with the day-to-day administration of their units. They would not have to administer their ORs because the well-established regimental training depots run by the 1st battalions would train them. This arrangement was also supposed to introduce them to the traditions and history of the regiments that they had joined.

In 2PPCLI, for example, the ORs went through their first stages of training at the PPCLI Regimental Training Depot, located at Camp Sarcee, southwest of Calgary. The 2PPCLI officers, in contrast, underwent refresher training under Stone's leadership at Currie Barracks in the city. In early September the ORs moved to Camp Wainright in Alberta for more advanced training, but still without their own officers.[45] Thus the ORs were separated from the officers who would command them and be responsible for unit discipline in the crucial early stages of 2PPCLI's life. This procedure also tended to spread the brigade out more than might have been necessary. By mid-August the brigade's units were training at Camps Valcartier in Quebec; Ottawa, Petawawa, Barriefield, and Borden in Ontario; Shilo and Sarcee in Alberta; Chilliwack in British Columbia; and at Currie Barracks in Calgary, Alberta.[46]

This training structure was badly conceived. The men who would eventually do the shooting were being trained by officers with whom they would not go into battle, while the officers who would lead them into battle had no direct control over them in training. The structure did not even solve the problem that it was meant to address, because 25 Brigade and the 2nd battalions' headquarters were daily bombarded with menial administrative concerns anyway.[47] Dextraze, for one, was determined to take command of his entire battalion as quickly as possible; he did so on 10 October,[48] and the other COs followed within days, as their units began to concentrate.

The Special Force's training syllabi were virtually the same as those used by the Canadian army during the Second World War, modified only slightly to meet what was known about the special circumstances of geography, climate, and the enemy's tactics in Korea.[49] Reports from the front indicated that the North Koreans (the Chinese had not yet intervened) were skilled at night infiltration and envelopment. Thus officers were to concentrate on communications training, especially to be able to work closely with the artillery to foil sudden enemy attacks. They were also instructed to be 'more proficient than their troops' in the use of their weapons.[50] Officers and ORs were to pay special attention to fieldcraft, weaponry, night fighting, anti-infiltration tactics, mountain fighting, patrolling, and fighting in extremes of temperature and weather.[51]

Since the North Koreans appeared well-stocked with Soviet-built T-34 tanks and had relied heavily on their armour thus far, the Canadians received anti-tank training on both the obsolete (and eventually discarded) PIAT (projector, infantry, anti-tank) and the 17-pounder anti-tank gun. The infantry also trained on the Second World War–era 2-inch mortar, a platoon weapon also subsequently discarded, and on the U.S. 'Bazooka' – the 2.36-inch and 3.5-inch rocket launcher.

Special emphasis was put on musketry, particularly on aimed fire in the standing position and firing on the move – a very difficult feat with the bolt-action Lee-Enfield 303 MK IV that was to be used in Korea.[52] This 'aimed-fire' doctrine was not obsolete in itself, but it did not reflect the newer approach in the world's major ground forces that used mass fire to supplement aimed fire in battle. The standard infantry weapon of the future was probably going to be some sort of automatic rifle, and the armies of Britain, the United States, and Canada knew it. They had not, however, agreed on a standard round, let alone on a standard weapon, in all the discussions that they had had on the issue since the end of the Second World War. So the Canadians would use the Lee-Enfield as they had in two world wars and would stress aimed-fire training.

The infantry concentrated on section training, especially fire and movement. All the men of the brigade were 'indoctrinated' as to the purpose of the Special Force, the principles of the UN, and the 'meaning of Communism and its objectives.'[53] The army wanted the men to receive battle inoculation through live-fire exercises during battle drill,[54] but army headquarters refused to relax peacetime normal safety regulations.[55]

Even before serious training began, Foulkes decided that the brigade would use a mix of Canadian, British, and U.S. kit.[56] The decision on the precise mix came in February 1951, only after months of investigating what was available, from whom, and what would be suitable for the brigade. Once again the need to raise the brigade quickly, and virtually from scratch, was the prime consideration. A large number of volunteers were Second World War veterans and used to British equipment and doctrine; using British weapons wherever possible would help cut training time and allow the army to dig into its still-ample stocks of surplus kit.

Even if sufficient American weapons had been available for the Special Force, a complete conversion at that late date would have thrown the entire enterprise of raising a ground force for Korea into chaos. One army study completed in March 1951 pointed out that although Canadian infantry battalions as then organized could be rearmed from top to bottom with U.S. equipment, 'the organization of such an infantry battalion would be very different in detail from both the present Canadian Army and the USA Army infantry battalion.'[57] One other key factor was the ongoing discussion with the British, Australians, and New Zealanders about the ultimate formation of a Commonwealth division to group their field formations together. If such a division were organized, it could be easier to maintain a special Commonwealth line of supply to keep ammunition, replacements, and spare parts flowing to the fighting formations.

The most important reason by far for using British-pattern kit was that not much else was available. For example, the brigade knew from reports from the front that good radio communications between companies, battalions, and brigade HQ were going to be even more crucial than usual, because North Korean infiltration aimed at cutting platoons off from companies and companies from battalions in the rough, hilly terrain. The Canadian army wanted U.S.-built radios, and the U.S. army planned to give the Canadian request 'first priority,'[58] but for the balance of 1950 and well into 1951 Canada's soldiers would have to rely on the by-then venerable 19 set radio of Second World War vintage. The 19 set headset could be worn only with the British-pattern, First World War–era 'tin hat' helmet. It gave its wearer virtually no protection for the neck and ears, but the much better standard-issue U.S. army helmet was not feasible for the Special Force because of the need to use the 19 set radios.[59] In Korea, the Canadians almost never wore their 'tin hat'–style helmets.

Much of the British-pattern kit was either outmoded or useless for the Korean hills. That included the PIAT, the 17-pounder anti-tank gun, and the 2-inch and 3-inch mortars. The brigade adopted the U.S. 60 mm and 81 mm mortar and the 3.5-inch 'Bazooka' rocket launcher. The 17-pounders were hauled to Korea, where most were discarded and replaced with U.S. 75 mm recoilless rifles, though a small number were used. By the time the Canadians got to Korea, they faced no Communist tanks; they used the bazookas, the 17-pounders, and the recoilless rifles for bunker-busting. The .303 Vickers MMG, an excellent weapon, was kept, as was the .303 Lee-Enfield rifle and the 9 mm Sten gun. The Browning .50-calibre was the preferred heavy machine-gun (it still is!). U.S. trucks, jeeps, and other vehicles were selected; the Second World War–era universal carrier was discarded as totally unsuitable. Canadian clothing was chosen, even though the basic wool battledress and greatcoat were unsuitable for the climate.[60]

The choice of what to use and where to use it affected organization, doctrine, training, and eventually performance in the field. It took more men to operate the U.S. mortars. Taking Canadian clothing and other equipment necessitated the inclusion of more personnel from the Royal Canadian Ordnance Corps and the RCEME in a formation that was already growing daily with the addition of non-fighting personnel.[61] These difficulties were minor administrative headaches, however, compared to the problem caused by the adoption of the Lee-Enfield, which eventually proved entirely unsuitable for Korea.[62]

On 15 September 1950, the military picture in Korea changed suddenly and dramatically when the 1st U.S. Marine Division made a daring landing at Inchon, a small port town on the west coast of Korea close to Seoul. The Marines took Inchon quickly and drove on to the nearby capital, outflanking the NKPA along the Naktong. To add to the Communists' woes, the U.S.–ROK forces launched a major offensive across the Naktong the day after the Inchon landing. The NKPA front deteriorated. On 27 September Seoul was recaptured after vicious street fighting; not long afterward ROK forces drove across the 38th parallel in pursuit of the fleeing Communists. The bulk of MacArthur's UN army soon followed. By mid-October 1950 it began to seem that the war in Korea was just about over.

The successful UN counterattack raised the question in Ottawa of what to do with the 25th Canadian Infantry Brigade (CIB) Group. Canada had just agreed to a NATO request to send a brigade group to Europe as its contribution to NATO's new Integrated Force.[63] To add another brigade group to the Canadian army within a year or so seemed all but impossible, and certainly very expensive. Since the Special Force had been offered to the UN for 'combat' in Korea, and since combat appeared to be just about over, maybe Canada could send only a small token force to Korea and the rest of the 25th CIB Group to Europe. Ottawa had no desire – and no budget – to provide the UN with substantial numbers of occupation troops for Korea. The United States, in contrast, was anxious that a Korean occupation be a multilateral effort.[64] Ottawa had to make some decisions quickly; if the 25th CIB Group were not going to Korea, there was little chance that the United States would cut corners to supply it rapidly with modern combat equipment.[65]

For almost five weeks, Ottawa tried to find out exactly what the United States and United Nations were going to insist on as fulfilment of Canada's pledge of 7 August. In the meantime, the brigade was scattered across Canada, winter was approaching rapidly, and the contingent's uncertain fate further undermined morale. Desertions increased. Something had to be done to concentrate the brigade in one place regardless of its final destination, but where? Japan? Okinawa? Fort Lewis, near Tacoma, Washington? All three destinations were considered, but the final answer was going to be determined in large measure by where the brigade was ultimately going to go. By the end of October the Pentagon made its decision – the Canadians would send one battalion to Korea as part of an occupation and pacification force, and the rest of the brigade could go wherever Ottawa wanted to send it.[66]

Claxton and Foulkes chose the sprawling Fort Lewis because of its good transportation connections, the opportunity it afforded for training in winter, and because a U.S. division bound for Korea had just recently left the post.[67] The concentration at Fort Lewis was not without its problems; a train wreck at Canoe River, British Columbia, on 21 November 1950 took the lives of seventeen soldiers of 2RCHA.

Foulkes sought Rockingham's advice on which of the three infantry battalions should go to Korea, and Rocky selected 2PPCLI. As he later recalled: 'Their training was as well advanced as any other unit in the Brigade and ... they were closest to the West Coast.'[68] Like the Canadians who had sailed out for Hong Kong at almost the same time of year, some nine years earlier, 2PPCLI was not nearly ready for combat when it left the west coast. But then the war in Korea was over, everyone agreed, and the bulk of the U.S. troops would be home by Christmas. Jim Stone's main difficulty was going to be maintaining morale, good order, and discipline while the men were doing mind-numbing occupation duty in a country that smelled like a cesspool.

By the third week in November 1950, a partially trained 2PPCLI made ready to sail from the Seattle docks for Korea, while the rest of the 25 CIB Group settled in for a long and rainy winter at Fort Lewis. No one in Ottawa took notice of reports that Chinese troops had clashed with ROK and U.S. forces in the steeply wooded, snow-covered hills near the frozen Yalu River. If five-star General of the Army and Commander of the UN Command in Korea Douglas MacArthur was not taking much notice of those reports, why should the Canadian army?

THREE

Preparing for Battle

Pusan Harbor, Republic of Korea, 18 December 1950. Most of the 917 men of Lt.-Col. Jim Stone's 2PPCLI crowded the deck of the U.S. troopship *Pvt. Joe Martinez* as it nosed slowly towards Pier 2. It was mid-afternoon; the strange sights, sounds, and smells of this busy port enthralled the new arrivals from Canada. Located near the delta of the Naktong River, Pusan was Korea's second largest city and its most important deep-sea port. The harbour was like an open bowl surrounded by steep hills, with the island of Mok-to almost like a bottle-stopper in the entrance. The docks, wharfs, and jetties could handle as many as thirty ocean-going ships at a time, offloading up to 40,000 tons a day.

On this day, it was a port at war. Tramp steamers and dark-grey U.S. navy cargo ships – most, like the *Martinez*, Second World War Liberty ships – were being unloaded by Korean labourers. Small Korean navy-patrol boats and a minesweeper were moored near the harbour's entrance. Dark green army trucks, jeeps, and half-tracks were being driven aboard olive-drab landing craft. Men in uniform filed down gangways; blanket-wrapped casualties were carried up gangways. Wooden cargo pads loaded with coffins were winched carefully into holds. Dockside cranes lifted cargoes of food supplies, cement, gasoline in jerrycans, crates of ammunition and small arms, even the occasional howitzer or tank, out of holds or off decks and deposited them on the docks. Seagulls cried as they swooped over the filthy water of the harbour, searching for food. Small craft buzzed back and forth as harbour tugs nudged empty cargo ships, riding high in the water, towards the harbour mouth.

The *Martinez*, with its Canadian and U.S. soldiers, was seventeen days out of Seattle. It had been a long voyage across the central Pacific. The 7,500-ton converted Liberty ship had been built to carry cargo, not soldiers, but for most of the voyage it was home to almost 1,500 troops, as well as its own crew. The below-decks bunk space had been hastily slapped together. The vessel was badly over-crowded. The cooking and eating facilities were inadequate. So was food storage. Fresh food and clean water were at a premium almost as soon as the *Martinez* left the west coast. Much of the crossing had been rough, and seasickness had been rampant. Below decks, it was either cold and damp or hot and steamy, and the vessel had smelled constantly of vomit, sweat, rotten food, and backed-up heads. The ship had pitched and rolled almost without pause.[1]

The *Martinez* had put into Yokohama and Kobe in Japan to off-load and take on U.S. troops and replenish supplies. The stops had been all too brief.[2] Some of the Canadians had managed to slip away to Japanese whore-houses and bars. There had been a few minor dust-ups with U.S. MPs or Commonwealth Red Caps, and a few AWLs, but Stone kept his men for the most part together and in relative good order with strong discipline and route marches around Kobe. When the time came to reboard the *Martinez* for Korea, almost everyone was there, sober, and ready for the short trip across the Tsushima Strait. Everyone hoped for quick relief as they neared the pier at Pusan; they crowded the rails and stood on the superstructure to get a look at this strange new world. At first glance, it did not seem auspicious, and almost half a century later Korea veterans would remember the 'shock,' the 'backwardness,' the sheer smell of the place.[3]

Although Pusan was not unlike all large ports, it and its surroundings were like nothing that the men had ever seen. The squalidness was everywhere. The hillsides were covered in broken-down squatters' shacks made mostly of corrugated iron. The warehouses and dockside buildings were in virtual ruin. The narrow streets were crowded and filled with garbage and rubble. Old men with long white beards, filthy children in rags, and women in thick padded clothing walked alongside military vehicles driving slowly through the crowds. The civilian cars and trucks were broken-down antiques. The harbour reeked of raw sewage, and the air stank of the human excrement used to fertilize the rice paddies. The dockside brothels and bars were doing a roaring business. More than one Canadian licked his chops in anticipation of a few days' leave before getting down to the business of training for war.

The men waited aboard the *Martinez* for four hours as their supplies were off-loaded by cranes and a long line of stevedores. The mayor of Pusan arrived with a group of ragged schoolgirls waving home-made Union Jacks; he offered his formal greetings to Stone. A small band cobbled together from the ROK army and navy played mostly unrecognizable music, but a U.S. army band played 'If I Knew You Were Coming I'd Have Baked a Cake.' After four hours, the 'Patricias' left the ship, formed up on the dock, and were then trucked to their new quarters on the island of Mok-to, in Pusan Harbor. The west end of the island was connected to downtown Pusan by a short bridge. There the 25th Brigade's advanced party, which had arrived several weeks earlier, had secured U.S. army tenting and erected it on a school playground at the base of a steep, 394 m hill.[4]

Stone had seen a lifetime of destitution and war damage in Italy in the Second World War, yet even he was stunned by the primitive state of Korean society and its people. He wrote Rockingham:

> Korea is a land of filth and poverty. Social amenities of a desirable type are lacking and nothing but hard work will alleviate the boredom that will soon set in. Lack of buildings will preclude the showing of movies, particularly in the winter. Beer is in fair supply, but the alcoholics in the battalion are already drinking the very poor liquor brewed in local bathtubs. Diseases, except venereal ones probably will not be a problem during the winter, but as all fertilizing of fields is done with human excreta there is no doubt that there will be a health problem in the spring and summer.[5]

Stone need not have worried much about how bored his troops were going to be in Korea, because the military situation had changed dramatically for the UN since 2PPCLI had embarked from Seattle almost three weeks earlier. The Patricias were going to be very busy, very soon.

Mao Zedong made the final decision to order Chinese troops into Korea on or about 5 October 1950. As early as the third week of September his government had threatened to intervene in the war to protect North Korea. On 3 October China's foreign minister, Chou En-lai, told the Indian ambassador to Beijing, K.M. Panikkar, in no uncertain terms that China would enter the war if U.S. troops crossed the 38th parallel.[6] But despite all this bluster, Mao was still somewhat hesitant; the Chinese civil war had ended only a year earlier, and the country was in no condition to fight a protracted war with the United States. Eventually Stalin convinced Mao that 'five or six divisions' of Chinese 'volunteers' at the 38th parallel would shield Kim-il Sung's regime long enough to allow the NKPA to regroup. Mao relented and initially agreed to send nine divisions.[7]

MacArthur betrayed no worry about Chinese intervention as ROK troops led the U.S. Eight Army across the 38th parallel on 30 September. The United States, at his urging, now seemed to shift its objective from repelling the invasion and restoring the Rhee regime to the military reunification of the Korean peninsula.[8] When the Chinese warned the Indian government that pursuit of that objective would bring in China, MacArthur concluded that they were bluffing. In violation of all that is holy in the laws of war, he split his forces in two. The bulk of his troops, under command of Eighth Army headquarters, drove northwestward towards Sinuiju, a key rail and road junction on the Chinese–Korean border, near where the Yalu empties into the Yellow Sea. X Corps, consisting of the 1st U.S. Marine Division, ROK troops, and other UN troops under MacArthur's direct command, headed northeast towards the Korean–Soviet border.

Mao's 'volunteers' began to infiltrate across the Yalu River in mid-October. By end of that month Mao's nine divisions had become some 180,000 troops in six field armies under the command of Gen. Peng Teh-huai. The bulk of these forces concentrated in front of the advancing U.S. Eighth Army in western North Korea.[9] They carried their supplies with them. They lived on a meagre ration of rice, millet, or ground peas. They packed their own spare ammunition. They had mortars, machine-guns, and some pack howitzers, but no larger crew-served weapons. They were armed with Russian, Japanese, American, and British rifles, pistols, grenades, and submachine-guns. They had very few radios. They moved on foot under cover of darkness. They stopped at dawn and hid themselves in the heavily treed slopes of the North Korean hills, using caves, railway tunnels, and abandoned farmhouses as cover. They began moving again at nightfall. They stayed far from the roads, invisible to the probing reconnaissance planes that regularly flew over them. If they did need to move by day, they started forest fires and advanced under the smoke. They were a huge ghost army flowing over the terrain – quiet, purposeful, relentless. They were intent on getting very close to the unwary enemy before striking.

It is not possible to hide completely a moving army of almost 200,000 men. The North Korean farmers knew that the soldiers were there. Disturbing rumours began to circulate among the UN front-line troops. UN commanders began to feel uneasy about their exposed flanks. The forests and the hills were too quiet. Why were those mysterious fires burning to the north? Were the North Koreans regrouping? Was it possible that Chinese or even Soviet troops were out there, waiting?

The answer came abruptly on 25 October, when the 4th Field Army of the Chinese Communist Forces (CCF) slammed into the ROK II Corps on the right flank of the U.S. Eighth Army. An entire ROK regiment was wiped out. Then the 8th Cavalry Regiment of the 1st U.S. Cavalry Division was hit near Unsan. It withdrew under heavy fire. The Chinese picked their spots carefully, hitting one regiment or one division hard, leaving the next alone. They used the same tactics on the eastern front on 2 November when they attacked X Corps, assaulting ROK troops and the 7th Marine battalion. Then, just four days later, they suddenly broke contact and melted back into the hills and forests whence they had come.[10]

Both sides learned lessons from these brief but savage encounters. The Chinese discovered the Americans' heavy reliance on roads, on tanks and artillery, and on tactical air support. U.S. attacks invariably used a combination of arms to prepare the ground for the infantry. U.S. infantrymen, when attacked, invariably withdrew to safe harbour to gain the cover of armour and crew-served weapons. The Chinese also found out that American units did not fight well at night unless they were in well-organized and strongly defended positions, that American automatic weapons could put out tremendous rates of fire, and that the beaten zone usually extended far forward of U.S. positions.[11]

For their part the Americans and other UN troops began to gain some familiarity with Chinese tactics, which had been tried and proven in the war against Japan and in the Chinese civil war. The Chinese infantry usually attacked at night, using the cover of darkness to neutralize the UN's superiority in crew-served weapons. In the advance, they used terrain very effectively, crawling along stream beds, moving through draws and ravines or through thick trees. They crept as close as they could to the UN positions on their rubber-soled sneakers, in a 'V,' with the open mouth of the V towards the defenders. The formation allowed the Chinese to outflank the enemy position on both sides before closing the V. The encircling attack began with the blowing of whistles and bugles, which gave the signal for the Chinese to rush from the dark throwing grenades and firing their Soviet-design 'burp' (submachine)-guns. When hit by defensive fire, the Chinese did not withdraw but instead went to ground to await a lull in the firing and resume the advance. Their object was to overwhelm the enemy at a given place by sheer weight of numbers. The Chinese 'human wave,' so often written about in the press of the day, was mythical. Like all sensible armies, the Chinese always tried to organize their attacks so as to outnumber the enemy at the point of attack. In fact, most Chinese attacks were in company strength. One U.S. marine officer defined the essence of their small-unit tactics as 'assembly on the objective.'[12]

MacArthur's two field commanders, Lt.-Gen. Walton H. Walker, commanding the Eighth Army, and Maj.-Gen. Edmond Almond, commanding X Corps, were momentarily stunned by the clashes with the Chinese troops. Walker had been having significant supply problems, and, given his new worries about what was in front of him, he brought a halt to his pursuit of the NKPA. MacArthur too seemed taken aback, his perpetual optimism fading quickly in early November as he demanded permission from the U.S. Joint Chiefs of Staff to bomb the bridges over the Yalu River. By mid-November, however, he was feeling positive once again. Although he ordered increased aerial reconnaissance in the wide gap between the Eighth Army and X Corps, he concluded that the Chinese threat was more apparent than real and was but a piecemeal intervention with limited goals.[13]

The ranking Canadian officer in the theatre was Brig. F.J. Fleury, commander, Canadian Military Mission, Far East. Based at Tokyo, he was responsible for contact with the Commonwealth Occupation Forces in Japan and with the UN Command, particularly Walker's Eighth Army, to which the Canadian contingent would be attached. He was also charged with overseeing the preparations and arrangements being made by the 25th Brigade's Advanced Water Party in anticipation of the arrival of Stone's battalion.

Fleury visited Pusan late in November to check on those arrangements and to find out about the situation at the fighting front. He filed his report to Ottawa late on 22 November. Although he went nowhere near the front, he fully endorsed MacArthur's view that the Chinese had only some 60,000 troops in Korea, half of them serving with NKPA units, and that they did not pose a serious threat to the UN position on the peninsula: 'It is my personal opinion that the Chinese intervention in NORTH KOREA had limited objectives and will not develop further. I consider the present position of enemy forces in NORTH KOREA untenable and I see no reason why the fighting should last more than a few weeks longer.'[14]

The apparent disappearance of the Chinese forces had convinced MacArthur that no significant obstacle lay in the path to a military victory, and he ordered his field commanders to resume the UN offensive on 24 November. They did. At first, they encountered little opposition. The Eighth Army pushed ahead 19 km through frozen mountainous terrain in the first thirty-six hours. Then, after dark on 25 November, the entire XIII Chinese Army Group swooped down from the snow-covered hills and the dark coniferous forests of northern North Korea and slammed into the right flank of the Eighth Army, where morale was already low. The extreme cold of the North Korean mountains in winter, shortages of warm clothing, hot food, and much else, and weeks of rumours of a possible Chinese attack had eroded the confidence of the troops. Now, the Eighth Army virtually broke. Under the Chinese hammer blows, tens of thousands of U.S. and ROK troops streamed south in panicked flight, losing contact with their pursuers.[15] The troops and the press called it 'bug out fever.'

To the east, much of X Corps was strung out along a road leading north on the western side of the Chosan ('Chosin' in Japanese) Reservoir. Maj.-Gen. Oliver P. Smith, commanding the 1st Marine Division in the lead of X Corps, had proceeded up the road with caution, establishing supply bases as he went. His corps commander had grown impatient with the slow progress. But Smith was proven right on 27 November, when his troops were suddenly attacked by the IX Chinese Army Group. Unlike the Eighth Army troops in the west, the marines were made of stern stuff. Most of them were older, and were better-trained and -equipped, and their numbers included many more battle veterans from the Pacific war in the non-commissioned ranks to stiffen their resolve. There was no flight, just a legendary fighting retreat from 'frozen Chosin.'[16] Under constant attack by numerically superior Chinese forces, the marines fought their way south, to Yudam-ni, through the Toktong Pass, through Hagaru and Pusong-ni and Koto-ri, to the port of Hungnam. From 15 to 21 December, the marines, the ROK I Corps, and the U.S. army 7th and 3rd infantry divisions hurried out of Hungnam. The Chinese were hot on their heels. The evacuation of the port was completed on 24 December; then warehouses and docks loaded with supplies were destroyed as the last UN ships departed. The UN retreat slowed as the bulk of the Eighth Army reached the Han River. There, Walker decided, the UN forces would regroup and make their stand. Every available soldier, every gun and tank and bazooka, would be needed to defend the river line and hold the South Korean capital. That effort would, of course, include Stone's half-trained battalion.[17]

When the Patricias had left Seattle, the Directorate of Military Training in Ottawa had estimated that the battalion would need at least until mid-March 1951 to get ready for action. Stone had tried to organize physical training (PT) aboard the *Martinez*, but conditions had made that all but impossible. The long voyage had taken its toll on the men's physical conditioning and had allowed no further operational training at all. The battalion was, if anything, probably in worse shape when it arrived in Pusan than it had been when it left Fort Lewis.

There was much to do. The men had to be brought up to an acceptable standard of physical fitness. They had to absorb new American weaponry. They had to study the hard lessons learned by those UN troops who had come to Korea earlier and who had been blooded. That meant that they had to learn the art of both defence and attack in Korean terrain, in the Korean winter, against an enemy much different from the one that the battalion's veterans had faced in the European war. Stone estimated that it would take at least eight weeks of intensive training before the Patricias would be ready for operations.[18]

That was not what Walker had in mind. As early as 3 December, Eighth Army HQ told the staff of the PPCLI advance party in Pusan that 2PPCLI could not stay long in the port area because Eighth Army HQ would be moving there. In any case, the Canadians would probably be moved as close to the front as possible while completing their preparations. On 17 December, Fleury was officially told that Stone's battalion would be given three days in Pusan to unpack its equipment and get organized and would then be trucked to Suwon, just 32 km south of Seoul. The Canadians would form part of Walker's reserve until they were ready to join the 29th British Infantry Brigade Group on operations.

Once more the spectre of Hong Kong raised its head. Was an undertrained and poorly equipped contingent of Canadian troops to be led to the slaughter in Asia once again?[19] Stone's command instructions had been framed in such a way as to avoid such a disaster, if at all possible: 'In the event that operations are in progress when you arrive in Korea you are not to engage in such operations except in self-defence until you have completed the training of your command and are satisfied that your unit is fit for operations.'[20] This dispensation gave Stone the last word on deciding when his battalion was ready. A copy of these instructions had been sent to Walker's command weeks earlier. Had no one read them?

On 8 December the Canadian cabinet revisited the issue of 2PPCLI's disposition in the light of developments at the front since the men had left Seattle. It decided not to make too much of a nuisance of itself and that 'no further communication [would] be made to the U.S. authorities concerning the disposition of Canadian troops bound for Korea.'[21] Maj.-Gen. H.A. Sparling, vice-chief of the General Staff, relayed the essence of that discussion to the Far East, telling Fleury: 'The Cabinet decided ... it would be improper for the Canadian Government to make further representations regarding areas of training and deployment in Korea.'[22] It was going to be up to Stone to decide what to do.

There is some mystery about what happened next. The official history of the Canadian army in Korea relates how Stone flew to Seoul to confront Walker with his instructions after failing to convince Walker's staff in Pusan to cancel the order to send 2PPCLI to Suwon. During the meeting in Seoul, Stone is supposed to have produced his instructions, forcing Walker to back down.[23] Stone wrote much the same version of the event in 1992.[24]

That was not, however, what he told Ottawa in December 1950. In that report he described meeting one of Walker's officers to explain the condition of his troops and then flying to Seoul the next day:

The morning of 21 Dec, I was granted an interview by Lt-Gen. Walker ... and explained in detail the state of training of the battalion. He kindly stated that although he was disappointed that we were not ready for immediate commitment, he would not ask us to go into action until our training was completed. It was apparent that the result of my interview with Lt-Col Lancaster had been communicated to General Walker, for his attitude was quite different to the one I had been advised to expect. General Walker was very gracious and discussed points of training for the rest of the interview.[25]

Two days later, Walker was killed in a traffic accident, and his place was taken by Lt.-Gen. Matthew Ridgway, paratrooper veteran of the Second World War.

The accommodations for 2PPCLI in Pusan harbor were 'primitive and limited.' Now that the move to Suwon had been cancelled, a better place was needed for dwellings and for training. The latter was especially important. Stone's first objective was to get the men toughened up, and he aimed to do that with hill-climbing and route marches around the Pusan area.[26] That proved quite a chore: 'Bad legs, wheezy lungs and faint and weak hearts were exposed,' Stone later wrote, 'and many sorry specimens of manhood were returned to Canada.'[27]

While the physical training was stepped up and Stone's second-in-command, Major H.D.P. Tighe, scouted out a more permanent location for the battalion, the men began to draw their new U.S. equipment.[28] The once-standard 2- and 3-inch mortars gave way to 60 mm and 81 mm mortars. The U.S. mortars had much greater range than the British-pattern ones that they replaced, were more accurate, and were capable of a much greater rate of fire. The 81 mm was considerably heavier than the 3-inch mortars that it replaced, however, and the six allotted to 2PPCLI were mounted on M3A1 half-tracks, a U.S. piece of kit also new to the Canadians. The battalion received twelve half-tracks, each armed with a .30 Browning medium machine-gun and a .50 Browning heavy machine gun. The 60 mm mortar was far superior to the 2-inch mortar in range but had a number of drawbacks. Its flare-illumination ammunition was unreliable and usually in short supply, so the Canadians kept at least one 2-inch mortar for each rifle company. The Canadians also initially found it more difficult to sight. More serious for the Canadian rifle companies, it took more men to carry and fire than the 2-inch, thus cutting down on the number of active riflemen.[29] Most company commanders eventually decided to 'man-pack' only one of the three assigned to each company when moving and carry the two others in half-tracks.[30]

The Canadians discarded their greatcoats for winter parkas, their universal carriers for jeeps,[31] and some of their 17-pounder anti-tank guns for 3.5-inch 'bazooka' rocket launchers. In action the bazooka was most often used for bunker-busting. The Canadians also received 75 mm recoilless rifles, which had proven useful to the Americans when fighting from the roads but were too heavy to be easily hauled up the Korean hillsides. The most important new piece of kit taken into the 2PPCLI inventory was the U.S.-pattern SCR 300 radio set. It had much better range and a far greater operating capability in mountainous country ·than the Second World War–era radios still in use by the army in Canada. The battalion's twenty SCR 300s were used to link the rifle companies to each other, to battalion tactical HQ, and to the 81 mm mortar platoon in the support company. British-pattern No. 88 radio sets were supplied to company and platoon commanders to form the 'company net' linking company HQs with its platoons.[32]

On 27 December 1950, the Patricias left Pusan for Miryang, a village on the Miryang River about 50 km north of Pusan and about half-way between Pusan and Taegu. Intensive training began, with commanders having one eye on the calendar, the other on the training syllabi. Stone knew that even though Walker had given him eight weeks to whip the Patricias into shape, that situation could change anytime if the UN's position worsened drastically at the front. He, Walker, and the Canadian cabinet knew well that although the Patricias needed lots of toughening and learning, they were not any worse prepared for combat than many of the UN units already in-theatre.[33]

Four days after the Patricias arrived at Miryang, the Chinese launched their Third Phase offensive. This time, with X Corps having completed its withdrawal through Hungnam on Christmas Eve, the full weight of the Chinese fell on the Eighth Army north of Seoul and along the Han. The Chinese pushed the UN forces relentlessly back. On 4 January, Seoul was abandoned; the next day, Inchon. But even though there was some initial panic among U.S. and ROK troops streaming back through Seoul, there was no mass 'bug out' as there had been at the end of November. Ridgway was everywhere, with his two grenades dangling from his webbing,

cajoling the troops, putting spine into his officers, teaching them
anew the fundamentals of defence, urging them to study the hard
lessons that they had already learned about how the Chinese
fought and how they could be defeated. Gradually the Chinese
attack was slowed, then stopped. By mid-month the Chinese had
suffered enormous casualties and the UN troops were holding on
to a well-organized defence position roughly 80 km south of the
38th parallel.[34]

The Chinese attack made the task of bringing 2PPCLI up to
operational status that much more urgent. One key to accomplishing that task was gathering as much information as possible on
how the enemy fought its battles and how to prepare for the enemy
in the cold and mountainous Korean terrain. Stone relied on
several sources of information. The previous November, in anticipation of 2PPCLI's arrival, Capt. J. Bowie of the Canadian
Armoured Corps and Lieut. J. Campbell of 2PPCLI had been
detached from the advance party and sent north to join the staff of
the 29th British Infantry Brigade. They were instructed to send
weekly reports to Major R.M. Bourgeois, Officer Commanding the
advance party, to help 2PPCLI prepare for operations. Bourgeois
was especially interested in tactical lessons learned in operations,
in how various pieces of equipment performed, and in specialized
training.[35] In addition to the reports from Bowie and Campbell,
Stone received 'Notes on Fighting in Korea' prepared at army HQ
in Ottawa from information gained from both U.S. and British
sources in the field. The notes covered a wide range of topics from
enemy-attack tactics to UN administrative requirements.[36]

Unfortunately, much of the information was outdated even
before it arrived at Stone's HQ. Bulletins circulated to the field in
January 1951, for example, reflected field conditions from the previous October, when the main enemy, the climate, and the tactical
situation had been very different. An especially serious omission
was lack of information on Chinese artillery. When the Chinese
had attacked UN forces near the Yalu in late October, they had not
had any appreciable artillery support, and in late November things
were little different. But as the Chinese pushed the UN further
south through December, they were able to use the North Korean

rail and road net to bring up supplies, ammunition, reinforcements, and artillery. Thus even as Stone's battalion was preparing
to fight an enemy that lacked artillery,[37] the Chinese were beginning to integrate artillery into their attacks.

Still, some of the lessons that the UN forces had learned earlier
in the war against the North Koreans were valid. The terrain dictated much. The steep hills demanded excellent physical conditioning by the men and care in planning who was to take what into
battle. Infantry commanders were warned to make sure that their
men carried as little as possible and took the lightest effective
weapons on patrols. Constant patrolling was stressed because the
North Koreans always flowed around points of resistance, seeking
out flanks, and penetrating as deeply as they could into UN positions before revealing themselves by firing. It took vigilant patrolling to defend against these constant outflanking efforts. The UN
forces also had to keep careful track of where their own men were
at all times, lest they mistake North Korean infiltrators for 'friend-
lies' and waste valuable reaction time in trying to identify people.
In Europe, Canadians had faced an enemy that used the tried and
true tactic of fixing the opponent with the fire of section light
machine-guns while outflanking the opponent with its riflemen.
That was also the basic section or platoon attack plan in the Canadian, British, and American armies. The North Koreans and the
Chinese did not play by these rules.[38]

There was not enough time for the Canadians to accomplish
everything that needed to be done because the battalion had been
raised in great haste and sent to Korea unprepared. As the war
diarist put it: 'Lack of training in Canada has meant too much
time on basic training in Korea and too little on movement and
fieldcraft.'[39] But what choice was there when some of the men
had never fired their rifles and others could not load their Sten
submachine-guns properly?[40] 'D' Company was still conducting
Tests of Elementary Training!

It was not until the second week in January that the platoons
began to practise advance-to-contact and setting up defensive positions in mountain terrain. Stone considered the latter especially
crucial, given the circumstances at the front. In discussions with

the commander of the 29th British Infantry Brigade, he had
learned that 'resolute men, dug in, in proper islands of defence
can kill at will, the hordes that rush the positions ... There can be
no administrative tail stretching back for miles ... Everything must
be tied up in Battalion defensive localities ... Infiltration between
localities must be expected, but with all areas defended such infiltration is not serious ... Such should be a defenders paradise, provided troops are all trained marksmen and realize that if they run,
they will certainly die.'[41] In the field this strategy involved setting
up heavily wired company defensive localities on dominating terrain features such that there would be interlocking fields of fire
and artillery sited to deliver rapid fire when necessary.[42]

One of the most valuable lessons to learn, but difficult to do in
the steep hills of Korea, was the basic advance-to-contact. In the first
six months of the war the American and ROK troops had been
extremely reluctant to get out of their trucks and jeeps and move up
to the ridge lines. That was partly because they had not been strong
enough to endure the climb in the heat of the Korean summer. It
was also because they relied too greatly on road-bound armour. The
NKPA and the Chinese had been left to the high country and had
used the height advantage with devastating effect. Stone was well
aware of the necessity of troops' keeping off the roads and advancing along the ridges. The trick was to teach the men how to advance
near the tops of the ridges without exposing themselves above the
skyline. This meant using rocks, scrub, and trees as cover, with sections leapfrogging each other as they pushed ahead, always ready to
bring the Brens forward as a firebase if they ran into enemy troops.

Training was well under way by 13 January when a sudden guerrilla attack on the nearby training camp of the 16th Field Regiment, Royal New Zealand Artillery, disrupted the routine.

The guerrillas killed two New Zealand gunners and wounded
two others. A second attack on a 2PPCLI platoon three days later
pushed Stone to action. With the permission of the UN Command,
he sent 'B' Company after the elusive enemy. It was aided by a
mortar platoon and several hundred Korean police who acted as
guides and stretcher-bearers. 'C' Company was also detailed to
help if necessary.[43]

Communist guerrillas had been infiltrating into South Korea since before the June invasion; retreating North Korean troops augmented their numbers and added to their supplies of arms and ammunition. The guerrillas formed bands of various sizes in the mountains of South Korea and descended from the hills to raid supply dumps, disrupt road traffic, and kill as many unwary UN troops as possible. In late 1950 the UN Command and ROK army estimated that there were some 8,000 operating in the far south. At one point in the spring of 1951 there were in excess of two ROK divisions hunting them down. By the end of the war some 19,000 guerrillas had been killed or captured.[44]

'B' Company headed out of the training area late on the morning of the 16th. Guided by the Korean police, and with the aid of a Piper Cub from X Corps Artillery, it proceeded to a range of craggy hills where the guerrillas had last been seen. Then the men began to climb. They took little with them except what was essential to feed themselves and to keep warm. They came on deserted villages and searched them for guerrilla hide-outs, ammunition, spare weapons, and food supplies. They found nothing. They climbed higher in the cold Korean sun. They searched caves and crags and peaks; they still found nothing. Night fell. They set up a defensive position on a hilltop, then spotted a ragged line of men moving against a ridge less than a kilometre away. Amid much shouting and pointing, they opened fire. The guerrillas scattered, some wounded. It was too dark for pursuit.

The Patricias set out again at first light. The guerrillas were gone, but they had left behind food and weapons and at least one blood trail. The Patricias tracked them out of the high country and called for help. Two platoons from 'C' Company joined in the search. They flushed small groups of guerrillas from fields and caves in the hillsides and opened fire. Most of the guerrillas escaped, but some did not; at least two were killed and several more wounded. All that day and for two more, the hunt continued. It was cold but sunny, and the clear mountain air, the hill-climbing, and even living on basic rations seemed to pep up the soldiers and pick up their morale. The only real problems that the Patricias had in their four days of guerrilla-hunting were their worn-out leather-soled boots and the inexperience of the radio operators. At the end of the expedition, 'B' Company's commander, Major C.V. Lilley, wrote: 'I consider hunting guerrillas the best company exercise for companies in the battalion as it brings out all the tactical and administrative lessons that have to be learned ... If this area is left alone for 3 or 4 days and then a company is put in I feel certain that more enemy can be killed.'[45]

During this period Stone sent sixty men home from Miryang as 'non-battle' casualties. The difficult training and the great physical exertion needed to hump the hills while carrying extra ammunition, hefting weapons such as the Bren, or hauling field rations bore heavily on the weak and the incompetent. There were still too many of those, despite the large number that Stone had already sent home from Japan and Pusan. He called them 'non-battle' casualties, but Fleury knew that many of them were simply soldiers whom Stone thought of as unfit for combat. He thought that Stone was being overly cautious in judging his men and sending too many back. In Ottawa, army HQ was alarmed at the very high wastage rate; Adjutant-General Macklin wanted Stone (and Rockingham at Fort Lewis) to be more judicious in deciding who might be salvaged and who was incorrigible.

It is difficult to see how Stone was supposed to salvage men with flat feet, chronic bronchitis, atrophy of the leg muscles and spine, traumatic arthritis of the spine, hernia, and hypertension.[46] A thorough medical examination of all recruits in Canada in August and September would have weeded out many of these men and saved enormous costs in wasted training time. Units cannot train properly or in good time when men are constantly leaving because of physical difficulties and being replaced by new arrivals.

In the last two weeks of January 1951 Stone stepped up the training. Companies practised advance-to-contact against 'enemy' troops from other companies. They set up defensive positions and tested them. They practised radio procedure and practised again. Cooperation with the field artillery and tactical air observers was added to the training regimen. Live fire exercises were conducted,

Lt.-Col. J.A. Dextraze, CO, 2 Royal Vingt-deuxième Régiment (2R22eR), 9 Nov. 1951

Brooke Claxton (second from right) meeting Gen. J.A. Van Fleet and Brig. J.M. Rockingham (second and third from left), Dec. 1951

Major E.J. Williams, 1 Princess Patricia's Canadian Light Infantry (1PPCLI)

Chairman of the U.S. Joint Chiefs of Staff, Gen. Omar Bradley, presents Brooke Claxton with Presidential Unit Citation for 2PPCLI.

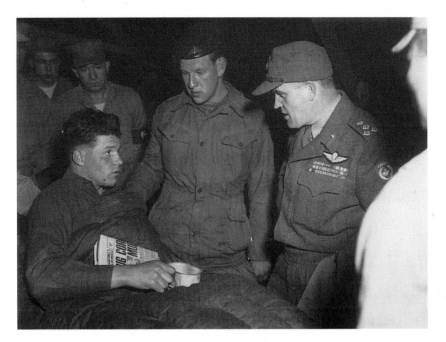

Brig. Jean Allard, with L/Cpl Paul Dugal, first Canadian prisoner of war released by the Communists at Freedom Village, Panmunjom, 12 March 1953

Members of PPCLI being instructed on U.S.-built 75 mm recoilless rifles

L/Cpl Réal Lebeau and Pte Armand Davignon, 3R22eR at 'stand-to' (on guard), June 1952, both wearing unauthorized American helmets

Member of PPCLI wearing a U.S.-pattern helmet practise-fires a bazooka anti-tank rocket.

Royal Canadian Corps of Signals (RCCS): Lieut. Paul Ranger checks Pte Jean-Guy
Lacroix's wireless set as he prepares for night patrol with soft shoes, dark clothing,
and black face make-up, 14 June 1952; Lacroix carries an unauthorized American
M2 carbine.

Canadians wearing U.S. armoured vests on patrol, 24 June 1952

From left: E.R. Duroche, I.R. Smith, and Cpl Ouellette, sniper. Duroche is holding an M2 carbine. To his right are five standard-issue Lee-Enfields.

A PPCLI soldier with two rifles – his officially issued Lee-Enfield (with bolt) and his U.S.-built M2 rapid-fire carbine.

Lieut. Robert Peacock, 3PPCLI, with his U.S. 'Tommy Gun' outside 6 Platoon HQ, Christmas 1952

Lieut. Brian Munro (left) and Pte Ron Bouregon, 2PPCLI, at horseplay, 1951, Munro with American M2 carbine over his shoulder

Ptes Bill Boshman and Art Cassidy, 2PPCLI, manning a Bren-gun position, 7–9 April 1951

Sgt Tommy Prince (second from left), one of Canada's most decorated soldiers and an Aboriginal veteran of the Second World War. To his left is Major George Flint. Virtually all the soldiers are carrying American rifles, including Flint.

Pte Ernie Howard of Cape Breton takes shelter under a poncho while serving with 'C' Company, 1 Royal Canadian Regiment (1RCR), in front lines, 30 June 1952.

Dug-out shelter built for 2PPCLI soldiers, with slanting roof to ward off rain and bazooka-bomb tube as chimney. Rain capes cover entrance for warmth and to prevent light from escaping at night, 7–9 March 1951.

Checking Chinese trenches for occupants: Pte Vernon Burke, 2PPCLI, April 1951

Observation post of 25 Canadian Infantry Brigade; left to right: Lt.-Col. E.G. Brooks, Lt.-Col. Norman Wilson-Smith, Brigs. M.P. 'Pat' Bogert and John M. Rockingham, April 1952

Three members of the 3R22eR maintaining lookout for the enemy from their front-line machine-gun position; left to right: L/Cpl Guy Raby, Pte Gérald Girard, and Lieut. Guy Robillard, 13 June 1953

Ptes Gérald Lapointe and Maurice Ethier of R22eR, positioned behind their Browning machine-gun, observe Korean Hills, June 1953.

Gunners of 2RCR firing a Vickers Medium machine-gun across a valley; left to right: Pte George Ellsworth of Cape Breton, NS, Pte Bill Climey of Hamilton, Ont., and Cpl Bill Coburn of Kingston, Ont., Dec. 1951

Lt.-Bdr D. Robertson, Sgt W. Malcom, and Gunners R. Flemming and J. Gaudet
(left to right), Royal Canadian Horse Artillery (RCHA), ready to fire 25-pounder,
26 Sept. 1951

Site of a Canadian field-artillery battery after night of heavy shelling: more than
5,100 rounds fired to protect Canadian infantry position near Hill 210, Nov. 1951

Two members of 2PPCLI control indirect mortar fire over an inter-company communications radio set.

Members of PPCLI steadying themselves after mortar firing; left to right: Ptes John Joyal, 28, and Henry Hayward, 24, of The Pas, Man., and Donald Beebe, 23, of Regina; near Miryang, Feb. 1951

Members of R22eR under fire and going to ground, during raid on Hill 166, 23 Oct. 1951

Personnel of 'B' Company, 1RCR, who survived Chinese attack on Little Gibraltar (Hill 335), 13 Oct. 1952; left to right: L/Cpl Wally Jones and Ptes Alan Markus and Doug McCallum

and massive amounts of TNT exploded to simulate the sound of heavy shells and rockets. 'Battle inoculation,' designed to get the men used to the sounds, sights, and concussion of shell fire, took place at the company and platoon levels.

On 2 February, a battalion-sized, five-day exercise designed to cover the basics of advance, attack, defence, and withdrawal began in the hills near Miryang. Dubbed 'Maple Leaf,' it was to be the battalion's final test before going into action. Stone seemed satisfied with the result. On 8 February he informed Fleury that 2PPCLI would be ready for combat in a week. On 15 February the battalion left Miryang to join IX Corps of the U.S. Eighth Army at the front, assigned to the 27th British Commonwealth Infantry Brigade.[47] Back in Canada the question of whether or not the rest of the 25th Brigade would follow it into action had still not been settled.

The Chinese attack of 25 November on the Eighth Army in northern Korea, and the near-collapse of that army, had had an immediate impact on the policy-makers in Washington and in most Western capitals, Ottawa included. The Chinese success had led to a tentative U.S. move to have China branded an aggressor at the UN and had raised fears of a general war between the UN and China.[48] In Ottawa, Claxton and Pearson warned their cabinet colleagues of the imminence of all-out war.[49] A Gallup poll released in early January 1951 showed that 53 per cent of Canadians believed them and thought that the threat of war was the nation's most serious problem, up from just 4 per cent the previous year.[50] The largest peacetime mobilization in Canadian history had begun. There would be more planes, ships, and soldiers for NATO and the defence of North America. The effort was going to be very costly. Finance Minister Douglas Abbott told the cabinet that defence expenditures could easily climb to 'some 10 per cent of the gross national product, or 12 per cent of the national income.'[51]

There followed weeks of agonizing in the cabinet and especially at DND headquarters. Claxton hoped that the UN Command might quickly recover from the Chinese offensive and that the balance of Rockingham's troops could be diverted from Korea to Europe, for NATO. The prospect of doing that waxed and waned

with UN fortunes at the front. As long as the political decision
remained unmade, however, Rockingham's troops training at Fort
Lewis had no real idea of where they were headed, or what to prepare for. That uncertainty placed additional and largely unnecessary training and equipping burdens on a brigade that had been
hastily recruited and was not physically or emotionally ready for
the rigours of the Korean War. As late as mid-November 1950 the
brigade's establishment and reinforcement structure had still not
been finalized because no one knew where it was heading.[52]

On 1 February 1951, Charles Foulkes became chairman, Chiefs
of Staff Committee, a new position created by the National
Defence Act of 1951. A little more than two weeks later, he went to
Washington to try to wriggle out of the Canadian commitment to
send a full brigade to Korea. Gen. Omar Bradley, chairman of the
U.S. Joint Chiefs of Staff, was distinctly unsympathetic. He laid
things on the line: Canada had made a promise of troops for Korea
and should fulfill that promise without further delay. Canada had
also obligated itself to send a brigade group to the NATO Integrated Force and should carry out that commitment as well.[53] That
settled the issue. On 21 February the cabinet finally approved the
dispatch of the remainder of the 25th CIB to Korea.[54] It was not
until then that Rockingham's troops knew where they were going.

Fort Lewis was and is a sprawling army base of some 90,000 acres
not far from Tacoma, Washington. It was born as Camp Lewis in
1917, when the citizens of Pierce County voted to donate $2 mil-
lion to their government to buy a package of 70,000 acres for an
army base. In 1943 the base was expanded when the Rainier Training Area was opened south of the Nisqually River. One of the busi-
est west-coast army bases throughout the Second World War, Fort
Lewis was home to the U.S. army's 2nd Infantry Division in the five
years between war's end and the outbreak of fighting in Korea.
When the Korean War began, the 2nd was the first division to leave
the continental United States for the Far East.

In the autumn of 1950 Fort Lewis was a beehive of activity as
reservists reported for duty, draftees were trained, and units
departed for Korea. Everywhere the sounds of hammers, saws, and

heavy construction equipment filled the air, as sewers and street-lights were put in, roads and sidewalks paved, and barracks, offices, gymnasiums, training fields, warehouses, and motor-pool garages built. The fort was a small city. It had its own stores, coffee shops, schools, enlisted men's and officers' clubs, military police facilities, and post office. It had a permanent population of almost 40,000. There were very few bases in Canada that could accommodate and train an entire brigade group in the autumn of 1950; Fort Lewis could accommodate and train the equivalent of an entire division.

Fort Lewis had every comfort and facility imaginable, but it was not a great place to be in the autumn and winter of 1950–1. There was rain almost all the time. It was difficult to maintain basic and acceptable levels of sanitation and cleanliness when the constant precipitation turned so much of the base into a morass of mud. The rain and the fog hampered training. The Canadian field artillery had to move some 200 km east to Yakima, which had a range large enough for live fire training. The base's facilities were overtaxed. There were shortages of food and almost everything else. The 25th Brigade was underequipped when it arrived, yet it still had to give up almost 450 vehicles that it had borrowed from the U.S. army.[55]

Since Rockingham was at first not sure where the brigade was going, training in December and January was more generic than mission-specific. For example, the armoured squadron initially received Second World War–era, U.S.-built M-10 self-propelled anti-tank guns. The M-10 was totally unsuited to Korea. For one thing, it was useless; by December the NKPA and its T-34s were history, and the Chinese never used armour in Korea. For another, it was dangerous; its open turret invited any enemy soldier with even a mediocre arm to lob in a hand grenade. Rockingham was uneasy about using the M-10s. He soon shifted the armoured squadron from anti-tank training to armour–infantry cooperation. But that too was useless, because the Korean terrain would not allow infantry and armour to advance together, while using armour in the attack forced an army to stay road-bound.[56]

The brigade began serious sub-unit training at the start of

November despite shortages of both equipment and weapons. It was Rockingham's responsibility to oversee this training, and he took that charge very seriously. It was a rare day when he did not visit some area of the fort to watch his troops train and, when he thought necessary, to give them a few pointers himself. On one occasion, for example, he watched a platoon of 2RCR execute an attack movement, then discussed the tactics used with the platoon sergeant, telling him to keep things as simple and direct as possible.[57]

By the start of February, training had advanced to the stage where each company could be tested on battle drill and battle procedure. The Canadian army had officially adopted battle drill in the Second World War as part of battle training, despite more than a little scepticism on the part of Gen. Montgomery. Battle drill combined battle inoculation with the teaching of pre-set drills designed to cover most of the eventualities that small units might encounter on the battlefield. Battle drill no doubt helped prepare soldiers for combat, but it was no substitute for basic advance-to-contact and fire and movement training, and it did not especially encourage independent thinking and decision-making by junior leaders. It tended to prepare soldiers to react to situations, rather than to initiate them.[58]

By mid-February company training gave way to battalion training. On 14 February, 2RCR successfully assaulted an 'enemy' position with two companies up and the support of 2RCHA. The assault was 'well controlled and consolidation [on the position] was made with the minimum delay.' The troops dug in and defended the position from an 'enemy' counterattack, again with the support of the artillery. These battalion exercises revealed very real differences in the state of training and preparation of each of the battalions. Rockingham was more than satisfied with 2RCR's performance on 14 February but noted 'many weaknesses' in the exercise conducted by 2R22eR three days later.[59] And 3PPCLI, which had replaced 2PPCLI at Fort Lewis so that the brigade could train as a brigade, did better on 20 February, proving itself 'battleworthy,' even though it had been formed only a month earlier.[60]

On 21 February, Foulkes informed Rockingham that the federal cabinet had finally made the decision to send the brigade to

Korea. Now mountain training began in earnest. Rockingham scouted out locations within the fort's boundaries where units 'could carry out hardening training and assault practise up steep gradients.'[61] A major exercise was laid on to pull together everything that the sub-units had learned from the beginning of December. Before that operation – Exercise Scramble – began, Rockingham learned that the brigade would leave for Korea on 17 April.

On 15 March, Rockingham signed his application for an active-force commission; eight days later he flew out of Vancouver to Japan and Korea to smooth preparations for the brigade's arrival. This was crucial, because when the brigade took the field, Rockingham was going to have several masters at the same time. Rockingham was a national contingent commander and as such would enjoy 'no limitation' in what he was allowed to communicate to army HQ in Ottawa, on 'any matter.'[62] His administrative 'tail' in Korea and Japan, however, was under the ultimate direction of Australian Lt.-Gen. Sir Horace Robertson, in Tokyo, who was commander of the British Commonwealth Occupation Forces in Japan and in charge of all Commonwealth support functions. Robertson was little more than a figurehead – a rear-area administrator – and in any case it was Fleury's job as commander, Canadian Military Mission, Far East, to report to him and to MacArthur.

Without doubt Rockingham's main role was going to be that of a field commander, and as such he would fit into the chain of command that ran from the lowest private to MacArthur himself. His immediate superiors in the field would be his divisional or corps commanders and ultimately the commander of the U.S. Eighth Army. Thus, in a tradition that had been established in South Africa and continued in the First World War and through the Second, army HQ in Ottawa was in administrative, but not operational, control of the Canadian field force.

Rockingham's visit to Tokyo was not especially auspicious. He was not awed by MacArthur, who lived like an emperor, he later remembered. In their brief meeting, the American talked about the politics of the war in a manner that Rocky thought highly inappropriate for a soldier. Rockingham did not get on well with Robertson, but that hardly mattered, given the latter's administrative status.[63] The real question was how he would relate to the other Commonwealth field commanders, to the corps commander, and – as a national commander – to Ridgway himself.

Rocky then went on to Korea. He found 'the wartime atmosphere together with ruined villages and other evidence of devastation of war ... very strange after five years back in untouched Canada.' He went first to see 2PPCLI at the front. When he arrived at the battalion positions, Stone was not there, temporarily evacuated to hospital because of smallpox. On a visit to one company's defended locality, Rockingham was impressed by the ruggedness of the mountain terrain: 'The approach to the company was through fairly thick cover of low trees and brush, then up a hill that was almost vertical. It was a far cry from the country I had fought over in Europe.'[64] Before leaving Korea, Rockingham had a brief visit with Ridgway at his headquarters at Taegu. He found the American general 'most welcoming and friendly' and 'full of praise for 2PPCLI.'[65]

Rockingham returned to Fort Lewis on 3 April. Preparations for the move to Korea were well in hand, and he spent much of his time during the next two weeks on ceremonial occasions. The governor general of Canada, Field Marshal Viscount Alexander of Tunis, visited, followed by Minister of National Defence Brooke Claxton on 14 and 15 April. On 13 April, Rockingham received his final command instructions. He was reminded that as a national contingent commander he had a special responsibility to maintain the Canadian fighting forces in theatre as a single entity: 'While the grouping of forces is a matter for the operational command to decide, it is anticipated that in the normal course of operations or other activities of the United Nations Forces, your tasks and undertakings will be so allotted or arranged, having regard to the size of the Canadian Force, that its Canadian entity will readily be preserved.'[66] On 19 April, the first contingent of the brigade sailed from Seattle aboard the *Marine Adder*. The rest of the brigade followed in two more ships on the 20th and 21st; they arrived together in Pusan on 4 May.

FOUR

Kap'yong

The situation at the front was in a renewed state of flux when the Patricias (2PPCLI) began preparations to join 27 British Commonwealth Infantry Brigade (27 BCIB) in mid-February 1951. On 11 February the Chinese launched their Fourth Phase Offensive on the central front. They intended to split the U.S. Eighth Army away from X Corps, but Ridgway's reinvigorated troops were ready for them. At Chipyong-ni, south of the 38th parallel, a torrent of well-organized defensive firepower and determined U.S. infantry held fast in their positions, killed thousands of attackers, and stopped the Chinese cold. The offensive collapsed; six days later, on 21 February, Ridgway struck back with a massive two-corps attack dubbed Operation Killer. It aimed to drive the Reds back over the Han River and recover the South Korean capital.[1]

Ridgway's approach to the war was simple – to kill as many Chinese and North Korean troops as possible within a short period. It was attrition warfare taking full advantage of the UN Command's dominance in airpower and heavy artillery. That was the only way, Ridgway reasoned, to negate Communist numerical superiority and test the bottom of the supposedly bottomless well of Chinese troops. The U.S. soldiers who did the killing called the new tactic 'the meatgrinder': 'You began with the long-range artillery from ten miles away enveloping the hills in tall columns of dust flung up by tons of high explosive, followed by the quicker shell-bursts from the more accurate lighter guns, at a shorter range. You bombarded the positions further with tank guns, while swooping aircraft plastered them with napalm and rockets.'[2]

That was the reality of the war that 2PPCLI was about to join, but it had little attraction for Minister of National Defence Brooke Claxton, who saw it all from the far-away comfort and safety of Ottawa. Claxton especially objected to the way 'some operations in Korea have been handled or reported,' including the use of heavy bombers and heavy artillery 'against defenceless villages,' dubbing attacks with such names as Operation Killer and describing the war of attrition as 'putting the Chinese through the meatgrinder.'[3] Foulkes, who ought to have known better, passed Claxton's complaints on to Simonds and added: 'Mr. Pearson also raised this matter with me ... in which he was concerned about the general effect on the Canadian public if we follow the American example of emphasizing brutality, in what may be close to barbarism, in these operations in Korea.'[4] Had Big Jim Stone read these comments back at the front, he might have given a scornful chuckle while thanking the powers-that-be that his battalion would be going into action under the protection of Ridgway's massive air and artillery support.

At first light on 15 February, the close to 900 men of 2PPCLI mounted their U.S. army–supplied 6x6 trucks and set off towards the front, some 240 km to the north. With only the heavy canvas of the trucks to protect them from the dead of winter and the numbing cold, the men sat on hard, straight-backed benches for hours at a stretch while the trucks carefully negotiated the hairpin switchbacks of the icy mountain roads. This was the central Korean winter in all its glory, threatening men with frostbite, numbing their dog-tired brains, and freezing the gun oil and lubricants on their weapons. They would soon learn that this season was as implacable and dangerous an enemy to them as were the Communist men whom they had been sent to kill. The ice and hard-packed snow slowed the long convoy to a crawl; it took more than forty-eight hours to negotiate the route from Miryang to the brigade concentration area at Changhowon-ni. The battalion arrived at 1500 on 17 February.[5]

The 27th BCIB was under command of the 2nd U.S. Infantry

Division, part of IX Corps of Ridgway's U.S. Eighth Army. The British brigade had been hurriedly dispatched to Korea from garrison duty in Hong Kong the previous autumn and then been augmented by Commonwealth troops; 3 Royal Australian Regiment, 16 New Zealand Field Artillery Regiment, and 60 Indian Field Ambulance. Its British core consisted of 1 Middlesex Regiment (1MX) and 1 Argyll and Sutherland Highlanders (1A&SH). When they first arrived in Korea at the end of August, 1950, the British had called themselves 'the Woolworth Brigade' because of the pathetic state of, and many shortages in, their clothing and equipment.[6]

The General Officer Commanding (GOC) was Brig. Basil Aubrey Coad, a tough professional and Second World War veteran who had had some difficulty in converting his formation from a strictly British unit to a mixed Commonwealth one. As well, there were growing morale problems among his British troops, who had been in the thick of the fight from the start of September 1950 and who were aware that sometime soon they would be rotated back to Hong Kong. But when? No one knew, and the uncertainty weighed heavily on them. As early as the previous December the War Office in London had suggested to Coad that he might 'best maintain morale by reminding [his] troops of the outstanding reputation they [had] made for themselves.'[7] That no doubt helped, but the British soldiers at the sharp end had little real understanding of the cause for which they were fighting, despised the South Koreans in general, and were not interested in what they saw as a Korean civil war.[8]

Coad's difficulties did not end with morale. In fact, he had little overall confidence in his U.S. divisional and corps commanders and little faith in the fighting ability of U.S. troops.[9] In early February 1951, he reported that he rarely received visits from his U.S. superiors and that when they did come around their intentions seemed purely social, 'and no information of the general situation could ever be obtained. In fact I was generally asked what I thought was going on. This state of affairs has always made it quite impossible to keep my Battalion Commanders in the picture and for them to let their soldiers know what they were trying to do.'[10]

Coad had a serious operational problem as well. Since 27 BCIB was in effect an artificial amalgam of personnel from four armies, it lacked some of the basic support and supply units on which normal British and American brigades counted. The most serious lack was in motor transport; on the move the troops had frequently to march, especially in withdrawals, when they received U.S. transport only after U.S. requirements had been met. As one senior British officer pointed out, this was hardly the fault of the Americans. U.S. transport was integral to the Americans' formations, and if they made their trucks available to the British first, it would be difficult if not impossible for the U.S. commanders to carry out their own movement orders. But whatever the cause, the brigade was likely to be relegated to rearguard duties and subjected to the possibility of 'being cut off' by a rapid Chinese advance.[11]

A heavy blizzard dumped about a metre of snow across the brigade positions on the morning of 18 February. The deep snow made climbing difficult the next morning as the Patricias set out from the hamlet of Chuam-ni, at the centre of the brigade front, for Hill 404, about 5 km to the northeast. The Canadians were flanked by 1MX to the left and 1A&SH to the right as they made their way across a broad valley and up its steep eastern slope. 'The key to defensive tactics in this country is to seize the high ground and hold it,' the British had reported.[12] That was the key to infantry advances also. Stone's wartime experiences in the mountains of Italy had taught him the wisdom of the doctrine that the British army first learned in the rough hills of the Northwest Frontier of India – that troops who moved down valleys placed themselves in grave danger. Stone's soldiers could never get high enough on the ridgelines, as far as he was concerned, because he who dominated the heights had the best chance of dominating the battle.[13]

The Patricias encountered no opposition at all as they trudged up the ridgeline towards Hill 404. Nor did the British troops to their left and right. The Chinese had broken contact and withdrawn into the hills further north, but not before leaving grim evidence behind about the dangers of defensive lapses in this frozen country. Atop Hill 404 the Patricias came on the stiffened corpses of more than sixty American soldiers laid out for a graves-registration party. Their sentries apparently asleep, or surprised, the Americans had been caught out in the middle of the night and machine-gunned in their sleeping bags.[14] Stone later remembered: 'This was the greatest lesson my troops ever had ... They saw the bodies and the sight sure made an impression.'[15] Stone ordered all sleeping bags sent back from the front.

On 21 February Ridgway's offensive on the central front resumed with Operation Killer, intended to take his forces closer to the 38th parallel. 27 BCIB was to attack northeastward in concert with the 1st U.S. Marine Division (recently transferred from the eastern front), 6 ROK Division, and 1st U.S. Cavalry Division. The plan was to trap large numbers of Chinese troops to the northwest of Hoengsong, some 16 km away. Air reconnaissance had revealed that two landslides had blocked the key pass through which the brigade would have to advance in the first phase of its offensive. Motor transport would have to take a circuitous route to keep up, and, worse, the towed field guns would have difficulty staying within range of the forward troops.[16]

At 1000 on 21 February, the Patricias left their start line at the small village of Sangsok and trudged north through a steep valley with hills on both sides rising from 240 to 450 m. Ahead and to their flanks they could hear the sounds of exploding bombs and mortar and artillery fire. Fog, rain, the deep, wet snow, and the steep rocky hillsides hindered their progress and made it nearly impossible for the infantry to move along the sides of the ridge lines. Two officers were severely injured when they lost their footing trying to negotiate the hillsides and tumbled tens of metres down the slopes.

The battalion's lead company had advanced but 1,500 m north on the hard-packed mud of the narrow road on the valley floor before coming under enemy fire near the hamlet of Chohyon. Cpl Karry Dunphy was in charge of a nine-man section advancing slowly through fresh snow on a nearby slope. It was wending its way through the small pine trees that dotted the hillside in late afternoon when suddenly, from up ahead, a light machine-gun opened up. Bullets whizzed high above the men, shaking the pine needles and cracking the air as they went by. Two or three of the men sprawled on their bellies, others went down on one knee, rifles to shoulder, or rolled into the trees, scattering, as they had been taught. Dunphy carefully exposed himself for a few seconds to get an idea of where the fire was coming from. Then, when he realized that the gun was far away, he began to urge his men forward, slowly, reminding them not to bunch up. Suddenly one man spotted a Chinese sniper, got down on his knee, and, as he had been trained, squeezed off three shots. The enemy soldier went down. Then the Canadian stood up, a strange look on his face, and began to run through the trees, shouting 'I'm in no shape for this! I got to see somebody.' His company commander, Major Vincent Lilley, soon arranged for him to be sent home on a medical discharge.[17]

The battalion took up night defensive positions in and around the village of Wol-li, then moved out again at 1100. 'C' Company led on the north side of the valley slope, with 'B' Company moving directly up the valley and 'D' Company clearing the high ground on the right.[18] It had turned bitterly cold in the night, the temperature dropping to –15°C, and the men's sweat-soaked parkas had frozen to their bodies. But the air warmed up fast after the sun came out, bringing a late winter thaw. As the temperature climbed, the snow started to melt rapidly, adding to the mud and making the footing even more treacherous than usual. The road on the valley floor became nearly impassable to jeeps and trucks alike; the soldiers had to walk on the verges to avoid the mud.

As the battalion approached a pass guarded by Hill 419 to the left and Hill 614, about 1,500 m to the right, the Chinese opened fire from the top of 419, and the Patricia advance stalled. Stone ordered Major J.H. George's 'C' Company to assault the enemy position, and George sent two platoons up in what was supposed to be a classic fire and movement pattern. But the terrain confounded textbook operations. The rocky defiles, steep slopes, narrow trails, and thick brush severely restricted movement; platoon advances were rarely possible in more than single file, giving Chinese defenders well-defined targets and an easy job of holding up the Canadians with a few well-sited machine-guns and rifles.[19] Thus four Patricias were killed and one severely wounded for no gain at all. A second attack later in the day by Major Lilley's 'B' Company also failed, and the battalion was forced to dig in at nightfall in the deep snow atop Hill 444, about 2,000 m southwest of the pass. The plan for the following day was that the Patricias would mount a two-company attack against Hill 419 while 3RAR would assault Hill 614.[20]

The Commonwealth brigade (27BCIB) had run into a strong Chinese defensive position laid out to deny the UN forces entrance to the pass. Two battalions of Chinese troops were entrenched on Hill 419, and another on Hill 614. To the north of them an entire Chinese division stood in reserve, preparing additional defensive positions on the next range of hills. The three Chinese battalions on 419 and 614 had been ordered to hold fast until the new defences were ready, and then to withdraw. The Chinese were well camouflaged, and their defences laid out for enfilade. They carried the usual assortment of small arms and grenades as well as machine-guns and mortars. The approaches to the two hills were steep, slashed by deep ravines, and covered with scrub. The Commonwealth troops were also hindered by interruptions in the flow of ammunition and POL (petroleum, oil, and lubricants) caused by washouts of temporary bridges thrown up by the UN forces over the Han River.[21]

The Patricias attacked Hill 419 again on the morning of 23 February, while the Australians attacked Hill 614 to the right. The soldiers found 419 a 'very difficult feature to approach either from left or right flank.'[22] An air strike went in ahead of the assault, and then, at 0900, 'C' Company moved off. It took an hour to climb upward through the narrow ravines and thick growth to the ridge leading to 419, thirty more minutes to begin edging along the spur towards the summit. Suddenly the Chinese opened up with heavy and accurate small-arms and automatic-weapons fire. Two Patricias were killed outright, one was wounded, and 'C' Company's advance stalled. For seven hours the men stayed in the cold on the exposed ridge, making two more vain attempts to inch along to the objective. They never made it. In the fading light they withdrew part way down the ridge, taking five dead and five wounded with them. 'D' Company, trying to get at the summit from another direction, was equally unsuccessful, suffering one killed and three wounded.[23]

After nightfall Capt. R.K. Swinton, the battalion's battle adjutant, led a company of Korean porters onto the slopes to the forward companies. This was the first time the Canadians had used these 'rice burners,' as they called the members of the Korean Service Corps, but it would not be the last. The porters were often the only way to carry food, supplies, and ammunition up the slopes to company and platoon positions. Swinton's porters stampeded briefly when they came under Chinese fire as they made their way to 'D' Company, but Swinton got them together and they reached their objective at 2330.[24]

At first light on the 24th, the sides and summits of Hills 419 and 614 erupted with smoke and flame as the New Zealanders pumped 25-pounder high-explosive shells at them and U.S. fighter-bombers hit them with napalm from all directions. Then the Canadians and Australians tried again; the Patricias' 'D' Company, led by Capt. J.G. Turnbull, advanced slowly towards the summit of Hill 419 from a ridgeline to the right. The Australians tried a similar ridgeline approach to Hill 614. In both cases the sharpness of the ridge feature limited advances to no more than a section at a time, easy pickings for the Chinese mortarmen and machine-gunners. The Patricias took fire from ahead, from the left, and from the right, and went to ground. The company commander later recalled: 'Although we called down mortars, artillery and air rockets, the Chinese were still there when we attacked ... Never in Italy or Germany were we under fire as intense as that. It was incredible. It chopped off bush briar at the six-inch level. Only fieldcraft carried us through.'[25]

The 2PPCLI attack, and that of the Australians, were called off at midday. Then Coad suspended offensive operations entirely for the next twenty-four to thirty-six hours. The supply shortages caused by the Han-bridge washouts, combined with news brought by a Korean deserter that at least three Chinese battalions were dug in on 419 and 614, decided the issue for the time being. Coad did instruct Stone and the Australian CO, Lt.-Col. F.S. Walsh, to patrol aggressively towards the Chinese lines.[26]

The Patricias carried out their patrol tasks for the next three days; on the 26th an Australian patrol almost gained the heights of

614, but it was quickly pushed back. The next morning a 3RAR platoon, supported strongly by mortar fire and air strikes, finally gained the top of 614 and held it; the Chinese withdrew after a short fire fight. Either that made Hill 419 untenable for the Chinese, or they were in the process of withdrawing their three battalions anyway. The next morning Stone's infantrymen took Hill 419 without serious opposition. There they discovered the stripped and frozen bodies of four Canadian soldiers.[27] Three days later the Patricias went into reserve.

The Patricias had suffered ten killed or dead of wounds and more than twenty wounded between 21 and 28 February. Compared to the fierce fighting that 1PPCLI had endured in Italy in the spring of 1944 these were relatively light casualties when spread over the four rifle companies. But it did show a disturbing pattern of losses taken when men bunched up under fire in this very difficult terrain. The realities of war were finally dawning on the troops. Bill Lee was a section leader in 'D' Company in the fight for Hill 419: 'Following that engagement, morale was extremely low,' he remembers. 'It was hard to convince the men to continue on, as this was their first real test, and mine.'[28] Don Urquhart was a sergeant with 'C' Company: 'The toughest part of being in command was dealing with casualties ... The trick was to keep the men motivated and keep them alert ... and not too anxious if they knew someone who got hit.'[29]

These first encounters with Chinese began to give the Canadians some idea of the sort of enemy they were fighting. Much of the information that they had already received from briefing notes was contradictory and confusing. One report on the fighting prepared at the British War Office in early April, for example, claimed: 'There [is] nothing surprising about the enemy; their concealment, mobility, poor marksmanship, stamina and boldness [are] all characteristic of the Japanese,'[30] which was simply false.

What was true, as the Canadians were learning painfully, was that the Chinese were excellent at siting automatic weapons along possible approach lines and using the terrain to conceal their defensive positions. They held long frontages. They built dummy

positions on hilltops to attract enemy fire but positioned their
main defences just below the summits. They defended reverse
slopes to pick off enemy troops appearing above the ridgelines.
They patrolled aggressively forward of their positions, and they
almost always fought at night and at close quarters.[31] Although the
Canadian soldiers, like other UN troops, called the Chinese
'chinks' (all Koreans were 'gooks'), those 'chinks' had already
earned more than a grudging respect from the Canadians for their
toughness and stamina. Cpl Dunphy told war correspondent
Pierre Berton that he thought the Chinese 'sporting soldiers,' and
was convinced that if they wanted to they could '[hold] the hills of
Korea indefinitely.'[32]

During the first week of March the brigade sat atop its positions
about 3 km north of the pass and waited for the 6th ROK Division
to fight its way up on the brigade's right flank. This gave Stone sufficient time to rotate the men in the rifle companies to the rear for
clean-up, a hot meal, and some recreation. The experience of the
Second World War had demonstrated the positive impact on
morale of hot showers, clean battledress, regular mail, and plenty
of good food. There was no time for an extended rest, but the men
blew off what steam they could with their beer ration, then
returned to their positions after a night of quiet, sleeping in tents.[33]

The bitter cold of the winter was beginning to abate, although
night temperatures still dropped to freezing or below, but in the
daytime, when the sun came out, the insects and birds were a
sure sign that spring was coming to the mountains. The view to the
north, up the valley, was breathtaking, with the mountains on the
horizon and rice paddies and orchards stepped down to the valley
floor. It was almost possible to forget for a moment that the Chinese were out there somewhere and that the battalion would soon
be on the move towards the dragon's lair. On 4 March, Ridgway visited the brigade and spent some time at the HQs of the Patricias
and 3RAR. It was plain that a new UN offensive on the central
front was just a day or so away.

Operation Ripper had the same basic objective as Ridgway's previous offensive, and there was nothing fancy about it – the UN

troops were to push across the 38th parallel to what the UN Command had named Line Kansas. In doing so they were to use their firepower advantage to kill as many of the enemy as possible and destroy its equipment.[34] The continuing UN build-up had just about evened the front-line troop strength on both sides, and although classic military theory held that an attacker ought to have at least a three-to-one advantage over the defender in personnel, the UN forces had the advantage because of their domination of the air, their supply train, and their ample artillery. As long as Ridgway and the UN forces dictated the battlefield agenda with daylight attacks in at least battalion strength, supported by lavish use of air power, artillery, and unit fire-power, the Chinese would continue at a distinct disadvantage.

Ripper was originally set for the morning of 6 March but was postponed for twenty-four hours, partly so that more supplies could be brought up and partly to give the air force and artillery another day to pound the main Chinese positions just across a lateral road that ran perpendicular to the northern end of the pass. Prior to the advance, Stone positioned the battalion's Vickers machine-guns and 81 mm mortars. The heavier 4.2 mortars were also sited. At 0500 on 7 March, Stone and the rest of his tactical headquarters set out by jeep for the north end of the pass; they then took their place behind 'D' Company in the line of march. The road was muddy, and many of the vehicles bogged down, delaying the attack by an hour. The battalion objective was Hill 532, about 1,500 m beyond the lateral road; 3RAR was to attack Hill 410, some 2,000 m southeast of Hill 532, at the same time.[35]

At 0700, 'D' and 'A' Companies crossed the lateral-road startline to advance on Hill 532. 'D' Company moved cautiously through the abandoned hamlet of Hagal-li, then went straight up the steep slope of the hill while 'A' Company swung left after crossing the road. 'A' Company went about 1,000 m westward, then turned north to hit the Chinese in the left flank. About forty-five minutes later, 'D' Company came under heavy Chinese machine-gun fire from bunkers well hidden in the brush that covered the rocky slope. 'A' Company had better going until it too began to climb the hill. The brigade's war diarist later recorded: 'Due to the difficult and hilly country [the enemy] was extremely difficult to close with. Not only were the hill slopes steep and in part covered with thick undergrowth, but the enemy's positions were well sited, dug and camouflaged and were extremely difficult to locate.'[36]

The Australians ran into similar heavy fire in their advance against Hill 410, and both battalions made liberal use of mortars, artillery, and air strikes to try to blast out the defenders. The Chinese answered with heavy mortar fire. The rugged slopes made it virtually impossible for Canadians or Australians to concentrate men against any particular Chinese position. The forward companies found themselves fighting section battles. It was even difficult to coordinate these section fire fights, and some of the riflemen and Bren gunners in the front sections fired away individually at whatever they could see of the enemy, which was not much.

Stone did what he could to run the battle from his tactical headquarters. As soon as the lateral road was clear of enemy fire he called on the tanks of the 72nd U.S. Tank Battalion to move forward and open direct fire against the Chinese on Hill 532.[37] He sent his intelligence officer to guide them into position and help them spot their targets. Stone later reported that he found the American tankers 'very bold in their tactics'[38] – they did not wait for preliminary mine removal from the ground between the lateral road and the hill but drove right up to the base of the hill and opened fire.

Tanks, mortars, and air cover could not help the individual riflemen on the slope, who were pinned down by the Chinese machine-guns and mortars. Casualties mounted. The men tried to shoot back with their Brens and bolt-action .303s, but the effort was mostly useless. It was out there in the rocks, under the Chinese fusillade, that the lack of automatic weapons was so critical. With only one Bren per section, there was no way the Patricias could lay down enough fire to force the Chinese to keep their heads down and give the riflemen a chance to move up. The Canadians were out-gunned.

As the bullets cracked above their heads and the Chinese mortar bombs exploded among the rocks and brush, it was all the Patricias could do to hang on. Still, they tried to get forward. After three-and-a-half hours on the slopes, a 'D' Company platoon made another try at getting to the top. As soon as it emerged from cover, previously hidden Chinese machine-guns joined the fire fight. The platoon was hit almost immediately, the Chinese slugs ricocheting off the rocks. To the left, 'A' Company was also taking heavy fire but continued to move slowly along a ridge leading to the summit. Then it ran into a series of rock pimples that blocked its path. The Chinese fire intensified, and it too dug in.

At 1400, 'D' Company began its final effort to gain the hilltop. The Patricias moved forward from rock to rock, seeking out the dead ground, then lurching ahead. They reached the first ridge held by the Chinese and pushed them out, but they came under fire from the upper slopes about 100 m higher up. Fire was coming in from three sides. Man after man was being hit. The company became scattered about, disorganized, under the Chinese onslaught. Stone ordered the men out, and they inched back, dragging some of their dead with them. The Chinese quickly flowed back into the ridgeline positions, and the Patricias had to leave some of their dead on the hill. By nightfall, 'D' Company had been pulled back to the rear, 'A' remained in place, and 'C' moved up to re-establish contact with the Chinese. All night the stretcher-bearers and porters tried to get the wounded off the hill. One party was ambushed by a small Chinese patrol but managed to escape without casualties. 'B' Company passed a fitful night, the Chinese lobbing grenades at its positions, but it suffered no casualties. The battalion's losses that day included seven killed, most in 'D' Company.

In this sector the first day of Ridgway's attack had been a disaster. The Australians on the right, the Canadians in the centre, and a Greek battalion under command of 1st U.S. Cavalry Division on the left had all been stopped after a short push. Even so, the progress of the two lead 27 BCIB battalions was better than that of the 6th ROK Division to the east. Once again the Koreans lagged, and the Commonwealth brigade's right flank lay exposed for about 6,000 m. It was a perfect opportunity for a Chinese counter-stroke, but the Chinese had other plans. On the morning of 8 March, 2PPCLI and 3RAR moved forward once again, but this time they met no opposition – the Chinese had withdrawn from Hills 532 and 410. In fact, intelligence filtering in from other UN units soon confirmed that the Chinese had broken contact all along the front. No one could understand this sudden withdrawal from excellent defensive positions, especially since the Chinese left behind them quantities of small arms and mortar ammunition, as well as other equipment. The brigade intelligence officer thought that they might have pulled out because of heavy casualties; eighty-two Chinese bodies were found on the slopes and summit of the two hills.[39]

For the next five days the brigade pushed after the withdrawing Chinese but made no contact. The ruined villages, the valleys, the hills, the newly thawed rice paddies were empty. The days grew warmer and the nights shorter, and the advance continued, but still no enemy. Finally, on 13 March, the brigade went into reserve. In the three weeks of fighting since 21 February, the Patricias had lost fourteen men killed or dead from wounds and forty-two wounded. On 15 March, ROK forces recaptured Seoul and UN troops again approached the 38th parallel. One week later South Korean troops crossed that portentous line across Korea.

Jim Stone was generally satisfied with the performance of his men since the start of the two offensives; he had after all weeded out most of the unfit, the unwell, and the unwilling, at Miryang. But he also told Ottawa that major gaps in training and preparedness remained:

[Our] own troops show lack of basic training, particularly in caring for weapons and equipment. Much 'scruff' that was hastily recruited has now been returned to Canada. Troops here are fit, morale high, show lots of guts in close contact ... Officers are generally good but junior ranks show need of a company commander's school. Practical experience will help but certain basic principles of military thinking are lacking. Troops are very well led and the aggressiveness they display in attack under very difficult circumstances is a great credit to the officers.[40]

To remedy these lingering problems, Stone resorted to three

measures that would soon pay substantial dividends. He shipped home eighty-six non-battle casualties. Some were no doubt victims of battle fatigue, but the majority were clearly unfit for soldiering.[41] Stone also stepped up the training in fieldcraft and weaponry and launched a battalion NCO school under Major Lilley.[42] Finally, he made sure that the men were cleaned up, got plenty of hot food, and had their worn-out battledress, boots, and other kit replaced. On 17 March, the regimental birthday, an extra beer ration was issued, but some of the men also resorted to spiking their beer with 'canned heat,' and two died from alcohol poisoning.[43]

Although Stone was not apparently concerned about morale in the Patricias, the United Kingdom's military attaché in Tokyo continued to worry about the state of mind of the British troops. In mid-March he wrote the War Office: 'I consider the question of the maintenance of morale of the troops to be a matter for serious consideration.' The British soldier was not much attracted to UN operations, which seemed to have the killing of Communists as their only objective. 'Already many British and American officers and other ranks have asked such questions as "When will the war end?" "When do you think the U.N. forces can be withdrawn from Korea?" "What is our object in Korea?"' He added: 'I have only included British and American troops because generally speaking the relatively small numbers of troops from other nations represented are adventurous mercenaries who are as content to serve as part of an international fighting brigade in Korea as elsewhere.'[44] Here was that unique, almost-genetic arrogance that marks some British officers, which Canadian officers could never tolerate in an American!

When he had arrived in Korea, Stone already knew from his war service as much about fighting as just about any Canadian soldier alive, but the three weeks of action against the Chinese in central Korea in late winter of 1951 taught him even more. He had taken the measure of the terrain, of his enemy, and of his allies, and he had devised new and different ways of fighting. He had opened a school to teach prospective NCOs the art of command in-theatre and to give refresher training to those new to the rank of sergeant or corporal who had not had sufficient preparation in Canada. He had directed the lavish use of the Vickers medium machine-guns as barrage weapons when insufficient artillery was available (the Vickers were also effective in defence near battalion headquarters). He had instructed his company commanders to warn their men against approaching enemy positions in single file or on tracks where the climbing was easiest. Instead, he forced them to attack from three or four ridges at once, no matter how hard that was, to force the Chinese to spread their defensive fire.[45] Innovation – knowing when to retain standing practice and when to discard it and develop something new – is the mark of an imaginative commander. Stone was that kind of leader. Although some of his men found him both arrogant and aloof, he was also brave, even contemptuous, in the face of the enemy. At one point later in the year Stone and his intelligence officer, Lieut. Mike Levy, went to visit front-line positions. Levy walked along the reverse slope of the ridge line, keeping as low a profile as possible, but Stone walked on the crest, in full view of the Chinese. The incident made a lasting impression on Levy.

On 24 March, the day the brigade went back into the line, Stone was evacuated with a mild case of smallpox, picked up probably in one of the abandoned Korean hamlets through which the battalion had passed in February. Major H.D.P. Tighe took over as acting CO. The brigade too went forward under a different commander, since Coad had been replaced by Col. (soon to be promoted to brigadier) B.A. Burke, former deputy commander of 29th British Infantry Brigade. The day after arriving at the front, the entire 27 BCIB was trucked some 70 km to the northwest in pouring rain to join two U.S. units – the 5th and the 21st regimental combat teams (RCTs) – north of the Pukhan River. Orders were to advance up the valley of the Chojong River, with 5 RCT on the left, 27 BCIB in the centre, and 21 RCT on the right, to Line Benton, which connected a number of towering hills roughly 7 km south of the 38th parallel.

The advance began on 27 March. Brigade HQ moved down the centre of the valley, while the Patricias were assigned to cover the eastern slope. All that day and into the next the Patricias trudged the ridgelines, being careful not to present their silhouettes to Chinese gunners waiting in ambush. But there were no Chinese gunners to be found, just the sound of crunching snow and running water and the ever-present rumble of far-away artillery. The fields of deep snow among the thick woods, the rocky slopes, and the complete lack of roads made the advance almost wholly dependent on the Korean porters. That was not too serious a matter, but important, because there was almost no way to bring the field artillery up close behind. If the Patricias ran into serious opposition, Tighe could count on only his 81 mm mortars for support.

Hour after hour the men carried their weapons through the thick woods on the slope of the valley, over steep and rocky terrain, and through deep snow. At nightfall, they set up defensive positions, kept as warm as they could, ate their rations, then slept fitfully in the cold. The next day, they did it all again. Towards nightfall on the 29th some Chinese far ahead pumped long-range fire at the Patricias, but the bullets cracked harmlessly over their heads and hit no one. The next day, another Chinese soldier fired at the advancing companies and was killed for his trouble.

Finally, on 31 March, action. As the three UN formations approached Line Benton at the head of the valley, they ran into Chinese defenders. The 27 BCIB was assigned to capture Hill 1036, and 21 RCT was to take Hills 974 and 834 some 6,000 m to the east. The Patricias came under fire from Hill 1250, just ahead of them. Burke wanted a coordinated attack on the hill positions to wait for first light, which was done. But when the attacks began, they came up empty. The Chinese had pulled back in the night.

On 1 April the brigade shifted some 5,000 m to the right into the Kap'yong River valley to begin an advance to Line Kansas, some 3,000 m north of the 38th parallel. As in the previous few days, it had little contact with the enemy along this new line of advance; Chinese troops would fire a few bursts in its direction, sometimes even stand fast in the dusk, but melt away by dawn. As usual, the thick undergrowth, the rocky outcrops, the patches of coniferous forest, and the steep climbs provided the most serious obstacles. For three days the Patricias covered the left flank of the advance before going into brigade reserve on 4 April.

The 27 BCIB was now the left flanking formation of IX Corps; 6th ROK Division was on its right; the formation on the left was the 24th U.S. Infantry Division, under command of I Corps.[46] In the first week of April the brigade crossed the 38th parallel and moved steadily towards Line Kansas, which was achieved on 8 April, the same day the Patricias came out of reserve and just in time for a further advance to Line Utah, not far north of Line Kansas, where the brigade was to be pinched out along the X corps boundary. The new advance began on 11 April, with the Patricias and the Middlesex Regiment in the lead. The British battalion ran into the Chinese on a hill code-named 'DAB' and was stopped cold. Chinese and British fought at close range with grenades, rifles, and automatic weapons; on their first attempt the Middlesex men almost reached the hilltop before they were driven off. A heavy mist then settled over the hills, killing any prospect of success. The Chinese were still entrenched in their positions at nightfall.[47]

The night was quiet; the fighting for DAB resumed in the morning, this time with help from air-force fighter-bombers, heavy artillery, and mortars. The Middlesex men moved up once more, only to be thrown back again by showers of grenades and heavy machine-gun and automatic-weapons fire. The deep defiles, the heavy brush, and the rocks made movement almost impossible; one Middlesex platoon became lost in the undergrowth. Battalion HQ had only the dimmest picture of who was where. The entire brigade would remain blocked as long as the Chinese held firm, because there was no way to outflank the embattled position.

Sometime on the night of 12–13 April, the Chinese pulled back from DAB, and the brigade resumed its advance. This time it was the Patricias' turn to take on a well-entrenched Chinese position as they moved to capture a long ridge that ended on Hill 826. As a platoon from 'D' Company moved along the ridge towards the hill, Chinese mortars rained smoke cannisters on the Canadians; when the Patricias emerged from the smoke, Chinese machine-gunners from nearby Hill 785 opened fire. The bullets whistled and cracked through the rocks and ricocheted off into the air as the Canadian infantry scrambled for cover. The rest of 'D' Company then set out. It took Hill 795, but its positions there were under observation and fire from Hill 826, about 1,000 m to the north. At nightfall, it was forced to pull back.[48]

At dawn on 15 April, the hills to the north of the Patricias blossomed with towering explosions as heavy artillery rained down on the slopes and summits. Then USAF Thunderjets blasted the Chinese with napalm. The Patricias moved. They climbed steadily up the steep sides of the hill, pushed through the thick brush, worked around the rocky outcrops. The Bren gunners fired to keep the defenders down while the riflemen moved close to pour rifle fire and grenades into the Chinese positions. Within an hour or so they had retaken Hill 795 with only light casualties, but the Chinese still looked down on them from Hill 826.

At 0800 on 16 April, the Patricias moved out to take Hill 826. They executed the attack, in the words of the brigade war diarist, 'with dash and precision,' as did 3RAR on its own, neighbouring objective. Both battalions met only scattered resistance, and both were on their objectives before noon.[49] Only one Patricia was killed in the fight to gain Lines Kansas and Utah; the Canadians were learning the difficult art of how to attack a well-hidden and resourceful enemy over this most inhospitable ground. Two days later the brigade pulled back into corps reserve north of the village of Kap'yong. The New Zealand gunners stayed put to support the 6th ROK division, which took over the brigade's positions.

When the Chinese armies began to disengage from the forward thrusting formations of the UN Command in mid-March 1951, they were following a long-held military strategy of the Chinese Communists to withdraw in the face of strength and then to regroup to force a decisive engagement. The aim of that decisive battle would be nothing less than the recapture of Seoul and, in the process, the destruction of the Eighth Army. Eighth Army intelligence estimated about seventy Communist divisions facing it, most Chinese, with about half the troops – more than 300,000 – on a 65 km front between the Imjin River and the Hwachon Reservoir.[50]

The main Chinese offensive opened on the night of 21–2 April with an attack south on the Hwachon–Chunchon axis. The plan was to split IX Corps on the right from I Corps on the left. The Chinese armies could then pour through the gap, outflank the defences of the South Korean capital, and force the collapse of the UN front. In the IX Corps sector, the main weight of the Chinese assault fell on the 6th ROK Division. Through the night and into the early morning of 22 April the South Koreans tried to consolidate their positions, but by midday they broke; men and vehicles began to stream to the south through the Kap'yong River valley.

First reports of the fighting around the beleaguered ROK division filtered back to 27 BCIB HQ not long after midnight on the 22nd. It took several hours to determine the full extent of the disaster that was shaping up some 25 km north of the brigade, but as the morning of 22 April wore on, it became clear that the Chinese had once again unerringly selected the weakest point on the UN line and smashed through it. This posed two immediate dangers: first, that the Chinese would pour through the hole in the UN front and advance rapidly to the southwest and behind the Seoul defences; second, that UN troops outflanked by the Chinese attack would be encircled. Suddenly the Commonwealth Brigade was no longer in corps reserve. Suddenly the brigade was IX Corps's only real hope to stem the Chinese advance on its front and hold the front open long enough to allow the soldiers of the 6th ROK Division and other UN troops to escape. At 1200 on 22 April, the New Zealand gunners were released from the by-now collapsed ROK division and ordered back to the brigade as quickly as possible.[51] They limbered their 25-pounders, loaded kit and shell aboard the 6x6s sent to pull them out, and drove south towards Kap'yong on the single dusty road, choked with refugees. They stopped and unloaded about 6 km north of Kap'yong, then were ordered back about half that distance when it appeared momentarily that the ROK troops might re-form. The Korean troops did not, so the New Zealanders pulled back again, reaching their position near Kap'yong by dark on the 23rd.

On the night the South Koreans were attacked, the Chinese opposite the I Corps front, some 30 km west of Kap'yong, slammed into the 29th British Infantry Brigade, holding a 12 km front on the south bank of the Imjin River. The brigade front was defended primarily by a Belgian battalion, the 1st Royal Northumberland Fusiliers, and the 1st Battalion of the Gloucestershire Regiment with attached armour and weapons units. The Royal Ulster Rifles were in brigade reserve about 10 km south of the river. When news of the attack reached brigade HQ, the front-line units prepared their defences for the inevitable onslaught, and they spent most of the daylight hours on the 22nd watching the Chinese build-up on the north bank of the river. By nightfall, the Chinese had forded the Imjin on a wide front, and all three battalions were heavily engaged.[52]

The Chinese quickly penetrated the positions of 'A' Company of the 'Glosters' on the left of the front and began to work their way around to the south of the Belgian battalion on the right. Already by the afternoon of the 23rd the positions of the three battalions were precarious, with the Glosters cut off and Chinese troops well inside the brigade area. Despite heavy air and artillery support, the beleaguered British could not be reached, nor could they regain contact with the rest of the brigade. On the night of 24–5 April, orders were given for a general withdrawal of the brigade, but it was too late for most of the Glosters. They were unable to break out, and attempts to reach them failed. Virtually every man from 'A,' 'B,' and 'C' Companies was killed, wounded, or captured as the Chinese closed in. Commanding officer Lt.-Col. J.P. Carne, later awarded the Victoria Cross, evaded capture for twenty-four hours with a small group of men but was eventually taken prisoner. Only thirty-nine men of 'D' Company escaped disaster. Virtually the entire battalion was lost at what soon became known as 'Gloster Hill.'

Kap'yong village is situated about 25 km south of the 38th parallel and some 40 km northeast of Seoul. It not only controls the north–south road through the Kap'yong valley, it also lies astride what was at the time a main east–west lateral road south of the front. The village lies about 1,000 m northwest of the junction between the Kap'yong River, which is not much larger than a stream, and the Pukhan River. Brig. Burke had established his brigade HQ about a kilometre north of the village. From there the Kap'yong meandered in a generally northeasterly direction for about 5,000 m, before swinging northwest near the hamlet of Chuktun-ni. About 1,000 m along that swing to the northwest, the Kap'yong was joined by a small stream known as the Somoktong, which began as a trickle some 3 km to the northeast. The junction of the Somoktong and the Kap'yong created a Y-shaped depression in the rugged, scrub-covered hills that climbed steeply away in all directions. From the valley floor to the highest peak to the west the elevation increased by some 800 m over 3 km; to the east of the Y-shaped valley, the hills were somewhat lower, with the tallest reaching just over 500 m. The terrain and the direction from which the onrushing enemy was coming dictated Burke's battle plan.[53]

Burke knew that the main Chinese advance must come down either or both arms of the Y. He was also aware that if the Chinese could be denied the heights along both the Somoktong and the Kap'yong, they could not push through the valley below. To that end he ordered 3RAR, backed by a company of the 72nd U.S. Heavy Tank Battalion, to dig in on the peak and forward slopes of Hill 504 – the highest position to the east of the Y – and positioned Stone's Patricias on Hill 677, to the west of the Y, about 5 km across the Kap'yong from the Australians. There were a number of serious weaknesses in Burke's plan: the brigade had no protection on either flank, there were no troops between the Australians and the Patricias, and the brigade would remain weak in artillery support until the New Zealand guns could be positioned, dug in, and sited.[54]

Jim Stone had returned to resume command of the Patricias only days before the Chinese offensive. When he received Burke's order to concentrate his battalion on Hill 677, he organized a complete reconnaissance of possible Chinese attack approaches. Stone, his intelligence officer, his company commanders, and the commanders of his support and communications units went to the north side of 677 while the intelligence officer examined the terrain to the southeast. Stone would later remember: 'Hill 677 is about a mile and a half across, gullied, wooded, and impossible to defend in the classic manner of deploying companies to support each other. Each company had to develop its own individual defended locality, the platoons being mutually supporting. The gaps between the companies would have to be covered to some extent by defensive fire tasks of the MMG section, the battalion's 81 mm mortars, the U.S. mortar company, and the New Zealander 25 pdr Regiment.'[55] Stone assigned defensive positions to his company commanders in a rough semi-circle, with 'A' Company on the lower slopes of the hill facing the Australians, 'C' on the north side of the hill, 'B' just to the west of 'C' and 'D' south of 'B.'

On the western side of the hill, 'D' Company was commanded by acting company commander Capt. J.G. Mills. Mills either did not understand what Stone wanted his company commanders to do or thought better of Stone's orders on how to deploy his company. In any case, he did not do as he had been told. He placed his company headquarters from 100 to 200 m to the rear of his platoons, out of sight on the reverse slope of a steep knoll. From that spot he could not effectively manage his company under fire, and he could not direct mortar, artillery, or machine-gun fire in defence of his platoons because he could not see them. Nor were his platoons placed in mutually supporting positions. Lieut. Michael Levy's 10 Platoon was dangerously isolated about 300 m in front of, and below, the other three platoons; 11 Platoon, on the far right flank of the company position, was 200 m to the east of 12 Platoon, too far away to offer effective support fire. All four platoons were positioned on forward slopes, where they were especially vulnerable to the enemy. Levy argued unsuccessfully with Mills to have his platoon relocated farther back and up the slope, but Mills refused until a burst of machine-gun fire from 12 Platoon almost hit his position. Mills then relented.[56]

In the afternoon and evening of 23 April the Patricias prepared their positions. 'A,' 'B,' and 'D' Companies got a section of two Vickers machine-guns each. The mortar platoon, with its half-tracks mounting Browning .30 and .50 machine-guns and Stone's tactical HQ, was placed about half-way between 'D' and 'B' companies. Burke also assigned two companies of 2 Chemical Heavy Mortar Battalion, with twelve 4.2-inch mortars, one to the 3RAR and one to Stone's Patricias. In addition Burke had at his disposal one battery of U.S. 105 self-propelled guns and a battery of the 213 Medium Artillery Regiment firing U.S. 155 mm 'Long Toms.'[57] It

was warm and dry as the Patricias dug their gun pits and sited
their weapons – the best weather that they had had for weeks; on
the road below them the remnants of two shattered Korean regiments and thousands of Korean refugees went streaming past to
the rear.

Just after midnight on 24 April, as the Patricias were starting to
put the final pieces of their defence into place, the Chinese hit the
Australian positions on Hill 504. Blowing whistles and bugles, the
Chinese infantry rose out of the dark and rushed the 3RAR slit
trenches behind a shower of mortar rounds. Close behind the first
line of attackers came a second, hurling hundreds of grenades and
carrying explosives to breach the Australian wire. The Australian
CO called for defensive fire before losing radio contact with the
brigade. As they hit the 3RAR positions, the Chinese swarmed into
the New Zealanders' gun lines, forcing Burke to pull the regiment
back to the proximity of his HQ.[58]

Back at brigade HQ and in the Patricias' positions to the west,
the loss of contact with the Australian battalion headquarters
caused confusion and anxious moments. A cacophony of automatic-weapons fire and exploding mortar and artillery shells could
be heard from Hill 504 as the Patricias saw the sky lit by tracer fire
and explosions. But what was happening in the platoon and company positions? After close to two hours of radio silence, 3RAR
made contact through 1MX and reported a pitched battle around
battalion HQ and in front of Hill 504. In fact, the Chinese had
penetrated to the centre of the Australian positions, were swarming around the slit trenches of the forwardmost platoons, and were
climbing on to the American tanks helping to defend the north
side of the hill. Tanks were being hit, Australian and Chinese infantrymen were firing at each other at point-blank range, and Chinese
mortar and machine-gun fire was raking the slopes. Retreating
ROK soldiers were still trying to move through the area; the Australians could often not tell who was ROK and who was Chinese.

Daylight brought no respite for the Australian defenders. The
fighter-bombers dropped their lethal loads, the 155 mm shells of
the corps artillery thundered in from 15 km away, and the New
Zealanders, stripped to the waist, fed their 25-pounders like men

possessed, firing thousands of rounds an hour at the massing Chinese. But still the enemy troops came: they had been cleared out from inside the Australians' positions, but their attacks on the battalion perimeter continued and intensified through the day. By mid-afternoon it was clear to Burke that the RAR could not hold out another night. He ordered it to withdraw; at 1730 the Australians, accompanied by the American tanks, began to pull back. They came out under constant mortar and machine-gun fire, their vehicles protected by the U.S. armour, but by 2240 the withdrawal was complete. The Australians had suffered thirty-one killed and fifty-eight wounded and had lost three men prisoner. Now it was the Patricias' turn.

Stone had observed the battle closely across the valley and by morning had decided that an attack on his position would most probably come against his eastern slope. He ordered 'B' Company to move from its position and prepare new defences south of 'A' Company, where it could protect the 'back door to the battalion area.'[59] As 'B' Company dug in, it reported seeing large numbers of Chinese infantry moving in and around the hamlet of Naechon, about 300 m below its positions.

Stone's prescience in shifting 'B' Company saved the Patricias from disaster. At 2130, just as the Australian withdrawal was being completed, about 400 Chinese infantrymen were observed forming up in a valley near 'B' Company. Company commander Major C.V. Lilley called for artillery and mortar concentrations, but the Chinese attacked en masse. The forward Patricia platoon, commanded by Lieut. H. Ross, battled them off as long as it could but was soon partially overrun and forced to pull back into the 'B' Company area. The other platoons of 'B' Company were less beleaguered and held their ground.

The fighting at close quarters was deadly. One sergeant later told Canadian war correspondent Bill Boss: 'They're good. They were on top of our positions before we knew it. They're quiet as mice with those rubber shoes of theirs and then there's a whistle. They get up with a shout about 10 feet from our positions and come in. The first wave throws its grenades, fires its weapons and goes to the ground. It is followed by a second which does the same, and then a third comes up. They just keep coming.' That sergeant threw his bayoneted rifle like a spear at the attackers when his ammunition ran out.[60]

In one of the Patricias' Bren-gun pits, the situation was desperate almost from the first moment of battle: 'We sat there and held them off as long as we could until we pulled back and Wayne [Mitchell] and I got separated. I don't know how long we were there before Lt. Ross gave us the order to move out. Just as we jumped up Ross added that anyone with any ammo left should cover the retreat of the wounded. I had three [bullets] left so I dropped back down and fired them off. Just as I jumped up again I fell over a Chinaman who was running up the side of the hill. He let fly and got me in the neck then ran into the end of my bayonet.'[61]

There was bravery on every part of Hill 677 that night. Bren gunners Ken Barwise, Jim Waniandy, and several others found themselves in front of an onrushing tide of Chinese grenadiers. 'We opened up with our Brens,' Waniandy later recalled. The Chinese started 'falling all over.' 'They kept coming in waves.' Barwise remembered. He killed at least six in one of at least five attacks directed at 'B' Company.[62]

As 'B' Company came under attack, a small group of Chinese tried to get inside the battalion area by infiltrating up the valley behind Stone's tactical headquarters. The Chinese were silhouetted against the Kap'yong River as they approached. Stone later described what happened: 'The mortar platoon, located with HQ, was mounted for travelling on twelve half tracks. Each vehicle was equipped with one .50 and one .30 calibre machine gun. ... Fire was held until the Chinese had broken through the trees about two hundred metres away. Twenty-four machine guns cut loose together. Only those who have experienced being under the fire of a heavy concentration of tracer bullets can appreciate the terror induced by that kind and volume of fire.'[63]

As the night wore on, the Patricias held to their positions, but their situation became increasingly desperate. Heavy fighting continued to swirl around 'B' Company, but at 0130 hours 'D' Company's 10 Platoon, on the western tip of the hill, became the focal point for another heavy Chinese attack. Despite the artillery and mortar fire pouring down around its positions to keep them safe, about 200 Chinese came at it from the west. Platoon commander Lieut. Mike Levy reported to Capt. Mills that his men were engaged on three sides. The Chinese attacked a 12 Platoon Vickers supporting Levy's men and killed the crew with a belt still in its gun.

By 0300 Levy's men were barely holding on while 12 Platoon had been overrun, leaving a gaping hole in the company's defence perimeter. Levy called for close-in fire support from the mortars and the field artillery. Back at 'D' Company headquarters, Mills had no real idea of what was transpiring in the dark a few hundred metres from his position. Because he could not observe the fighting, he became in effect a messenger passing radio or land line traffic from his platoon leaders to the supporting arms. All he could do was pass on Levy's request. The shells rumbled in, at first exploding about 50 m from the well dug-in men of 10 Platoon. In one forty-minute period the New Zealand gunners fired some 2,300 rounds.[64] The shrapnel bursts, set to explode just below tree-top height, sent clouds of hot, jagged, and twisted metal into the Chinese ranks; below ground the Canadians were protected. Levy called in instructions – left 20 m, right 10 m, down 15 m – directing the fire about thirty or forty times as his men, pressed on three sides and heavily outnumbered, fought for their lives for more than five hours. At about 0300 Mills concluded that his company could not hold and asked Stone if he could pull back. Stone refused: 'I told him to stay there, that nobody could pull out, if we ever lose that hill, we lose it all.'[65] The early morning attacks were broken up, although the Chinese continued to engage 'D' Company until dawn, when they slackened off and 12 Platoon regained its positions. According to the 27th BCIB war diary, the calling down of the artillery on 10 Platoon's position 'was completely successful inflicting heavy enemy casualties and daylight found the Canadian Company still in position and holding their ground.'[66]

Still in position it was, but although it held the hill it was cut off and, after a night of hard fighting, almost out of ammunition and short of almost everything else. Ten platoon was also still exposed at the far western edge of the battalion perimeter and suffered harassing fire all day. There was no way in which supplies could get through overland, so Stone radioed for an air drop; six hours later a flight of USAF C-119 Flying Boxcars swung over the Canadian positions as loadmasters kicked their payloads out the rear. Food, ammunition, and water floated down onto the slopes of Hill 677. Virtually all the supplies fell within the Canadian position. The battle for Hill 677 was over; on 26 April, the Patricias were relieved by a battalion of the 1st U.S. Cavalry Division and went into reserve. Ten Canadians had been killed and twenty-three wounded, and several, including Barwise and Mills, were decorated for bravery.

In the words of one American chronicler of the Korean War: 'The holding action of the Commonwealth Brigade at Kapyong had been decisive. It plugged the hole left by the ROK 6th Division and blocked the [Chinese] long enough for the 24th [U.S. Infantry] Division to withdraw.'[67] In fact, that holding action also allowed the UN Command to bring up additional units of the 1st U.S. Cavalry Division, place them to the south of Kap'yong, and block any further Chinese advance down that axis. To the west, the Glosters were lost, but the damage that they and the rest of 29th British Infantry Brigade had inflicted on the Chinese attackers slowed the Communist momentum on that front as well. The reprieve gave the Eighth Army's new commander, James Van Fleet, time to set up a new defensive line running just to the north of Seoul, withdraw his units to that line in good order, save the capital, and prepare for a massive counterattack back to the 38th parallel when the Chinese eventually ran out of steam.[68]

The Patricias had held off a Chinese force at least three times its size through factors rooted in both good luck and superb preparation. The luck came from the Chinese decision to hit 3RAR first. Had it been the other way around, it is unlikely that the Patricias could have held Hill 677 for at least another full day. Because they were attacked after the Australians, the Chinese hit the Patricias with a somewhat depleted force and were clearly unable or unwilling to press their attack home against the Patricias in the daylight hours of 25 April as they had against 3RAR the day before.

The good preparation was the result of the presence of tried veterans of the Second World War in the persons of Stone and his officer cadre. He and some of the others had fought in the mountains of Sicily and Italy and knew how to defend a hill. Stone had noted the early British reports to the effect that well-led men, if they were provided with a good defence, lots of ammunition, and no way out, would fight and die where they stood rather than break. He had faith in his battalion. Stone and his senior officers laid out the defence from the enemy's point of view and planned for strong, mutually supporting fire between the platoons in each company. That, plus quick and accurate response from the medium and heavy mortars and the field artillery that drenched the inter-company locations with fire, gave the battalion a chance to survive as a coherent unit. Whether Stone was lucky or showed great skill in placing all his half-track–mounted, heavy .50 machine-guns in a concentration near his tactical headquarters, that move weighed heavily in beating back the Chinese. For his solid leadership and imaginative planning, Stone received a bar to his DSO. For the crucial forty-eight hours they bought Van Fleet at Kap'yong, 2PPCLI, 3RAR, and the 72nd U.S. Heavy Tank Battalion received a U.S. Presidential Unit Citation. To this day, the PPCLI is the only regiment in Canadian history to be so honoured.

FIVE

The Brigade

0800, 4 May 1951. The SS *Marine Adder* docked in the crowded harbour at Pusan carrying most of the soldiers and some of the equipment of the 25th Canadian Infantry Brigade Group. The Canadians crowded the railings and peered at the warships, harbour craft, lighters, oilers, and troop transports lined up at the piers or anchored in mid-harbour. They watched Korean dockhands manhandle the ropes tying *Marine Adder* to her place of rest after long weeks at sea. They wondered what lay ahead.

Rockingham had flown from Fort Lewis, Washington, to make sure that preparations were completed for the arrival of the brigade. Now, as the gangway was set in place, he scrambled aboard to be reunited with his troops. Jacques Dextraze, who had commanded the brigade aboard ship, was presented with flowers from the wife of a Korean dignitary. Everyone smiled for the cameras. Then, the brief ceremonies over, the men hefted their kit and wound down the gangplank as dockside cranes swung into action to unload vehicles, ammunition, and other necessities. The Americans marvelled at the sheer volume of supplies that the Canadians had brought with them; there was almost as much here, they observed, as for an entire U.S. division. They were right, but it was all a mistake. Several tonnes of supplies ought to have been offloaded in Japan but were brought to Pusan in error; it took six ships to carry all the Canadian gear, and six days to unload, organize, and prepare it for use.

The brigade's home for the next week or so was to be an unused prisoner-of-war camp about 15 km from Pusan; a large, empty warehouse next door would serve as the main supply depot.[1] It was warm as the men boarded trucks for the drive through Pusan's crowded streets. The heat brought out noxious smells of poverty and human waste. The trucks nosed slowly through the milling crowds. One Canadian soldier later remembered that it was 'hard to realize over a million people live in such a cramped dirty community.'[2]

Rockingham wanted the brigade ready for fighting very soon. The UN forces had halted the first phase of the Chinese spring offensive, aimed at smashing the Eighth Army and outflanking Seoul, but there was no hint that China was prepared to abandon its goal of military victory in Korea. That meant that the brigade could be called on to move to the front at almost any time. Unlike 2PPCLI, which had arrived the previous December wholly unprepared for combat, 25 Brigade had been through rigorous training at Fort Lewis. But long weeks at sea had softened muscles and lulled senses, and there was still much to learn about fighting the Chinese in Korea from those who had already done so.

The serious work began on 5 May in a tropical downpour. Rockingham arranged for the replacement of most of the brigade's 17-pounder anti-tank guns with U.S.-built 75 mm recoilless rifles, which had proved effective at providing the infantry with close, direct-fire support. Each of the battalion's anti-tank platoons received six of the 75 mm weapons. Several days later, Ottawa authorized Rocky to arrange to swap the M-10 tank destroyers of C Squadron, Lord Strathcona's Horse, for Sherman M4A3 tanks, supplied by the U.S. army and equipped with the 76 mm high-velocity gun. These two major changes of equipment were not complete until mid-May,[3] delaying the training schedule.

The configuration of the Canadian infantry battalion in Korea was essentially unchanged from that employed by Canada in the Second World War. 'A' echelon was the rear battalion headquarters, which gave direct support to the battalion's tactical headquarters at the front, to the line rifle companies, and to the support and heavy-weapons companies and platoons. 'B' echelon contained the battalion's logistics and supply facilities. 'F' echelon was responsible for transporting supplies and men from 'B' echelon to the front. The standard Second World War 'LOB,' or left-out-of-battle, arrangement was also usually followed. This involved the rotation to 'B' echelon of a core of NCOs and officers every twenty-four hours, not only for rest and a hot meal, but to ensure continuity of command in the event of a disaster.[4]

While Rockingham's staff saw to the equipment, he himself oversaw a rigorous program of training for the soldiers. Hill-climbing with full packs was designed to get the men into shape.[5] To bring the lessons of the field directly to his officers and NCOs, Rocky borrowed Patricia Major R.K. Swinton, who had commanded 'D' Company of 2PPCLI since mid-April. Swinton taught the new arrivals the specific lessons that the Patricias had learned about the Chinese enemy and how to defend against it: defence should always be laid out in tight perimeters, with companies allotted a section of the mortar platoon (two 81 mm mortars) and a section of the Vickers platoon (with two Vickers machine-guns each) inside the company wire; defensive localities had to be as mutually supporting as possible; and when the Chinese approached, the defenders should hold fire until the enemy was within 10 m of their wire, then open up with Brens and machine-guns. The Chinese were not often dissuaded by Bren-gun fire alone but seemed mightily impressed with the noise of the Vickerses. The Patricias had learned to use lots of wire and were prepared, if necessary, to call their own artillery fire down on their heads if they were overrun. At night, they made sure that one man slept while the other stood guard, but everybody was kept up and alert when the moon rose – this was the Chinese's favourite time to attack. By day, one section was assigned to guard while two sections rested. It was crucial to do everything possible to make sure that the men got sleep whenever they could, even when they were reluctant to do so.[6]

Until the Canadian brigade joined up with other Commonwealth units to form 1st (Commonwealth) Division, Rocky's formation would operate as an independent infantry brigade with attached supporting arms. In essence, it was like a small division. For much of the next few weeks, therefore, Rockingham would deal directly with Lt.-Gen. James A. Van Fleet, who had assumed command of Eighth Army on 14 April, following Ridgway's promotion to Commanding General, UN Command, when MacArthur had been relieved by President Truman on 11 April. Truman fired him for violating a presidential order prohibiting officers from making public pronouncements about higher UN strategy.

Van Fleet's overall strategy for dealing with Chinese offensives was similar to that of his predecessor. He believed that the UN's superior fire-power should be liberally used not only in the attack but also to defend. He wanted his troops to set up killing zones of integrated small-arms, machine-gun, mortar, and artillery fire, supplemented by close air support, in front of well-established and well-sited defensive positions. Then they could let the Chinese attack and dash themselves to pieces.[7]

Rocky was a 'hands-on' commander, and with his troops spread out over several dozen kilometres in the hills near Pusan, he was determined to see for himself not only that the training was moving ahead with all possible speed but also that it was being carried out according to the requirements of this strange battleground. By jeep, helicopter, and aircraft, he covered hundreds of kilometres to observe training, confer with HQ Eighth U.S. Army Korea (EUSAK), make arrangements for equipment transfers, and talk to his battalion commanders. On 10 May, for example, Rockingham flew to Taegu from Pusan to discuss the tactical situation at EUSAK and finalize arrangements for the delivery of the Sherman tanks. The next day he attended the first serial of Exercise Charley Horse, aptly named because it involved a 600 m hill climb for the men of 2RCR, who carried their 81 mm mortars and 3.5-inch rocket launchers with them for good measure. That afternoon he flew by helicopter to Ulsan, where 2RCHA was encamped, to watch a road move exercise. At dawn on the 12th, he returned to the main brigade staging area for another round of Exercise Charley Horse. Later he paid a surprise visit to Dextraze's encampment while the battalion was on a road-movement exercise. He noted that several vehicles had been left behind and made sure that he returned later in the day to find out why.

On 16 May, the training complete, the men boarded trains for the north and the front; their heavy weapons, major pieces of kit, and vehicles went by road. Already 2RCHA had departed to add its guns to the fire-power of the 28th BCIB along the Han River. Rockingham was distinctly unhappy with the arrangements for the move. He had wanted to keep men and equipment together so that they might form up as soon as they reached Kumnyangjang-ni, about 16 km east of the railhead at Suwon. As it was, the men, moving by rail, would reach their destination much earlier than the roadbound equipment. Rocky was also unhappy about assembling his brigade near an active front.[8] But just before the brigade moved out, the Chinese launched the second phase of their spring offensive, and Rocky's objections were lost in Van Fleet's determination that every available UN soldier in Korea should be available to throw back the assault.

It rained as the brigade headed for its concentration area near Kumnyangjang-ni. The Korean countryside was ablaze with the glory of the season. Green spring wheat was already ankle-high in the fields. Peach, apple, and pear trees were heavy with blossoms. Even in the rain, peasants stooped in the fields and paddies, doing the work that they and their ancestors had done for centuries, oblivious to the war and to the endless stream of troop trains and flatcars laden with tanks, guns, trucks, and all the other accoutrements of modern war.

Van Fleet's intelligence had long predicted a second phase to the Chinese spring offensive, and as mid-month approached, warning signs multiplied. Van Fleet postponed his own plans for an offensive back to the Kansas Line because of his desire to meet the Chinese on ground of his own choosing, ground well prepared in advance to chew up Chinese lives.[9] When the attack came on the night of 15–16 May with twelve Chinese and six North Korean divisions, its full weight fell on the eastern front in the X Corps area, but the impact was felt all along the front.

Once again the Chinese concentrated on portions of the UN line held by ROK troops, and once again the defenders collapsed under the sheer weight of Chinese and North Korean manpower. This time, however, the orderly withdrawal of U.S. troops and Van Fleet's quick action in shortening the X Corps boundary and sending reinforcements from the western part of his front contained the attack.

The U.S. enlisted men (GIs) fought tenaciously as they pulled back kilometre by kilometre; they inflicted heavy casualties on the attackers. X Corps artillery, augmented by batteries of 155 mm 'Long Tom' medium and 8-inch howitzer heavy guns, inflicted a frightful slaughter on the Chinese troops. Within days, at Ridgway's urging, Van Fleet began to plan a counterattack of his own along the western portion of the front to force back the Chinese. In the event, the attack was not necessary; Chinese losses were so heavy – some 17,000 killed in action and 36,000 wounded[10] – that they could not sustain their offensive. By 21 May they had once again broken contact and pulled back.[11]

Rockingham's brigade played no immediate part in helping to hold the UN line. On the 16th he and part of his staff left for Suwon – a distance of approximately 270 km over appalling roads, some virtual bogs after days of heavy rain. He arrived at Suwon well after dark and the next day attended an impromptu noon-hour conference at a nearby airstrip with the commanders of I and IX Corps and of 3rd, 24th, and 25th U.S. infantry divisions and Van Fleet, who flew in for the meeting. Van Fleet explained what has happening along the front to the east and his plans for holding the line in the I Corps sector. He intended to move the 3rd U.S. Infantry Division and its 65th Regiment, then holding part of the south bank of the Han River, eastward as part of a strengthened X Corps reserve. He wanted Rockingham's brigade to take the 65th Regiment's positions and asked when the Canadian formation would be ready. Rocky pointed out that the brigade was still in transit but assured Van Fleet that it could be in place by last light three days later. Van Fleet was satisfied. Rockingham arranged to have Keane, Dextraze, and his other unit commanders picked up from the road convoy by air and flown to Seoul to begin making plans for the deployment.[12]

Writing some years later of this meeting with Van Fleet, Rockingham claimed that Van Fleet had actually asked him to use 25 Brigade to 'fill in' the hole torn in the UN lines by the Chinese attack as soon as the brigade arrived at its concentration area. He wrote that he had refused, pointing out that his troops and equipment could not be married up in time for such a deployment and that it would not do to have his troops 'only expend their 50 rounds of rifle ammunition, then perhaps leave as big a hole as existed now ... I felt thoroughly miserable refusing my first task ... However, I was determined my troops not be put into action when they were missing so much of their essential equipment.'[13] This story is repeated in Col. H.F. Wood's *Strange Battleground: Official History of the Canadian Army in Korea*[14] and in the British official history.[15] At face value, this was just another occasion when unfeeling U.S. officers were prepared to sacrifice Canadian troops as Walker had been prepared to do with 2PPCLI shortly after it had arrived in Korea the previous December.

Rockingham's account of this episode is at variance with the known facts. The war diary from 25 Brigade HQ records no such incident. It is very precise as to the chain of events: Rockingham accepted his assignment without demur at around noon on the 17th, and, accompanied by Van Fleet, the 65th Regiment's CO, and other officers, he flew to the 65th Regiment sector for a reconnaissance. When Van Fleet and his entourage left, Rocky stayed behind to tour the ground and look over the defensive positions. The next day he and his battalion commanders made final preparations for deployment, along with Major Donald Rochester, who commanded the Canadian field-engineer squadron. On the 19th, Rockingham received orders cancelling the brigade's move into the 65th Regiment's positions because of the commencement of Van Fleet's western-sector counterattack, dubbed Operation Piledriver.[16]

The record is clear; at no time did Rockingham refuse any assignment. It is also highly unlikely that Van Fleet ever had any intention of using the Canadians to help stem the Chinese attack, since the Canadian brigade was far from the main Chinese penetration and other reserves were much closer. Why did Wood uncritically accept the events as related in Rockingham's memoir? No doubt he did so out of respect for Rockingham. Why did the official British historian, Sir Anthony Farrar-Hockley, accept Rockingham's version of the events? No doubt out of respect for Wood. Such are the pitfalls of following official histories too closely.

Just as 25 Brigade missed out on the fighting, so too, for the most part, did the Patricias who were still under command of

28 BCIB. Although thousands of Chinese troops were spotted near 28th Brigade's positions, and some skirmishing took place between the Commonwealth soldiers and the Chinese, the brigade itself was spared a major assault and suffered only minor casualties. As Lieut. C.W. Crossland of the West Yorkshire Regiment later recorded: 'The attack against this Brigade's positions never materialized. Although there was quite a build-up in front and quite heavy probing attacks on both flanks he never actually got to grips with us in strength.'[17] The Patricias eventually left 28 BCIB on 27 May and moved due south to Sambi-ri on the north bank of the Han River to rejoin Rockingham's main body.

Thursday, 24 May 1951. It was clear and very hot as the men of the 25th Canadian Infantry Brigade took their places in the line of march from Uijongbo north, to the Kansas Line astride the 38th parallel, and possibly beyond. For this first advance to contact, the brigade was under command of the 25th U.S. Infantry Division and followed a trail blazed across the valleys and hills of central Korea by Task Force Dolvin. The task force consisted of three tank companies and an infantry battalion. The strategy for the advance was simple; the UN Command's front-line formations would move ahead, in line abreast, protecting each other's flanks from enemy attempts to infiltrate between the UN formations.

Rockingham decided to move his headquarters along the dusty and narrow valley road that ran alongside a small stream. Because 2PPCLI had not yet rejoined the brigade, he had under command the Philippine army's 10th Battalion Combat Team; 2RCHA, which had been attached to the 28th BCIB, reverted to his command in time to take part in the advance. Dextraze's 2RReR, accompanied by one troop of Sherman tanks of 'C' Squadron, Lord Strathcona's Horse (Royal Canadian), or LdSH (RC), would lead on the right; Keane's 2RCR, with a second troop of Shermans, would lead on the left.[18]

The brigade crossed the start line at 0930 and moved ahead cautiously. There was virtually no opposition because the Chinese were retreating rapidly in order to concentrate to protect the village of Chorwon and its surrounding plain. Chorwon was a major rail and road junction and the main Chinese military supply and trans-shipment point in central Korea. It was the key to Chinese logistical support; the Chinese were determined to defend it. Their tactics called not for a fighting retreat or a defence in depth after the failure of a major attack such as the May offensive, but for a virtually complete break in contact and rapid withdrawal, leaving behind only small, well-hidden fire teams to harass the advancing enemy.[19]

Australian war correspondent Derek Pearcy, working for Reuters-Australia, described the first hours of 2RCR's advance:

After a hectic night of preparation and celebration they set off at 6 a.m. down a valley thatched with paddy fields and dotted with farms and out buildings.

Keyed up with training and waiting behind the lines, they started out carefully ... Their small arms were at the ready, their eyes alert for the slightest movement ahead of them.

The first shot rang out. The infantrymen ducked for cover, fanned out, and opened fire at a hill on their flank.

There was a short silence, then a rattle of Sten guns, then silence again.

The Canadians emerged cautiously from shelter and closed in warily on a camouflaged dugout not far from the crest. A young Canadian looked intently into the dugout, laughed a little, then waved the others on.

By mid-afternoon the Canadians were under heavy harassing fire ... From the gnarled mountain on their left came the continuous crack of small-arms fire ...

The infantrymen crossed a field to scale the mountainside from the north. Chinese entrenched on the razor-backed ridge opened up a wild barrage of machine-gun, rifle and mortar fire and the Canadians climbed up, jumping out from behind rocks and trees. For an hour the valley resounded to the crack of rifles, the crash of grenades and the thump of tank guns and mortars.

Allied fighters added to the din as they wheeled and dove to rocket and drop napalm on the Chinese.[20] The RCR had run into a small Chinese fire team atop Hill 407 armed with rifles, light machine-guns, and a light mortar. The fire fight continued until nightfall, when the battalion hunkered down into a tight defensive position. This was the last dispatch that Pearcy ever wrote; he was killed the next day.

Early the next morning the valley reverberated to the sound of low-flying jets and rocket and napalm explosions, as fighter-bombers of the 5th U.S. Air Force tried to blow apart the Chinese position atop Hill 407. There was a moment of comic relief after the smoke cleared and the roiling flame of the napalm died away when Rockingham saw three men emerge from their holes atop 407, hurriedly roll up their blankets, grab the remains of their breakfast, and scurry down the far side of the feature.[21] After the air attack, the Canadian advance continued over rugged mountain country bisected by razorback ridges and small, fast-flowing streams. On 27 May the brigade reached the Kansas Line; a combined Canadian–Philippine tank-infantry team then pushed about 10 km beyond and dug in. At this point the entire brigade was situated in a salient because it had advanced some 4,000 m beyond its flanking formations – the 35th U.S. Infantry Regiment on the left and the 24th on the right.

This type of warfare was slow and plodding, where sections, platoons, and occasionally a company assaulted the rearguard Chinese fire teams, invariably well entrenched. One of the Chinese defensive techniques was to dig holes under large boulders, leaving only enough room for themselves to clamber in and fire on the Canadians from near the bottom of the boulders. The Chinese were hard to spot and harder to dislodge. There was little here of the sweep and movement that modern warfare was supposed to be all about. One Second World War tank veteran told Canadian Press correspondent Bill Boss: 'The whole thing makes you think of Italy, doesn't it?'[22]

It may be that the natural desire of the Canadians to get the enemy out into the open and then fight led to the near-disaster that befell 2RCR on 30 May as it tried to capture Kakhul-Bong (Hill 467). This high, craggy, twin-peaked feature dominated the north–south valley through which the brigade would have to pass in the next phase of its push north; it was directly in the way of 2RCR's axis of attack. Rockingham was somewhat reluctant to push ahead with the 2RCR attack, since it would further expose the brigade's flanks, but the divisional commander, Brig.-Gen. Bradley, assured him that the two laggard regiments would 'be able to conform in time to secure the flanks.'[23] In the event, they did not.

Keane's plan was to move his battalion through the Royal 22nd Regiment shortly after first light on 30 May and deploy three of his four companies in a sweeping attack to outflank the feature on the left, isolate it, then take it by direct assault of the fourth company. 'A' Company, mounted in half-tracks and accompanied by tanks, was ordered to move quickly over the start line, through Kurunjumak, a tiny hamlet about 1.5 km to the north, then follow a rough track on the valley floor between Hill 467 to the right and a series of rice paddies to the left. It was to advance some 5 km ahead of the main battalion positions straight into the village of Chail-li, about 2.5 km north of Hill 467. 'A' Company's main task was to secure Chail-li, especially a small bridge on the north side of the village, which Keane considered the back door to Hill 467. Following 'A' Company, 'B' Company would cross the start line, then veer left and secure a small knoll known as Hill 162, about 2.5 km west of Hill 467. 'C' Company would follow 'A' Company's path through Kurunjumak but would veer right after passing Hill 467 to occupy Hill 269, about half-way between Chail-li and 467.[24]

Daylight brought heavy rain, fog patches, and mist swirling around the heights of Hill 467; the battle would be fought in conditions of low visibility not unlike a night attack. The planned air strike was called off. Two regiments of Long Toms and one regiment of field artillery opened their designated firing tasks at 0600, hitting various suspected enemy strongpoints on the route of attack and bombarding Chail-li itself for about fifteen minutes. Then 'A' Company pushed off, followed by 'B' and 'C.' At first all went well, and the infantry easily secured its respective objectives. When 'D' Company began the arduous climb up the rain-swept crags of Hill 467, however, it came under concentrated Chinese fire from up the hill, especially from a machine-gun position at the very top. Then the Chinese counterattacked 'A' Company in Chail-li. The Canadians were hit with mortar and machine-gun fire as well as shells fired by low-trajectory, direct-fire guns. One 57 mm anti-tank gun disabled a Sherman with a hit in its suspension. At the same time Chinese troops began moving down from the north and working their way around both flanks of 'A' Company. The men of 'C' Company, some 20 m to the south on Hill 269, could see soldiers moving through the fields in the mist but could not be sure if they were Canadians or Chinese; they held off calling for a barrage. The troops were Chinese intent on closing a trap around 'A' Company. These Chinese soldiers were nothing like the ragamuffins whom the Canadians had been meeting since the start of the advance on 24 May. They were highly motivated, excellent in fieldcraft, and well-armed, and they were determined to hold Hill 467 until they were good and ready to pull back to the Chorwon area.

By midday Keane and Rockingham knew that not much was going as planned. Things got much worse, however, when large bodies of Chinese troops were spotted moving from the northwest right past 'C' Company's position on Hill 269, towards 'D' Company. They had found the brigade's uncovered right flank even while 'D' Company was still trying unsuccessfully in the heavy rain, and under fire, to reach the top of Hill 467 or destroy the machine-gun position there with bazooka fire. The Chinese reinforcements came within 300 m of 'C' Company, which tried to engage them with Bren and rifle fire, but the distance was too great for their fire to have any measurable effect.

By early afternoon Keane's entire battalion was in deep trouble. 'A' Company in Chail-li was under heavy fire including mortar fire and in danger of being cut off. 'D' Company was spread out on the slopes of Hill 467 and awaiting an onslaught of at least two companies of fresh Chinese troops. No air support was available, and the mist and fog made artillery-spotting too risky. At approximately 1300, Rockingham contacted Keane and ordered him to withdraw south of Kurunjumak hamlet.[25] That task was easier ordered than done. With the walking wounded being protected by tanks, and with the flanks of the withdrawal route being blasted by Canadian mortar and artillery fire, the men pulled back, with the Chinese harassing them all the way.

By 1900, 2RCR was back where it had started, but with five men killed and thirty-one wounded for virtually no gain. Two tanks had

also been lost, although one was recovered the following day. Rockingham later wrote that the men of the battalion had 'acquitted
themselves nobly,'[26] as they no doubt had, but they had done so
trying to execute an attack plan that was badly conceived from the
beginning. Keane's scheme was too complicated and depended on
split-second timing and excellent communications, all very difficult to achieve in a blinding rain, with fog and mist obscuring the
battlefield. By trying to outmanoeuvre the Chinese on Hill 467,
Keane had placed his companies too far apart for real mutual support. Keane had in effect turned half his rifle strength – 'B' and 'C'
Companies – into frustrated bystanders, while his other two companies, widely separated from each other, tried to deal with a
major Chinese counterattack. Worse, the Canadian attack had
overexposed the entire brigade's right flank.[27]

The brigade did not resume its advance past Hill 467; 2R22eR
and 2RCR remained in their forward positions on 31 May, and the
entire formation, save the Van Doos and 2RCHA, went into corps
reserve one day later. The two detached units remained to support
the 65th U.S. Infantry Regiment, which took over the brigade's
positions. While in corps reserve, 25 CIB moved to an area approximately 15 km south of the confluence of the Imjin and Hantan
rivers to link up with 28 BCIB and 29 BIB in preparation for the
formation of 1 (Commonwealth) Division in July.

President Truman and the U.S. Joint Chiefs of Staff had much earlier decided that the UN could not seek victory in Korea against
China, especially with the potential threat of Soviet intervention.
Korea would be divided eventually, but until the Chinese came to
the same realization the war would continue. Ridgway and Van
Fleet were determined to take advantage of the collapse of the Chinese spring offensives by pushing all Communist troops out of
South Korea, re-establishing a strong presence on the Kansas Line,
and pushing beyond it as far as their political masters in New York
and Washington determined. Once that was accomplished, the
UN's original aim 'to free South Korea of the enemy and to re-
establish and hold the boundary' would be achieved, and the
active phase of the war, if not the war itself, might end.[28]

Throughout the last days of May and into June, Van Fleet's Operation Piledriver, spearheaded by X Corps, rolled up the Chinese flank in the east, gaining some 70 km along the east coast of Korea between 22 May and 8 July. The overall strategy was to fortify the Kansas Line to make it virtually impregnable to any major Chinese offensive while pushing farther north in small jumps and establishing further defensive lines beyond the Kansas Line. Those forward lines would be much more temporary in nature, designed to absorb the first shock of a major attack. By early July the Wyoming Line had been established north of the Hwachon Reservoir in central Korea and through the base of the so-called iron triangle bounded by Chorwon on the southwest, Pyonggang on the north, and Kumhwa on the southeast. This was the same vital Chinese staging area, also known as the Chorwon Plain, that 2RCR had poked its finger near on 30 May, with near-disastrous results.[29]

On the western end of the Kansas line, in the I Corps sector, Van Fleet anchored his line along the Imjin River. Flowing southward, it formed a good defensive barrier as long as the Chinese were prevented from approaching it in strength.[30] Crossing the Imjin at this time was not contemplated, since the failure of the Chinese spring offensive opened up the possibility of cease-fire talks. Thus it was political restraint, not military incapability, that left the north and west banks of the Imjin River, near its junction with the Hantan River, beyond the UN's main line of resistance on the Kansas Line.

The cross-river area of several hundred square kilometres was essentially a salient of unoccupied territory in the northwest corner of the UN's main line of resistance. The salient was bounded by a great loop in the Imjin River on the south and east sides, but wide open to possible Chinese infiltration from the north and northwest. To prevent such infiltration in strength, EUSAK ordered regular patrols to be mounted across the Imjin. Each patrol was really a reconnaissance in force by armour/infantry teams mounted from forward patrol bases held by formations of at least a battalion in strength on the north side of the river. One could cross the river by cable-operated pontoon ferry, a footbridge, or a number of fords, where vehicles such as half-tracks could travel at low water. The patrols would be mounted largely by

the 25th CIB and the other Commonwealth units. Another generation in a later, limited war in Vietnam would call such patrols
'search and destroy' operations.

The 25th CIB's patrol activity increased after a change in position to the northeast, near the Chorwon end of the Wyoming Line,
in mid-June. The patrols were difficult to mount, used major artillery and air resources, and brought a steady stream of casualties –
fourteen Canadians were killed in action and two died of wounds
on patrol in June and July. The dead and wounded were a constant
drain on the brigade's manpower, and the patrols exhausted
the men, especially in the hot weather. The repetitiveness of the
patrols over the limited number of hard-packed roads in the
salient, and through thick undergrowth, gave the Chinese ample
opportunity for interdiction, which took many forms, from mining
to ambushes.

The Chinese grew bolder day after day, moving farther forward
with their ambush teams and raising the prospect of a significant
battle with serious consequences for the Canadians, whose lines of
supply and communications ended on the south bank of the
river.[31] At one point in late June, IX Corps decided to evacuate all
civilians living in front of the patrol bases and along all patrol
routes as a security measure against spies and saboteurs. Several
thousand were removed to a civilian collecting point 40 km south
of the 25 Brigade area.[32] Such 'relocation' intended to deny the
enemy access to civilians, was also similar to what happened in the
Vietnam conflict.

On 30 June 1951, at Washington's direction, Ridgway broadcast
an invitation to Chinese and North Korean commanders to send
representatives to discuss a cease-fire preliminary to a peace settle-
ment. The following day, the Communists agreed.[33] Both sides
decided on the small village of Kaesong, on the 38th parallel (then
in Communist-held territory) as the venue for talks that would
begin on 8 July. Van Fleet had issued orders on 30 June that the
invitation to talk was not to affect operations[34] – both sides were
determined to keep fighting for position despite the talks – but the
reality was quite different, at least on the UN side. As Ridgway later
wrote: 'It seemed to me, with a cease-fire faintly visible on the hori-

zon, that I should do all I could to keep our losses as a justifiable minimum. I notified our commanders therefore that we would conduct no major offensives but would seek to retain the initiative through the use of strong patrols and local attacks designed to seize key terrain which would extend our observations and curtail the enemy's.'[35]

The patrols across the Imjin continued, however, as did the casualties and the continuing strain on men and equipment. After one particularly harrowing patrol by 2PPCLI on 2 July, Rockingham's war diarist noted: 'The weather continued hot and dry with the temperature in the high eighties. The troops suffered considerably from the heat especially as most of their movement was climbing through dry and dusty bracken, in some places four feet high. The growth in this area is very dense and movement along the paths is very difficult. The cover afforded the enemy is very good and Chinese tactics are adapted to the terrain and cover, giving them a decided advantage in a patrol action like today's.'[36]

Fortunately for the Canadians, the Chinese were not always capable of recognizing the golden opportunities that these missions provided them to inflict great damage on the patrolling forces. One such missed opportunity presented itself between 18 and 22 July, when a major patrol effort was mounted by 25 Brigade to cover the withdrawal of the 1st Battalion, 5th Cavalry Regiment, from the salient. On this occasion Rockingham's tasks were set by the 25th U.S. Infantry Division, which instructed him to allocate a battalion to set up a patrol base deep into the salient, about 5,000 m from the main brigade positions along the river. Rockingham chose 2R22eR to make the main penetration, while three companies of 2RCR were to guard the pontoon ferry. Both battalions were to be supported by Strathcona tanks. Rockingham worried that 2R22eR might be too far out to help if the Chinese offered heavy resistance, and he prevailed on the division commander to allow him to locate the battalion's objective closer to the river.

The operation commenced on the afternoon of 18 July; that night the Chinese 'gave their first indication that they were prepared to make the occupation of the outpost position by 2R22eR as difficult as possible.' The fighting was not intense, but more an indication from the enemy that it was alert and biding its time. At midday on the 19th, heavy rains began, and they continued for the next forty-eight hours. The Imjin rose rapidly. Half-tracks attempting to cross the north ford were swamped. The footbridge was carried away, tearing out telephone lines to the north bank and smashing the cables supporting the pontoon ferry. Almost all the Royal 22nd radios failed, and the telephone lines to the south bank were ripped away by the rushing river. The Chinese attacks on the Royal 22nd intensified by the hour.

By midnight of 20–1 July, the situation across the river had reached a crisis. Rocky had the entire 2R22eR, three companies of 2RCR, and one company of 2PPCLI sent to the north bank to reinforce the Van Doos, and four Strathcona tanks 'completely isolated and without access by ferry, ford or footbridge to the east bank of the Imjin.' Also trapped were an American intelligence and reconnaissance platoon and some seventy-five vehicles. Rockingham ordered up powerboats as the troops worked feverishly to defend themselves from Chinese probes while re-establishing regular communications with the Royal 22nd. He also ordered Dextraze to abandon the battalion outpost and return to the river bank. The Canadians held fast along the river, and the Chinese failed to press home their advantage. The weather moderated, although the pontoon ferry finally broke its mooring and drifted downstream. At 0830 on 22 July the crisis passed when the commanding general of the 25th Division 'ordered all forces to be withdrawn across the river.'[37]

If the Chinese had mounted a coordinated attack in the salient in brigade strength on the night of 20 July, the Canadians would have suffered heavily. No one can know why the Chinese did not take advantage of their opportunity. But whatever the reason, Rockingham and his brigade were just plain lucky. The fortunes of war had smiled on Canada, allowing virtually half the brigade to survive to fight again.

The absence of major fighting in central Korea in July 1951 provided an opportunity to finalize the formation of the composite

Commonwealth division envisioned by the British, Australian, New Zealand, and Canadian governments as far back as July 1950. The 1st (Commonwealth) Division was born on 28 July in a brief ceremony near the small Korean town of Tokchong, less than 10 km south of the Imjin River. Maj.-Gen. A.J.H. Cassels, designated GOC, and the commanding officers of the Canadian, British, Australian, New Zealand, and Indian formations that were being joined, played host to Van Fleet at a ceremony that lasted only twenty minutes. As the brigade commanders stood at attention, Cassels and Van Fleet broke out the blue UN banner and the divisional flag – a UN banner with the word 'Commonwealth' across it in gold letters. Then, behind them, the flags of the five participating nations were also unfurled. Van Fleet read a brief message from Ridgway. There was no time for histrionics when the business of war was waiting.

The idea for the division was not rooted solely in a sense of Commonwealth solidarity. Soldiers fight best when their morale is good, and their morale is best when they receive a constant flow of the basics of war, such as food, ammunition, replacement weapons, reinforcements, and the essentials of civilized life – regular mail, hot meals, and a chance to wash up, clean up, rest up, and blow off steam. Soldiers also need to know that if wounded they will be evacuated as quickly as possible and will receive the best medical care available. These support services were vital to both the fighting power of the brigade and to the well-being of the troops. With Canada having sent only one brigade group to Korea, it would have been difficult, wasteful, and very expensive to set up a fully functioning support system. This was a major consideration behind the desire to combine with other, smaller national contingents in a single division. Thus the Commonwealth Division was mostly the result of practical necessity.

The division was composed of the 25th CIB, the 28th BCIB (itself made up of British, Australian, and New Zealand troops), the 29th BIB, and a number of artillery, armour, anti-aircraft, engineer, and medical units. The Belgian battalion was also part of the division. At the time of its formation, the division held a 10,000 m section of the front along the Imjin River, anchored between the

1st ROK Division on the left and the 25th U.S. Infantry Division on the right. Both 28th and 29th brigades were in the line, but not Rocky's, which was being held in corps reserve some kilometres back. This holding back of the Canadian brigade was to remain a minor bone of contention between Cassels and his corps commander for some weeks. Cassels continually emphasized the difficulties that he would have to overcome in any task assigned his division until 25 CIB was married up with it and transferred from corps to divisional control.[38]

Cassels had more than a passing acquaintance with the militaries of the Commonwealth partners. Prior to being named GOC-designate of the new division, he had served on the United Kingdom Services Liaison Staff in Canberra. During the war he had commanded a brigade in the 51st Highland Division to which Rockingham's 9th Brigade had been attached in the Rhine River crossing of March 1945. The official historian of the British role in the Korean War describes Cassels as a man with 'an open and engaging manner combined with an ability to speak his mind firmly on matters of principle without giving offence.'[39] These were invaluable traits, given the unique position of the Commonwealth Division in the UN Command's order of battle.

The division was one of five that made up I Corps, commanded by Lt.-Gen. J.W. ('Iron Mike') O'Daniel. In matters military, 'Iron Mike' was boss and passed orders down from Van Fleet to Cassels. It was then up to Cassels not only to assign tasks to his brigade commanders and/or to the supporting arms organically part of the division – the normal job of a division commander – but also to interpret those instructions in a way that was intelligible to his subordinates. This was vital, because American soldiers and those who came out of British traditions, and who had been trained in British doctrine, in effect spoke different languages. They had learned to fight wars in different ways, and in Korea the differences had contributed to the April 1951 disaster suffered by the Glosters on the Imjin.[40]

The formation of the Commonwealth Division put Cassels and his staff, Canadians among them, between the battalions that did the fighting and the American high command at corps and army levels. As Lt.-Col. N.G. Wilson-Smith, of the 1st Battalion, PPCLI, later put it: 'When 1st Commonwealth Division was formed ... its headquarters stood between U.S. Corps Headquarters and our forces. From this time on, at the Battalion level especially, the direct effects of serving under U.S. command were fairly well filtered out.'[41]

The formation of the Commonwealth Division was not an unmixed blessing for Rockingham or, for that matter, for the two other brigade commanders. As commander of an independent brigade group, and national commander, Rockingham had had complete control of his subordinate formations from the field artillery to the field ambulance. Now that he was a brigade commander in a division, he lost operational control, or command authority, over those supporting arms such as engineers and field artillery that normally fell under divisional control. He did, however, maintain administrative control of all Canadian formations attached to the brigade.[42]

Differences in battle doctrine and administrative systems between Allied armies were as inevitable as those in formation establishment, weaponry, and artillery procedures. The difficulties and the misunderstandings that might result had been somewhat anticipated when London, Ottawa, and Canberra gave their national commanders their command instructions. Even though Rockingham was operationally subordinate to Cassels, O'Daniel, and Van Fleet, for example, Ottawa had provided him with a secret means of communication to army HQ and the right to refuse an assignment if he deemed that course necessary for the safety of his command. He would have used this provision, referred to as 'waving the paper,'[43] only under the most drastic circumstances and in fact never did so, but it might have provided some measure of protection if he had ever been ordered to execute a command that he knew would lead to the virtual destruction of his brigade.

In the Korean fighting there were a number of significant differences between the way in which Americans conducted operations and normal British practice. In the British and Commonwealth armies it was usual to pass detailed orders regarding objectives and formation boundaries down the chain of command but to leave the method of carrying out those orders to the discretion of the subordinate formation commander. In the U.S. army, subordinate commanders received not only their objectives but also a set of instructions as to how to achieve them. This arrangement allowed for more centralized control from above, but less initiative from below.[44] Cassels chafed under it. At one point he 'put his cards on the table' and told his corps commander that Americans and British had different ways of doing things. In future he would appreciate it if Iron Mike simply give Cassels his task, explain why it was important, then let the divisional staff alone to do the job. In Cassels's words, 'The Corps Commander could not have been more helpful and, since then, things have been much better and both sides are happier.'[45]

Differences also extended to the front line. U.S. doctrine held that a hill should be defended from positions on the shoulder, so that defending troops could direct grazing fire at an attacking enemy. Grazing fire is high-volume fire directed low and parallel to the ground and more likely to make inadvertent hits than aimed fire or plunging fire – fire from hilltops that arced downward. The U.S. command believed that grazing was far more effective than plunging fire.[46] Commonwealth doctrine held that hills were best defended from the top. There were also differences in doctrine regarding patrolling, the mounting of counterattacks, and the imposition and maintenance of discipline.[47]

As well, there were personal differences between Cassels, calm and understated, and O'Daniel, who tended to be boisterous, rambunctious, and aggressive. Cassels was appalled by the 'cold steel' rhetoric that O'Daniel and other American officers loved to spout. Yet there was a method to the apparent U.S. madness. Aside from the 1st Marine Division, most U.S. troops in Korea were conscripts. During the long lulls between battles there was significant danger that these soldiers would lose their sharpness and the aggressive spirit that was so vital in the face of the enemy. There was therefore a definite place for this aggressive rhetoric and for the individual and unit refresher training, which emphasized the 'cold steel' approach to battle that went with it.[48]

One of the most crucial differences between the Canadian and the American efforts in Korea concerned rotation policy. In the Second World War, U.S., Canadian, and other Allied troops inevitably served in active theatres of war 'for the duration.' But that war was, from start to finish, virtually a fight to the death, to be waged until the enemy had unconditionally surrendered. It was certainly clear on the UN side by the late spring of 1951 that the Korean conflict was to be very different in objective, and this raised the question of rotation policy; if U.S. or Canadian soldiers were not to stay on the peninsula indefinitely, when and how would they be sent home and their places be taken by other soldiers? The U.S. answer was to rotate individual soldiers after a fixed period of time in-theatre, leaving existing formations in place.[49]

Guy Simonds, Chief of the General Staff of the Canadian army, disagreed with that approach. He recommended to Brooke Claxton that Canadian troops be rotated by whole units and that the 1st battalions of the parachute-trained Mobile Striking Force be dispatched to Korea to replace the 2nd battalions. He suggested that no Canadian unit remain in Korea longer than a year, or at most one winter. Simonds wanted the regular army units to rotate through Korea both for the morale of soldiers in the Mobile Striking Force (MSF) and in order for them to gain operational experience. He did not want the regular units to get into a 'home service' mindset, leaving overseas assignments only for special volunteers. He believed that it would be a 'serious blow to the interest and pride of the officers and men of the 1st Battalions' if the 3rd battalions, formed from the excess of volunteers for the MSF, were sent to Korea before them. After a scheme was worked out to assure Claxton that a core of trained parachutists would remain for the defence of Canada, Simonds's proposal was approved.[50] 2PPCLI was to be rotated back to Canada first, since it had been first to arrive in Korea.

On 18 August, 1PPCLI, commanded by Lt.-Col. N.G. Wilson-Smith, was given a warning order to begin preparations for the move to Korea. The first two rifle companies of 1PPCLI arrived in-theatre on 5 October, and the third came three weeks later. The actual rotation was carried out *in situ*, with the 2nd battalion still holding its front-line positions. After a short course in weapons and tactical training, the first two companies of 1PPCLI entered the line on 14 October and acquitted themselves very well when they first came under fire.[51]

Unlike the first contingent of Canadians, who had to learn about Korea largely by fighting in it, these troops were very well-trained in infantry fundamentals and had the great benefit of being able to learn the lessons of the previous year's fighting from U.S., British, and Canadian experience. By the summer of 1951 the Canadian army was serving up regular 'Notes on Training from Korea,' garnered from every possible source, which went into great detail in preparing officers and men for what they would experience at the battle front. One such circular, for example, not only stressed the extreme need for great physical toughness in order to climb steep hills with heavy packs and be able to fight as soon as the top was reached, it even instructed Canadian soldiers in the hill-climbing techniques used by Korean porters. Other key subjects included how the Chinese positioned their weapons inside their bunkers so as not to be observed except from very close, the construction of Chinese box mines and mine-laying techniques, and how to throw grenades up hill.[52]

The cease-fire negotiations at Kaesong put an end to major offensive operations along the UN front in the summer of 1951 and marked a definite shift to defensive operations. In the I Corps sector, Van Fleet had decided that the Wyoming Line was to become 'a main line of resistance,' although the Commonwealth Division was to maintain its positions along the Kansas Line. One consequence of this turn of events was the effort to enhance the defensive fire-power of the rifle companies by allotting a minimum of three extra Bren guns per company and, if possible, one extra Bren to every section.[53]

Despite the emphasis on defence, active patrolling in force and in daylight continued along the Commonwealth Division front. Vigilance in the salient across the Imjin remained important. Van Fleet rather suspected that a new Chinese offensive might begin at any time, and the UN Command carried out its planning at army, corps, division, and even brigade levels during these months with one eye on the possibility of such an offensive.[54] In mid-August, Cassels ordered his two brigades in line, 28 BCIB and 29 BIB, to mount a fighting patrol each day and at least two night ambush patrols each week. Rockingham's brigade, still in reserve, was to send one battalion forward in rotation every week to take part in the patrolling.[55] While in reserve, Rockingham decided to devote considerable staff time to planning for a possible Chinese offensive, since, if one developed, 25 Brigade would be rushed back to the Seoul sector to help defend the capital. One of the possibilities for which the brigade planned was a Chinese parachute attack against the bridges spanning the Han River, which formed the only route by which UN troops might withdraw in the face of a massive offensive against the South Korean capital.[56]

The patrols over the Imjin continued through the first three weeks of August; for the 25th Brigade, they climaxed with Operations Dirk (13–16 August) and Claymore (22–4 August), both battalion-sized raids. The first was mounted by 2RCR; the second, by the Royal 22nd Regiment and the Patricias. Both were supported by C Squadron tanks. Dirk began just before nightfall on the 13th, when the RCR's 'B,' 'C,' and 'D' Companies crossed the Imjin at the ferry site and moved about 2 km into the salient. The following day they set up a firm base for patrolling and reconnaissance about 10 km north of the Imjin crossing and fanned out to begin trying to determine Chinese strength across the base of the salient. This was the deepest penetration of the salient mounted by any formation of the Commonwealth Division and actually reached the Chinese outpost line, but the Chinese chose not to oppose the raid in anything other than desultory fashion.

Despite a number of fire fights on the 15th, there were no prolonged exchanges, and the Chinese did not bring heavy weapons to bear. The Canadian artillery, supplied by 2RCHA from across the river, and the accompanying Shermans no doubt helped keep the Canadian casualties down; no Canadians were killed, and very few were wounded, although they killed an estimated thirty-five Chinese. The Canadians were learning how to fight effectively in tank-infantry teams in this otherwise armour-unfriendly terrain.

The acting commander of 2RCR, Major C.H. Lithgow, thought the artillery and tank fire support 'superb.'[57]

Claymore, several days later, was mounted to reconnoitre the northern part of the salient, especially the hilly area about 3 km southeast of Little Gibraltar – Hill 355 – which dominated the country for kilometres around. Both 2PPCLI and 2R22eR crossed over the Imjin about 9 km north of its junction with the Hantan and moved west before splitting up to assault two hills – 208 and 187 – before returning across the river on the 24th, the Royal 22nd to the original crossing site and the Patricias to a ford several kilometres to the southwest. The operation was 'relatively uneventful,' in the words of one report, and 'few tactical lessons [were] learnt.'[58]

Through the hot, dry summer of 1951 the representatives of the UN Command and the Chinese and North Korean armies met sporadically at Kaesong. They accomplished nothing of any consequence because the Communist side was not yet interested in bringing the fighting to a conclusion on any terms but its own. On 23 August the talks were suspended indefinitely, not because either side had abandoned hope for agreement on the overall objective of dividing Korea, but because it was dawning on Ridgway that renewed military pressure on the Chinese was essential to getting any worthwhile results. But how much pressure was enough?

A great debate has raged in the memoirs of some of the UN military leaders, and in histories of the war, as to the wisdom of relaxing military pressure on the Communists after the collapse of the two phases of the Chinese spring offensive in April and May 1951.[59] There is no reason to relate the major arguments of that debate here, except to point out that the successful UN advance had convinced the Chinese to talk in the first place and that it ought to have been apparent to someone in higher authority that continuing to apply military pressure might be the only way to produce a quick result at the talks.

The breakdown of the Kaesong talks gave O'Daniel an opportunity to move his troops, principally the Commonwealth Division, across the Imjin, thus straightening out the Wyoming Line in his sector and eliminating the salient caused by the river's swing to the southwest. Cassels agreed with the move and may have suggested it to O'Daniel[60] because the patrols-in-force across the river were accomplishing very little. Cassels planned the move in two phases; on 8 September, 28 Brigade crossed the Imjin after securing the bridge and ford at map point 'Teal,' in the south, and the bridge at map point 'Pintail,' about 6 km to the northeast. After the brigade crossed, British and American engineers worked quickly to construct class-50 bridges, capable of bearing tanks, at Teal and Pintail and to improve surfaces, grades, and load capacity of the roads forward of the bridges. They completed the work in three days.[61]

On 10 September, 2PPCLI began its move across the river in advance of the rest of 25 Brigade, using the new bridge at Pintail; the other two battalions followed the next day, with the brigade then taking its place along the new front line. The 28th BCIB was to its north, and the 29th BIB to the south, about 6 km west of the river. On the northern section of the brigade front, the new Canadian positions were dominated by Hill 222, which lay about 1,500 m northwest of where the Royal 22nd was digging in. A reconnaissance patrol confirmed Chinese troops on the position, and Rockingham directed Dextraze to clear the enemy from the hill and from two smaller nearby peaks. Dextraze selected his 'B' Company for the task.[62]

'B' Company, accompanied by tanks, moved out from the main battalion position in mid-afternoon of 10 September, paused while the USAF executed a heavy rocket and napalm strike on the objectives, then moved out over the rugged terrain. The Chinese opened up with heavy machine-guns spattering lead among the rocks. The Canadians took cover while the company commander and the forward observation officer (FOO) who directed the artillery, crawled forward to get a better view. Within minutes the battalion's 81 mm mortars and the 25-pounders of 2RCHA opened up, raining explosives on and around the three hills. Larger shells from the medium 155 mm Long Toms soon joined the bombardment. Then two platoons advanced under cover of the Strathconas' tanks to assault Hill 215, a knoll at the southeast end of a ridge that ended at Hill 222. A tank observation officer went with them.

Wearing a cerise panel on his back and carrying a small 88 radio set, he directed the tank fire right in front of the advancing infantry and sometimes directly into the openings of the Chinese bunkers.

The Royal 22nd riflemen charged uphill. Enemy grenades, rifle, and machine-gun fire poured down. The Canadians pressed forward. One section led by Cpl J.G. Ostiguy was reduced to three men, but Ostiguy pushed into a Chinese platoon position and grenaded the Chinese out. By 1630, the Royal 22nd had reached the top, at a cost of two dead and two wounded, but it could not hold the peak in the face of intense Chinese fire from Hill 222. It was forced to pull back, but it had killed thirty-six Chinese soldiers.[63] The following day Dextraze tried again, sending 'D' Company out in a heavy fog. It encountered some resistance, but nothing of the intensity of the previous day, and secured Hill 222 by 0930.[64]

On 18 September, Rockingham learned that a second corps offensive involving the Commonwealth Division was in the planning stages for the near future.[65] Details of what was to be attacked, by whom, and when were still sketchy, but the only logical move was to push farther west to the base of the river salient and take control of the height of land overlooking the Nabu-ri valley, through which flowed a small, unnamed tributary of the Sami-Ch'on. Across that valley, intelligence believed, lay the Chinese winter defence line. The weather was still very summer-like, with hot, sometimes humid days and mild nights, but deep cold and heavy snowfall were now weeks, not months, away. If the Chinese were to be driven as far as possible from the UN Command's main lateral road and rail supply line, which ran through Chorwon and had been taken during Operation Piledriver by U.S. troops, time and good weather were running out. In preparation, Rockingham ordered a new location to be prepared for his brigade headquarters on the north side of the Imjin.[66]

In the interval between the push across the Imjin and the coming attack, the Canadians prepared their company defensive localities with the idea that their best defence was to patrol vigorously into no man's land, primarily at night. This would deny the

Chinese the time or space to mount attacks on the Canadian positions. During the last half of September each battalion in turn took part in the patrolling, the men generally leaving their forward positions in the early morning hours to return just before last light. In total, eleven Canadians were killed in action that September, most in patrol actions.

The push to the Jamestown Line – Operation Commando – was to be a five-division attack along the entire 60 km of the I Corps front to the new forward defensive positions. All available army, corps, and divisional artillery was to support the advance, and there was to be a constant allotment of fighter-bombers aloft at the disposal of divisional HQ. In the Commonwealth Division sector, Cassels planned the 10 km advance in phases, much as he had done in Operation Minden. D Day was set for 3 October, when 28 Brigade on the division's right front was to open the attack, with Hill 355 as the main objective. That was phase 1. In phase 2, to begin the second day of the operation, Rockingham's brigade and the 29th were to move forward, 3,000 m ahead of the Wyoming Line. In the last phase, all three brigades would advance to the Jamestown Line.

At 0600 on 3 October the divisional, corps, and army artillery opened up on pre-arranged fire tasks. They fired some 27,000 rounds of 25-pounder shells alone in the course of the day. F-80s and F-84s hit targets in front of the 28th Brigade positions as the British and Australian infantry advanced in a heavy mist across low hills to a small valley at the base of Hill 355. There they stopped in preparation for the next day's attack on Little Gibraltar itself. At first light on the 4th, the three battalions – from the Royal Australian Regiment (3RAR), the King's Own Scottish Borderers (1KOSB) and the King's Shropshire Light Infantry (1KSLI) – assaulted Hill 355 and Hill 227, which lay immediately west of 355 and was connected to it by a high saddle. They inflicted major casualties on the Chinese but suffered only two dead and eighteen wounded themselves.[67]

As the 28th BCIB, supported by the 57-tonne Centurion tanks of the 8th Hussars, pushed up the two dominating peaks in the northern sector of the attack, the 25th and the 29th brigades began their part of the offensive. The British brigade, in a somewhat weakened state because of the departure of one of its battalions to Hong Kong, advanced to the left of the Canadians, sliding in behind to become the divisional reserve. Rocky had disposed his attacking troops with the Patricias on the right flank – 2RCR in the centre and 2R22eR on the left.

The two southernmost battalions ran into little resistance.[68] The Patricias were not so fortunate. An advance patrol came under heavy Chinese fire about 300 m from Hill 187, the battalion's first major objective of the day. Stone ordered 'D' Company to attack the feature and arranged twenty minutes of neutralizing fire from 2RCHA before the start time, then ten minutes of a rolling barrage after the assault company had crossed the start line. One troop of Shermans was detailed to provide direct fire support from about 1,800 m behind the attacking company.

The Chinese had dug a deep trench at the base of Hill 187 connected to bunkers and slit trenches at strategic places on the hillside. Under cover of the tank fire and field artillery, the Patricias reached the bottom-most trench on the forward slope. Chinese infantry swarmed through their crawl trenches, pushing down towards the Patricias. Tank and artillery fire poured on to the Chinese attack routes, but they come on anyway. The Patricias at the bottom of the hill refused to be trapped; bayonets fixed, they shot, bayoneted, and grenaded their way up the hill. They cleared the hill and found twenty-seven Chinese dead. Many more may well have been buried in their bunkers. After two hours the hill was secured at a cost of one Patricia killed and six wounded.[69] The Canadians fought one more tough fight later that day when 2RCR's 'B' Company, moving along a spur towards its objective, came under heavy Chinese fire. The company commander and his wireless operator became separated, and movement became almost impossible. The leading platoon was pinned down for hours; the company could not evacuate its casualties until after nightfall.[70]

Brigade casualties for the Canadians' first day totalled four killed and twenty-four wounded.[71] On 5 October, the last day of Commando, the division reached the Jamestown Line and began almost immediately to establish effective defences. In the next few weeks, brigade and battalion HQs were sited and wired in to their forwardmost troops and to division HQ. Thousands of rolls of barbed wire were laid, and fortified company positions were dug, on the line of hills that overlooked the Nabu-ri. Each was like a small fort, with mines laid around it, wire in front and in the valleys between; circular trenches connected to outward-thrusting fire trenches; and areas of approach covered by machine-guns set to fire on fixed lines. Mortars and artillery were ranged on to possible attack approaches and forming-up places. Extra Brens were brought forward to increase defensive fire-power. On the rear slopes, command bunkers, ammunition depots, and supply dumps were dug and covered over. It was going to be a long winter, the men knew, especially now that they were face to face with the Chinese just a few hundred metres away.

October was a month of constant night patrols and the odd daylight attack in company (or greater) strength for limited objectives, such as capturing a prisoner or booby-trapping Chinese positions. It was a month of digging deeper and laying ever more mines and stringing ever more barbed wire – there was never enough out there. It was also the month when intelligence reports that the Chinese had moved hundreds of artillery pieces close to the front were confirmed. The first heavy shelling was suffered by 28th Brigade troops on the afternoon of 7 October. 'Heavy shelling of this type by the enemy is very unusual,' the brigade's war diary noted that day. The shelling became the norm by the end of the month, with Chinese barrages approaching the intensity of German artillery shoots of the Second World War. October was also the month when the Chinese began to mount regular night attacks on the Jamestown Line positions, creeping forward under cover of their own artillery to place explosive charges or bangalore torpedoes under the Canadian wire to blow it and then jumping into the Canadian trenches. It was a pattern with which the Canadians would become all too familiar in the months ahead. In October 1951, twenty-three Canadians were killed in action in Korea, one of the heaviest tolls by far for any month of the war.

On 25 October, representatives of the UN Command and the Chinese and North Korean military gathered at Panmunjom, not far from Kaesong, to resume the cease-fire talks. The start of the talks initiated the so-called static phase of the Korean War, which was to last for twenty-one more months. This phase was static only in that UN unit commanders, from battalion on up, were ordered not to launch anything larger than single-company raids on Chinese positions. This order was rooted in political considerations, not military ones. It was a direct outcome of Washington's unreasonable fear of provoking Chinese or Soviet retaliation and undercutting the talks. It was a policy conceived in timidity that tied the hands of UN military commanders, who were henceforth unable to disrupt Chinese attacks before they took place or despoil Chinese weapons positions, communications facilities, and supply dumps. From November 1951 until the end of the war the soldiers of the UN Command fought for their lives with one hand tied behind their backs. Although some 111 Canadians had been killed in action or died on active service in Korea up to the day when the cease-fire talks resumed at Panmunjom, close to 200 more would be killed in action before the fighting actually stopped on 27 July 1953.

SIX

The Saddle

2100, 9 November 1951. It was hard for the seventy men of 'C' Company and the Scout platoon of the Royal 22nd to be totally silent as they moved cautiously out from the main battalion positions on the Jamestown Line and crept down the forward slope towards Hill 166. Everyone knew that the Chinese held the hill in strength, but no one was certain of the exact disposition of their defences. If any of the men moving out that night had known the history of their regiment in the First World War, they would have seen the similarity between the venture that they were about to undertake and the night trench raids mounted by the Canadians on the Western Front. Despite the advent of the atomic bomb, faster-than-sound fighter jets, and all the other major technological strides that warfare had made since 1916, the Korean War had come down to small knots of men trying to surprise the enemy under cover of night.

Operation Toughy was typical. The men wore Second World War–era battledress, but with knitted caps on their heads instead of helmets. Most carried U.S. M2 semi-automatic carbines and had bunches of grenades attached to their webgear. Their faces were blackened. The basic strategy was simple; they were to creep as close as possible to the Chinese, get into their trenches, snatch a prisoner, and do as much damage as possible. Toughy was supposed to be a textbook fire-and-manoeuvre assault, but without any artillery- or tank-fire preparation. The artillery-fire plan was to be used only if the Canadians encountered opposition. The raid was intended as much to keep the Chinese on their toes as to gain intelligence, however, because the side that dominated no man's land at night had a distinct advantage in both position and morale.

As it moved through the dark, 8 Platoon crossed the valley in front of the Canadian positions and headed north, directly at the hill. Seven platoon followed, then swung west to attempt to move on to the objective from the left flank. The men tried to keep quiet, but heavily armed soldiers do not usually move in great stealth unless they are especially trained and equipped to do so. These men were not. Someone may have stumbled in the dark. Maybe pebbles were kicked loose, to tumble to the valley floor. Or a rifle butt knocked against a grenade. Whatever it was that alerted the Chinese, they opened fire on 8 Platoon about fifteen minutes after it crossed the start line. Machine-gun, burp-gun, and rifle fire exploded out of the dark. Grenades came sailing towards the Canadians.

The platoon scrambled into a crawl trench some 75 to 100 m short of its initial objective – a knoll below the summit of Hill 166. Setting two of his sections up as a fire base, the platoon commander tried to get on to the objective with his third section moving around to the left. That did not work, so he called for artillery support, and the knoll ahead was plastered with heavy mortars and 25-pounder shells. Then the platoon charged the knoll, 'firing from [the] hip, throwing grenades and yelling fiercely.' That worked.[1]

To its left, 7 Platoon also came under heavy fire from automatic weapons and grenades. The men took shelter wherever they could, but they had no crawl trench to give them sanctuary. The platoon commander sent two sections ahead in the dark to probe the approaches to Hill 166, but the men could find no clear path. He decided to go up the middle. On signal, the entire platoon rose from the ground and charged ahead, with the men firing guns and throwing grenades until they reached their initial objective. It was 0100 on 10 November.

The Scout platoon, working around the far left of Hill 166, was not discovered by the Chinese until about 0122, when heavy automatic-weapons fire stopped it in its tracks at the base of the hill. By this time, however, 8 Platoon was ready to go for the summit of the hill, and 2RCHA began to lay on its fire plan. The guns fired at the hilltop and at suspected Chinese mortar and machine-gun positions on the forward slopes. The platoon tried to move ahead under cover of the fire but made little progress. The Chinese had the range, and the Canadian artillery and mortars were obviously failing to destroy their fire trenches and weapons pits.

The danger now increased by the minute that all three platoons would be pinned down until dawn, when they would be completely exposed to the Chinese defenders. One platoon commander reported by radio that Chinese infantry had infiltrated his platoon and that his men and the enemy were all mixed up. This made it impossible for the Canadian Shermans to 'bring down tank fire on previously registered targets' because of the danger to the Canadian infantry.[2] Fearing the worst, Dextraze ordered a general withdrawal. The raiders were back in the forward defence positions by 0300. Two men were missing, four wounded.[3]

The raid was a complete failure, even though casualties were relatively light. It accomplished nothing of any value; it took no prisoners; it gained no intelligence. The Chinese could not have sustained many casualties nor suffered any real damage to their defensive positions. The Canadian casualties were low only because Dextraze could easily see that the raid was going nowhere and that his men might be trapped if he did not act quickly.

What went wrong? There had been too few raiders. They had not used artillery, mortars, or close air support to mask their approach and neutralize the defenders because they chose to attack at night. When the artillery did get into the act, it fired according to predetermined plans, but darkness made the selection of new targets of opportunity almost impossible. The tanks could not use direct fire for fear of killing Canadians. Instead of playing to their overwhelming firepower strengths, Canadian and other troops of the UN Command were starting to fight a Chinese-style war. It was the inevitable result of the political decision to do as little as possible to upset the status quo on the front line.

By the beginning of November 1951, 1st (Commonwealth) Division held some 12,000 m of front between 1st U.S. Cavalry Division to the right and 1st ROK Division to the left. The Canadian portion of the division was supposed to have amounted to one-third – one of three brigades. But because the 28th British and the 29th Commonwealth brigades were under strength, Canada's 25th Infantry Brigade was contributing three of the seven line battalions; each Canadian battalion had all four rifle companies up.[4] That amounted to about half of the line infantry and almost two-thirds of the front.[5]

The three Canadian infantry battalions in the line at the start of November 1951 were 2 Royal Canadian Regiment (RCR), 2 Royal 22e Regiment (2R22eR), and three companies of both 1 and 2 Princess Patricia's Canadian Light Infantry (1 and 2 PPCLI). They were directly supported by the 25-pounder gun/howitzers of 2 Royal Canadian Horse Artillery (2RCHA) and the 76 mm–armed Sherman tanks of 'C' Squadron, Lord Strathcona's Horse (Royal Canadians). They held about 9,000 m of north–south front along roughly a 100 m contour line. The land dropped suddenly some 75 m in front of their positions to a small stream flowing south to the Sami-Ch'on. The Sami-Ch'on fed into the Imjin River about 5 km farther south. The dominant peak in the region was Hill 355, Little Gibraltar. The highest feature in the UN lines west of the Imjin, 355 towered over the surrounding hills. It and Hill 227, 1,500 m due west, were held by the 1st Battalion, King's Shropshire Light Infantry (KSLI), of the 28th British Infantry Brigade (BIB).

The Canadians faced the 568th and 570th regiments of the 190th Division of the Chinese Communist Sixty-fourth Army. Although the Chinese troops suffered many hardships compared to the UN forces,[6] they were by then far better equipped than the Chinese who had suddenly appeared out of the mountains of North Korea a year earlier.[7] Liberally supplied by the Soviet Union, the Chinese infantry was now supported by numerous direct and indirect fire weapons, Katyusha rocket batteries, self-propelled guns, and large numbers of mortars, all well dug in to the north-west of the Canadian positions. The evolution of the equipment mix of the Chinese troops was reflected in the nature of Canadian battle casualties. Some 52 per cent of all Canadian casualties reported up to December 1951 were caused by fragment wounds; only 33 per cent by small-arms fire or automatic weapons.[8]

Ridgway's decision to go over to the defensive ought to have dictated thorough preparation of defensive positions and aggressive tactics aimed at denying the initiative to the enemy, but that did not happen on the Commonwealth Division front. The problem began at division HQ, which never established or enforced a standard defence doctrine whereby each battalion would develop its defensive locality according to a single plan. That failure was compounded by shortages of adequate materials for bunkers, trenches, and dugouts; uncertainty produced by the armistice negotiations; and the sheer ignorance of many junior officers in the matter of selecting ground for defence. The static nature of the war discouraged initiative; battalions, companies, and platoons rotating into front-line positions usually just occupied the defences already there, undertaking only minor repair work and little improvement.[9]

The defences themselves were largely patterned after those that the Canadians had used in Italy in the Second World War. Rifle companies were positioned on hilltops along the front in positions encircled by a minefield, a single row of concertina wire, and a single, circular main trench. Fire trenches radiated outward from the main trench. Platoons were usually positioned at the corners of these defensive localities in order to engage the enemy in defilade. The valleys between the hilltop positions were strung with wire, and mines were planted there too. To the high ground to the rear, powerful searchlights were sited so as to illuminate enemy troops trying to infiltrate between defensive localities.[10] There was much dead ground on the lower slopes, however, while the minefields surrounding the hilltops had only one gap, to allow access and egress for purposes of patrolling. Given the roughness and the hilly nature of the terrain, the platoon positions were often sited too far forward to be of much help to the other platoons and were easily isolated by the attacking enemy, which usually went after them in company strength.[11]

There was no defence in depth for these hilltop fortresses, either from other defensive localities close by or to the rear – from the Wyoming Line, some 8 km back, or from the Kansas Line,

about 12 km farther back from Wyoming. Wyoming was intended
as the UN's first main line of resistance should the enemy penetrate the Jamestown Line, and Kansas was to be the second. There
was thus virtually no chance that troops along the Jamestown Line
could count on heavy fire support from the rear, except for rare
occasions when corps medium artillery could be brought to bear.
To compound the difficulty of defence on the Jamestown Line,
bad weather often made the Lines of Communication (LOCs)
from the rear almost impassable.[12]

In the Second World War, Canadians had come to count heavily
on their artillery. The system by which forward observation officers
(FOOs) could call down 'Mike,' 'Uncle,' or 'Victor' targets had
allowed them to devastate concentrations of German troops when
they were spotted forming up for attack. When a 'Mike' target was
called for, the twenty-four field-artillery pieces of a single artillery
regiment such as 2RCHA – the normal complement attached to a
brigade (four batteries of six guns each) – fired at a single target.
An 'Uncle' target concentrated the fire of the seventy-two field
pieces of the three artillery regiments of a division on one target.
When an FOO called for a 'Victor' target, all available 216 field
guns of an entire corps zeroed in on the same coordinates. With a
good rate of fire, a 'Victor' shoot could literally place a thousand
shells or so on a German position inside of a minute.[13] The same
effectiveness was also possible in the attack, of course. In Korea,
however, the placement of the field artillery behind a strung-out
front line rendered it almost unable to deliver concentrations of
that magnitude; the best that it could do under even the most serious conditions was an 'Uncle' concentration.[14]

The type of rough-and-ready defensive positions used in Korea
had sufficed for the Canadians during the Italian campaign; the
Germans, after all, had been defeated there. Thus Italy seemed to
offer lessons for Korea because the terrain was somewhat similar
and infantry dominated the battle. What appears to have been lost
to the Commonwealth Division, and to the Canadian brigade, is
the fact that there was a significant strategic difference between
Italy and Korea. In Italy, the Germans were on the defensive,
engaged in a fighting withdrawal to the north from almost the start

of the campaign. When they were not withdrawing, they were engaging in active defence along well-fortified lines such as the Winter or Gothic lines. The Canadians, like the other Allies, were on the strategic offensive in Italy. The victory that they sought could come only from successful advances. So even when fighting tended to slacken in the Italian winter, the Canadians and their allies still had no real need of a defence in depth. Indeed, construction of such a defence could have undermined an offensive spirit among the soldiers and precipitated a garrison mentality.[15] None of that applied in Korea.

The Canadian defences on the Jamestown Line received their first serious test on 2 November 1951.[16] Large numbers of Chinese infantry were seen massing across the valley from the 2RCR positions at about 1300. The brigade artillery opened up with all twenty-four guns at 1520, but the Chinese continued to assemble on reverse slopes and in dead ground. At about 1800, Chinese howitzers opened up on the forward slope of the RCR's 'A' Company, while Chinese high-velocity shells struck inside the 'A' Company's perimeter. Two hours later, the Chinese infantry, supported by between four and eight heavy machine-guns firing from across the valley, moved up. With bugles and whistles blowing in the night, one company of Chinese infantry hit 'A' Company, tried to penetrate between 'A' and 'C' (about 250 m to the north), then attacked 'C' itself. It was followed in close order by two more companies.

These Chinese attacks, and the ones that followed throughout the night, were of a pattern. Chinese artillery landing to the front and sides of the Canadian positions forced the Canadians to keep their heads down while Chinese infantry with bangalore torpedoes blew gaps in the Canadian wire. Some Chinese cut the wire with hatchets. Still others, with thick padding on their coats, threw themselves over it to form human bridges for those behind. Once inside the wire, the Chinese tried to get into the trenches and firing pits. Canadian artillery and 4.2 mortars kept up a steady fire on the Chinese forming-up positions, but this did not remedy the problem caused by those Chinese already on top of the Canadian positions. At 0200, some fifteen Chinese were reported inside the wire of 1 Platoon, even though their own artillery continued to pound the Canadians. The platoon held out for an hour, then pulled back to the main company position, followed closely by two companies of Chinese. Within minutes the Chinese were seen advancing against 'A' Company HQ 'in waves'; 2RCHA fired 'Mike' concentrations on top of the position, breaking up the advance.[17]

The Chinese attack slackened towards morning; three air strikes were called on the Chinese forward positions as 'A' Company's 3 Platoon went out to reoccupy the positions abandoned in the early-morning hours. An overly exuberant RCR intelligence officer estimated three hundred Chinese killed or wounded in return for one dead and eleven wounded Canadians, but there was no way of verifying that figure because the Chinese made great efforts to remove their dead from the battlefield. The next day, the figure for Chinese casualties was finalized as eighteen killed, two wounded, and one prisoner of war confirmed.

The rest of 3 November was quiet on the Canadian front as the Chinese prepared to take on the 28th Brigade to the north of the Canadian positions. That attack began with heavy shelling in the early afternoon of 4 November, followed by an infantry assault on the King's Own Scottish Borderers (KOSB) starting at about 1630. Heavy fighting, some hand to hand, raged through the night, with the KOSB suffering severe casualties and the loss of the western slopes of Hill 317 at midnight.[18] The Chinese attack was accompanied by 'intense and well-coordinated' artillery fire. An estimated twenty to thirty self-propelled guns (SPs) delivered one round every two seconds on the bunkers and trench lines of the KOSB.[19] At about the same time, an eight-man Chinese wire-cutting party was spotted in the valley separating 25 and 28 brigades and driven off by 'D' Company of 1PPCLI. The Chinese attacks on the 28th Brigade continued through the night, their artillery destroying practically all the KOSB's line and signal equipment. The Patricias spotted Chinese infantry forming up in front of their positions shortly after first light and called for artillery fire, which drove off the enemy.

The Patricias endured shelling and mortaring for the rest of 5 November; nightfall brought another infantry attack. At 1815 the

Chinese mounted two assaults on 'D' Company. The Chinese infantry were equipped for a prolonged stay. Each carried an entrenching tool, spare ammunition in pouches and bandoliers, and extra hand grenades. They were armed with rifles, burp guns, and Russian-pattern light machine-guns, and they brought rice, tooth powder, cigarettes, an extra jacket, and North Korean and Chinese currency with them.

The fighting raged at close quarters. Land lines were cut almost as soon as the Chinese barrage started. The battalion FOO radioed for the searchlights to be turned on to pinpoint the enemy so that he could call their positions to the field artillery. Canadian gunners, machine-gunners, and mortarmen worked feverishly to put a curtain of fire between 'D' Company and the enemy and succeeded in driving off the Chinese. They returned under cover of a massive artillery barrage at 2020 and concentrated on 12 and 10 Platoons. The men in 10 Platoon fought to the last bullet, then withdrew down a crawl trench into the main company position, the Chinese hot on their heels. 1PPCLI's war diarist summed up the action that followed: 'Wave after wave of enemy charged at D coy's wire with bangalore torpedoes and small arms fire, to be beaten off by our small arms fire and grenades.'[20]

At 2300, the hills across from the Canadian positions erupted with a chain of massive explosions, as bombs from a B-29 radar-directed strike walked across the Chinese front. No one could tell how much damage the bombing had caused, but coming when it did it was a definite morale-booster for the beleaguered Canadians, who now knew that they could depend on air support even at night. Despite the bombing, the Chinese went at the Patricias one last time at 0130. Once again, they targeted 'D' Company. A massive concentration of 25-pounder shells from brigade artillery and 155 mm shells from the U.S. corps artillery was directed into the valley in front of 'D' Company. In spite of the barrage, at least two companies of Chinese infantry moved up to attack 10 Platoon, which had infiltrated back into its position during a lull in the fighting. The battalion directed its 81 mm mortars to within 50 m of the Canadian wire, which had a devastating effect on the Chinese. Those who managed to get through the wire were killed by small arms and grenades. Once again the fighting was done at close range until two red flares went up from the Chinese lines, signalling a withdrawal.

In three attacks through the night, the Chinese had pushed the equivalent of a full battalion at the green 'D' Company of 1PPCLI, but 'D' had held. The Canadians suffered three killed and fifteen wounded; the Chinese had left thirty-four corpses within less than 50 m of the wire, seven of them in the minefield, and had clearly carted many more away. The Patricias' war diarist chalked up the failure of the Chinese attack to defensive Canadian artillery and mortar fire, excellent communications between the forward positions and the rear batteries, the concertina wire, and 'the mettle of the men of 10 Pl in remaining in their slits to fight it out at close quarters with the enemy and the excellence of the leadership of the officers and NCOs in the company.'[21]

It is easy to discount the last of these observations. The war diary, after all, is composed by the battalion intelligence officer and approved by the battalion CO. But 'D' Company had done well in its first real battle, and no doubt part of its steadfastness can be chalked up to intense training, regimental pride, and professionalism. In fact 1PPCLI was part of Canada's professional army. It had begun conversion from an ordinary infantry battalion to Canada's first standing peacetime paratroop unit in the autumn of 1948 at Rivers, Manitoba. Although its first parachute drill, Exercise Eagle, held in August 1949 had produced mixed results because of inadequate numbers of transport aircraft, the battalion had itself done well. It had also received arctic warfare training and been part of Exercise Sweetbriar in the Yukon in January 1950.[22] The CO of 1PPCLI, Lt.-Col. N.G. Wilson-Smith, was a decorated veteran, who had been wounded in wartime action in northwest Europe.

On the afternoon of 6 November, the evacuation of the PPCLI casualties began. There were no mobile army surgical hospital (MASH) helicopters available. The Canadian casualties were carried from their hilltop positions on stretchers by Korean porters, then loaded on to jeep ambulances lower down. The stretcher parties quickly tired picking their way down the rocky and slippery slopes, so relief parties were almost always necessary. As the war diarist recorded: 'The Korean Service Corps personnel are generally as loath to carry our wounded as we are to trust our wounded in their hands, and in no circumstances will they carry our wounded down the hills, so for the most part the "rice-burners" are useless to us as stretcher bearers.'[23]

In the late summer of 1953, Major W.H. Pope, who had commanded a rifle company with both 1 and 3R22eR, analysed the pattern of Chinese attacks that had started to develop in the autumn of 1951 and offered his solution for a revised and more effective defence doctrine. It was Pope's view that the Chinese had developed a predictable pattern in their raids on the Canadian positions on the Jamestown Line.

The sequence of Chinese moves and Canadian countermoves that Pope discerned went something like this. First, the enemy increased its patrolling in front of the position to be raided. The Canadians would either counter with patrols of their own or cease patrolling and await events. When Canadian patrols were mounted, Pope believed they were invariably too weak to accomplish much because the companies had too much front to defend with too few troops. Instead, the Canadians were engaged and chased off by the Chinese, who maintained a stronger presence in no man's land at night and who were willing and able to take heavy casualties. The mere presence of these weak Canadian patrols hindered the defence of the main positions on the Jamestown Line, however, because heavy mortar and artillery fire could not be brought to bear on the Chinese forming-up positions for fear of hitting the Canadian patrol. If no patrols were sent, then there was little warning before the Chinese hit the Canadian wire.[24]

Next, Chinese shelling would intensify on the Canadian positions in a classic First World War–era effort to neutralize the defenders by forcing them to keep their heads down, disorganizing the defence, depressing morale, and keeping the Canadians bottled up in their defensive positions during daylight. The tactic worked well, as one PPCLI sergeant told Canadian war correspondent Bill Boss: 'The Communists are using much more artillery now and sometimes it gets hard to just sit and take it. My fellows are good, fairly new, and sometime they get jittery during the shelling, and if the Chinese come in and attack, they get excited during the grenade throwing.'[25] Not only did the Canadians get jittery, but they surrendered the initiative during daylight. And that was precisely when their overwhelming strength in field and medium artillery, heavy mortars, and, most important, tactical air power gave them a distinct advantage over the Chinese.[26]

Canadians positioned their defensive localities poorly. Instead of clustering defensive positions on selected hilltops in such a manner that platoons covered platoons, and companies covered companies, they almost automatically placed defences on every hilltop in the line. This was what they had done in Italy, good for troops planning to move up against an enemy who is not intending to advance, but tempting fate when used against a habitual attacker. The single line of defensive hilltops not only thinned the defences, it also forced the very concept of defence into artificial and ineffective patterns that made enfilade very difficult. But then, what choice was there when the Canadian brigade, indeed the entire division, had no effective reserve? Not much, according to 1PPCLI platoon commander Robert Peacock: 'There was no real reserve except artillery and mortars once the direction of the enemy attack was determined. The frontages covered by the Commonwealth Division on the type of ground in Korea opened the way for an undetected breakthrough by the Chinese if we didn't cover all the hills and passes. On one position our platoon was deployed on a ridge 200 metres long ... There was no other place to go! We made the best of it all.'[27]

Finally, the defensive localities were themselves poorly laid out, with a single encircling company trench, which, when beleaguered, offered its occupants little protection. Pope thought that there ought to have been at least three such encirclements, each offering fire protection for the other two, and much less use of mines, which made movement as difficult for the defenders as for the attackers.

What all this amounted to was that the Chinese were able to seize the initiative, select the time and place for the attack, make up for whatever fire-power deficiencies they had by using the cover of darkness, and attack virtually at will. When they did attack, they were often through the wire and into the fire trenches as soon as their shelling lifted. Then Canadian infantrymen, with their out-moded bolt-action rifles, had to deal at close quarters with Chinese in the trenches firing automatic weapons or on the open ground throwing volleys of grenades down into the trenches. As Pope wrote: 'Rifles at five paces at night, with or without bayonets fixed, give one no confidence against a burp gun.'[28]

Although the Canadians were not heavily tested again for some weeks, casualties in the line mounted daily. Chinese sniping, occa-sional sudden barrages, and patrolling took their toll, and few days went by when there was not a man killed. By the third week in November the toll of dead for the month reached seventeen. But the Canadian losses were small compared to those suffered by the 28th Brigade, which held that portion of the line from the Cana-dian positions to the divisional boundary with the 1st U.S. Cavalry Division. On 17 November, the Chinese pushed 1 KSLI off Hill 227. In the words of the 25 Brigade war diarist: 'This was a serious turn of events as it exposed [a] good deal of the Patricia's [*sic*] right flank previously dominated by the two platoons and company headquarters of A coy [of 1KSLI] on top of the feature.'[29] For three days, the hill changed hands as British counterattacked and Chinese responded. On 20 November, it was permanently lost to the Reds.

The loss of Hill 227 created a salient in the Commonwealth Divi-sion's lines, with potentially disastrous consequences, even though Hill 355, 1.5 km to the east, dominated the 227 feature. The exist-ence of the salient was particularly dangerous because of the weak-ened condition of the 28th Brigade, which had few prospects for reinforcement. The division was already covering too much front with too few men, and to remedy the situation partially Cassels ordered a repositioning of the brigades to enable him to take the 28th out of the line and shorten his front from 19,000 to 15,000 m. The 25th Canadian Infantry Brigade was moved to the right to occupy the saddle formed by the west slope of Hill 355 and the foot of Hill 227.[30] Then the 28th Brigade was relieved by the 7th Infantry Regiment of the 3rd U.S. Infantry Division (which had replaced the 1st Cavalry), which thereby inherited the summit of

Hill 355.[31] All three Canadian battalions were in the line with all four of their rifle companies – the RCR on the left, the PPCLI in the centre, and the R22eR on the right – with the last holding a section of line formerly occupied by most of a brigade.[32] There was no brigade, or divisional reserve; everything was in the shop window.

By his own admission, Dextraze was a 'meddler' who took a 'hands-on' approach to battalion command, even in battle.[33] He began to prepare his battalion for the move into the 227/355 area at an Orders (O) Group on 19 November. He told his company commanders that he would retain control of, and assign fire tasks to, the 60 mm mortars, the 75 mm recoilless rifles, and the heavy machine-guns. He urged a thorough check of all equipment, even as to the state of the Bren-gun magazines. He demanded a tightening up of discipline, with daily inspections, Tests of Elementary Training, and range practice. He insisted on strict five-yard intervals between men in the line, no one on forward slopes, and continuous observation of enemy positions. Above all, in the event of attack, there was to be 'NO withdrawal, No platoons overrun and No panic. All would be expected to perform their duty in a typical "VAN DOOS" manner.'[34]

The Van Doos began to move into their new positions on the night of 21 November after a hot Thanksgiving dinner of turkey and all the trimmings, courtesy of the U.S. army. Their task was to occupy and hold the saddle between Hills 355 and 227. The battalion took over a triangular-shaped defensive position formerly occupied by 1KSLI. The KSLI had held that position only briefly after inheriting it from an American battalion. The Americans, as was their fashion, had constructed 'hot dog stand' defensive positions – slit trenches and bunkers with low sandbag revetments and roofs several feet high. They were especially vulnerable to direct fire. The British troops had no time to reorganize their defences before they were moved out to be replaced by the Canadians, another example of the drawbacks that arise when armies with different defence doctrines constantly swap positions. Dextraze placed 'D' Company on a spur that ran north–south across the saddle at the front of the triangle. 'A' Company was sited about 500 m to the south, at the end of the spur, in the middle of the triangle. 'B' Company took the bottom left corner of the triangle, about 1,200 m, and across a ravine, from 'A.' 'C' Company was positioned about 1,100 m east of 'B,' with the same ravine between it and 'A.'[35]

These positions were inadequate for effective defence. The OC of 'D' Company, Major Réal Liboiron, later recalled:

> The K.S.L.I. had good positions until they lost Hill 227 and then their platoons were not mutually supporting and were much too crowded. My No. 11 Platoon, for example, was holding a position previously held by a K.S.L.I. section. The K.S.L.I. had also constructed 'hot-Dog stands' [*sic*] which were perfect targets for SPs and were responsible for many casualties. I intended to readjust the positions at the first opportunity but as events turned out there was never the time.[36]

What was true of 'D' Company's positions was also the case of the entire battalion. Although 'A' and 'D' could offer supporting fire to each other, both were too far from 'B' and 'C' to help in their defence. Given the terrain and the short period between moving into the line and coming under attack, it is hard to see what more Dextraze might have done.

The battalion was in place by 0630 on 22 November and quickly got to work improving the defences. Dextraze himself supervised the laying of additional wire and mines and the siting of the heavy .50 Browning machine-guns, the lighter .30 Brownings, and even the .303 Brens. By mid-afternoon his HQ was functioning with radio and land-line communication to the rifle companies and to brigade HQ to the rear. Not long afterward, Chinese shells began to rumble in from across the valley. The shelling grew more intense by the minute and was soon added to by heavy-calibre rocket fire. The Chinese concentrated on 'D' Company and on the American positions atop 355. One Van Doo private was blown to bits when a shell exploded in his slit trench. Others were wounded by flying shards of steel or by the dirt, rocks, and pieces of smashed bunker that rained down on them. The concertina wire in front of the company positions was shredded. Telephone lines were cut. The minefield was pulverized. As night fell and the cold penetrated into the very bones of the Canadian infantrymen, the shelling continued. It started to snow heavily, the first real snow of the winter,[37] but the Chinese did not come, and when morning dawned on 23 November, the shelling slackened.

The men of 'D' Company used the hiatus to repair damage and lay new telephone lines. In mid-morning a Chinese scout was captured near the pioneer platoon wire; minutes later shells began to fall once again, this time on 'D' Company's left flank. The shelling forced the men to ground. At 1350 an observation plane reported at least a company of Chinese infantrymen advancing from the northwest, about a kilometre away, and called down an artillery concentration. In response the Canadian and New Zealand batteries plastered the paddy land in a valley to the left and front of 'D' Company.

At 1620, Chinese rocket and shell fire began to strike the summit of Hill 355; less than ten minutes later, approximately two companies of Chinese infantry hit the 'D' Company wire. The fighting was close, intense, and desperate. The Canadian infantrymen threw grenades, worked the bolts of their Lee-Enfield rifles, and fired magazine after magazine of Bren-gun and belt after belt of Browning machine-gun ammunition at the onrushing Chinese. One Van Doo section broke, but the platoon commander led it back into position. On Hill 355, Easy, Fox, and George Companies of the 7th U.S. Infantry were under attack from an entire Chinese battalion. At 1735, word reached Dextraze that U.S. infantrymen from 355 were arriving in the 'A' Company area; the Americans had been forced off Hill 355.[38] This was a 'very grave and serious situation,' according to 25 Brigade's war diarist. Hill 355 was not only the highest position in the line, it also dominated the lateral road running through the American sector. The Canadian right flank was now completely open, and the Chinese could look down into the Van Doos' positions from their U.S.-dug trenches and bunkers.

The Chinese had taken 355, but they had not taken the saddle; they attacked the Van Doos' positions with renewed fury. At one point a single Canadian platoon was beleaguered by an estimated 400 Chinese soldiers. At brigade HQ, the Canadian tanks were ordered forward to support the Canadian infantry. At his own HQ, Dextraze worked the radio, ordering his company commanders to hold fast and directing mortar, tank, and artillery fire, sometimes bringing it down virtually on the 'D' Company wire. Four Chinese attacks were beaten off by morning; as the Canadians stubbornly defended their ridge, a U.S. counterattack retook most of Hill 355.

The Chinese attackers melted away at first light on the 24th, but intermittent shelling-continued. Dextraze ordered a platoon counterattack towards Hill 227. The advancing unit met little resistance and gained the summit of 227, which it held until it withdrew in the face of another massing of Chinese infantry at about 1700. Brigade and divisional artillery rained down on the Chinese forming-up positions but failed to stop a renewed assault on the Van Doos' 'D' Company. The Chinese came from all directions despite a hail of tank, mortar, and artillery fire. 'D' Company's left forward platoon collapsed back into the main company positions, but the company itself held fast. Just before midnight, the Van Doos' Scout platoon edged forward to retake the lost platoon position. It did but was then strongly attacked by at least two Chinese companies and forced to pull back to take cover in several shell holes. Dextraze then called down heavy mortar fire on the Chinese attackers. At about the same time, a forced withdrawal of U.S. troops on the western slope of 355 once again exposed the Canadian left flank until 355 was retaken before first light on the 25th.

In the morning, the Van Doos' Scout platoon once more made its way back to the lost platoon position to the left front of 'D' Company. Up on Hill 355 the Americans swept the entire feature from east to west, ferreting out any remaining Chinese. There were no more Chinese attacks on the Van Doos until dark, when a small probe was sent against 'D' Company from the direction of Hill 227. The Chinese were met with a volley of artillery fire and withdrew. That was the end of 'D' Company's ordeal. Just before dawn on 26 November, Dextraze ordered 'D' Company relieved by 'B' Company. In the words of the brigade war diarist, 'The troops of D Coy ... had reached the limits of their endurance. They had been exposed to the snow, the cold of the day, the freezing nights, and had had no sleep since the evening of the 21st.'[39] They had also received only minimal help from the other three companies of the battalion because the terrain, the woefully inadequate siting of the positions by 1KSLI, and lack of time for correction of the situation had not allowed it.

In the four days between 22 and 26 November, the Van Doos lost sixteen men killed – nine from 'D' Company alone – forty-four wounded, and three missing and presumed dead after a direct hit by a Chinese shell on a Van Doos bunker.[40] The division estimated 2,000 Chinese dead in the operations around Hills 227 and 355, but only 742 enemy dead were actually counted.[41] The division noted building defence in depth as one major lesson from the attacks, but little was done to improve defensive positions along the division front in the months, and indeed the years, to come.

One conclusion is inescapable: the Canadians had fought well, both officers and men, and the eighty-four-hour travail of 'D' Company, 2R22eR, was one of the finest defensive actions in the history of the Canadian army. But the magnificent effort of the troops was undermined by an improperly prepared divisional front and poor defence doctrine. This was a failure that ran from the brigade, through the UN Command, to the highest political decision makers in Washington and New York. The failure began with the political decision to prohibit major offensive operations on the UN front. It continued with the decision of the UN Command to fight a defensive war on the front line. This dictated the strategy of building the strong and well-defended Wyoming and Kansas Lines to the rear, while relegating the Jamestown Line to the status of a rough and ready 'tripwire' with no defence in depth and inadequate fire support. But there was failure at the divisional level also. Commonwealth Division HQ never imposed a uniform defensive doctrine along its front. Essentially, each brigade 'did its own thing.' This was not just a British failure, because divisional headquarters had representatives from all the contingents and the divisional commander sought the advice of his brigade commanders when formulating doctrine. None of the failures were to be remedied for the duration of the Korean War.

On the afternoon of 26 November 1951 two of the last Chinese shells fired in that month's struggles along the Canadian front on the Jamestown Line fell on one of the 2R22eR positions. One man was buried. When he was finally dug out, 'there was so little left of him he looked as if he had been pulverized by the force of the explosion,' his platoon commander, Lieut. Gerard Belanger, wrote in a letter home. That letter mirrored Belanger's dark mood: 'If we continue to lose men at this rate, the Battalion will be decimated in a few weeks ... The snow covered the ground today; there are snow flurries this evening; it's quite a sight to see, especially when you're living in a hole without a heater to keep you warm. We're living like rats and we'll probably die like rats ... It is now 0625; the day is just breaking and I haven't slept since yesterday morning. So much for the glorious life of a platoon commander.'[42] These were the thoughts of one Canadian soldier fighting the defensive battle along the Jamestown Line in far-away, frozen Korea in November 1951.

SEVEN

The Line

Jamestown Line: Canadian sector; a day between December 1951 and July 1953:

0630: First light stand-to

Don B. Urquhart spent a year as a platoon sergeant in Korea, virtually all of it on the line: 'A typical day in Korea never happened,' he would later remember. 'Most days were boring, some were hair raising, no two were ever the same.'[1] Nor were the experiences of all companies or battalions the same. But in many respects Canada's soldiers in Korea lived similar lives the entire time they held the Jamestown Line. At first light the front-line troops would 'stand to,' much as their predecessors had done on the Western Front in World War I. Everyone would be awake, alert, and fully manning defensive positions in the event of a Chinese dawn attack. For most of the period from November 1951 until the armistice of 27 July, 1953, the Canadians manned the Jamestown Line to the southwest of Hill 355. The sun always rose at their backs and set at their fronts, so there was little real danger of a Chinese attack at first light. Still, it was always best to be cautious.

At the 38th parallel, the differences in length of days between summer and winter is not nearly as pronounced as in much of Canada. The hours of the rising and setting of the sun and the moon – and the weather – were very important in determining the rhythm of a front-line soldier's day in Korea. The weather in central Korea varied little from day to day but was extreme over a season, as in most of Canada, with hot summers, very cold winters, and short springs and autumns. Tables of sun and moon rise and set were routinely distributed to battalion and company headquarters so the soldiers would have a rough idea of when their day would begin and end. The longer nights of winter brought additional hours of darkness, in which the Chinese might attack, while a bright moon shining over a snowy landscape made night patrols extra risky. Sometimes, when the Canadians held especially dangerous positions, the troops 'stood to' all night. That was the case with 1R22eR when it occupied Hill 159 in September 1952, when it faced enemy troops close in to the north and west. After a long night the men slept after breakfast, usually to be awakened by Chinese shelling directed at the Lord Stratchcona's Horse emplacements in the afternoon.[2]

0710–0740: Stand-down

If the dawn 'stand-to' was uneventful, as it almost always was, half the troops stood down forty minutes later, and the rest another half-hour after that. Depending on platoon strength, each platoon then assigned two men every two to four hours to watch the Chinese positions or to man platoon outposts.[3] Before the men cleaned up, shaved, or ate breakfast, they serviced their weapons. Weapons maintenance was especially important in the conditions prevalent on the central Korean front. Hot dusty summer weather, the heavy rains of monsoon season, and the extreme cold of the winter played havoc with automatic weapons, which were the keys to defence.

The troops used a carefully structured mix of weapons when setting up their defences. After the onset of the 'static' war in Korea in late autumn of 1951, the weaponry of the standard Canadian infantry platoon was considerably beefed up over what it had been at the outbreak of the Korean War. By the beginning of 1952 there were some two to three times the normal complement of light machine-guns (LMGs), with a second Bren and two U.S.-issued M1919A6 Browning .30s added per section.[4] The heavy machine-guns (HMGs) – Browning .50, belt-fed, air-cooled, tripod-mounted – and the medium machine-guns (MMGs) – the Vickers .303, belt-fed, water-cooled, tripod-mounted – anchored the hilltop positions. The light machine-guns (LMGs) – Bren guns and U.S.-issued Browning .30, belt-fed, tripod mounted – were sited to support the HMGs and MMGs. Riflemen armed with the Lee-Enfield .303 Mk IV, the 9 mm Sten and copious quantities of No. 36 fragmentation grenades were assigned the job of supporting the LMGs.

If the HMGs or the MMGs jammed during a fire fight because of dirt, or cold, or cartridges badly inserted in magazines, clips or belts, the whole burden of a battalion's defence might fall on a handful of LMGs and the riflemen. That was why the first thing the soldiers did after standing down was to strip, clean, oil, and reassemble their weapons and carefully check their ammunition. That was particularly true of the pesky No. 36 fragmentation grenade. British leftovers from the Second World War, many of these grenades had literally been in storage since the end of the war and unless constantly stripped and dried to prevent condensation were prone to misfire.[5] The task of caring for the weapons took even more time in winter than in summer, as the men worked with cold fingers on freezing metal parts, but it was even more crucial. Unless the weapons were lubricated with special arctic-weather gun oils, even the hardiest might fail in the heat of battle.

There was much dissatisfaction among the Canadian soldiers in Korea with their standard weapon – the Lee-Enfield .303 Mk IV, a bolt-action rifle. In the hands of an expert marksman, it was effective between about 500 and 900 m. The British army's infantry-training pamphlet no. 3 for rifle and bayonet, 1948 edition, required that a trained rifleman be able to shoot at least one round every twelve seconds when ordered to produce 'deliberate' fire or one round every four seconds in 'rapid' or 'snap' fire. The rapid-fire rate was unchanged from that called for in the First World War. An exceptional rifleman might exceed one round every two seconds with accuracy, but such a performance was very rare.[6]

The Lee-Enfield was no doubt a superior weapon for aimed fire at troops massing some distance away; but it was incapable of producing the high rate of fire needed to defend against Chinese 'hugging' tactics. Those tactics, designed to produce a quick assault under cover of darkness and shell fire to get rapidly into the enemy trenches, were designed to make up for deficiencies in crew-served weapons. Canadian riflemen in Korea quickly learned that firing with a bolt-action rifle placed them at a serious disadvantage in the close-in fighting of a Chinese night assault. They also discovered that the Lee-Enfield was ineffective on night patrol when an enemy ambush might require high rates of fire in defence. One report from the front marked the Lee-Enfield down as 'almost useless ... except as a personal weapon for troops not manning the defensive positions, for example, troops in the echelons.' What was needed was 'a fully automatic short range weapon of short overall length and with light magazines of a shape easy to carry.'[7]

There was a weapon available that could have significantly increased the fire-power of Canadian infantrymen – the standard U.S. infantry rifle known as the Garand M1. A .30-calibre, gas-operated, semi-automatic rifle, the M1 was slightly heavier than the Lee-Enfield – the former weighed in at 4.37 kg, the latter at 4.17 kg – but it had a much higher rate of fire. However, when reports from battalion COs reached Ottawa about Canadian troops unofficially arming themselves with the M1, those reports almost always disparaged the American weapon. Stone, for one, told his superiors that Canadian infantrymen invariably found the M1 far more unreliable than the Lee-Enfield, requiring 'more maintenance and attention' than they were able to give it. He also reported that they found its dependability to be 'markedly reduced' in winter conditions, when 'mud and frost show the advantage of a hand operated rifle.' Overall, Stone did not think 'an automatic desirable';[8] he was 'old fashioned,' he claimed, and liked 'a bolt which can be forced open if necessary.'[9] If Stone was correct and some Canadians did have unhappy field experiences with the M1, their problems may well have resulted from lack of training in that weapon's use and maintenance.

The Americans had virtually no problem with the M1, even in severe winter conditions. In his *Battlefield Analysis of Infantry Weapons (Korean War)*, U.S. Army Official Historian S.L.A. Marshall characterized the M1 as 'sufficiently accurate for the purpose intended,' highly serviceable, and 'of all the weapons carried by

the [U.S.] infantry ... least sensitive to heavy frost, extreme cold
and icing.' He reported that U.S. infantrymen reconciled themselves
to its weight because of its consistent performance. In winter conditions, the rifle misfired only some 2 to 4 per cent of the time.[10]

Some Canadian infantrymen did prefer the Lee-Enfield; it was
especially popular among snipers because of its accuracy over long
distances.[11] But snipers had no real need for a rapid-fire weapon.
The more common view among Canadian soldiers of all ranks was
that the bolt-action rifle had seen its day. The director of infantry
for the Canadian army, Col. Roger Rowley, for example, strongly
disagreed with Stone and reported to Ottawa: 'The No 4 [Lee-
Enfield] does not produce an adequate rate of fire,' while the M1,
carefully maintained and 'nursed,' would put out 'a much more
adequate volume of fire.' Rowley thought that asset far outweighed
any maintenance deficiencies that the M1 had.[12]

In the early years of the First World War, Canadian troops had
gone into action with the Canadian-manufactured Ross Rifle,
which failed repeatedly in combat. There is no way to measure
accurately the numbers of Canadians who were killed in that era
when their rifles failed to shoot. Since their army and their government took far too long to solve the problem, the troops took action
themselves by acquiring Lee-Enfields any way they could. The same
thing happened in Korea, except this time it was American rifles
they wanted. When a soldier's life depends on the reliability and
battle performance of a weapon, no power on earth is going to
stop him (or her) from getting a better piece of kit.

Stone's pronouncements against semi-automatic weapons not-
withstanding, there are dozens of photographs of Canadian officers in Korea armed with U.S. semi-automatic rifles. The semi-
automatic favoured highly by the Canadians was the Winchester
M2 Carbine, a .30 weapon developed as a semi-automatic rifle for
use in the Second World War by commando and other troops who
were thought to need a lighter, shorter weapon than the Garand.
Designated the 'US carbine M1,' it weighed about half as much
as a Garand but had nowhere near the hitting power because of a
much lower muzzle velocity. After the war it was modified to
shoot in either semi-automatic or fully automatic mode and re-
designated the M2. The modification was not a success. Although

it was light, and had a high rate of fire with a thirty-round clip, the M2 jammed constantly during heavy use, especially in winter conditions. Misfire rates of 30 per cent were not uncommon. Infantrymen with the 1st U.S. Marine Division also claimed that it was inaccurate.[13]

Despite the many complaints about the M2 from U.S. troops, the Canadians bartered for M2s in great number. 'There were a lot of guys who wanted to get their hands on US equipment, especially the automatics,' Stanley Carmichael of 1PPCLI later remembered, 'there was a lot of underground trading going on.'[14] James W. Morrice of 1RCR was one who 'grabbed a U.S. weapon' as fast as he could.[15] Both men were forced by their section leaders to revert to their Lee Enfields,[16] but overall the unofficial rearming was so pervasive that it amounted to mass disobedience. Canadian troops regularly and routinely disregarded orders not to use 'unauthorized' weapons: 'We were always trying to get our hands on US weapons and they were easily obtained,' David Cathcart of Lord Strathcona's Horse later recalled.[17] Don Bateman of 3PPCLI remembers that it was 'common in Korea for the members of [my] platoon to ... bargain with the Americans to get access to their weapons.'[18] Lorne E. Warner, a field engineer with the 23rd Field Squadron, 'personally used a US Army M1 and the carbine on most occasions.'[19] Even when forced to revert to the Lee Enfield, soldiers smuggled M2s out with them when they went on night patrol. They preferred it for its higher rate of fire than the Mk IV and for its much greater reliability than the standard-issue Sten submachine-gun.[20]

No weapon was more widely despised by the Canadian troops than the venerable Sten, a British Second World War stopgap somewhat updated in Korea and equipped with a wooden stock. Veterans routinely describe the Sten as having been 'dud useless,' 'totally fucking useless,' and 'a fucking useless piece of shit.'[21] The Sten failed habitually in action when the spring-operated bolt jammed with heavy use. Worse, it was outranged by the Chinese 'Burp' guns. In the spring of 1952, Lt.-Col. D.A.G. Waldock, deputy director of armament development for the Canadian army, visited Korea to check weapons performance in the field. He had this to say about the Sten: 'Almost without exception, personnel complained that this weapon was generally unreliable ... The mere appearance of the weapon had a poor psychological effect on the men and the men had no confidence in it.' As one officer put it: 'This was a cheap "backs to the wall" weapon produced to meet an emergency situation, so let's put it away until we have our backs to the wall again.'[22]

On patrol Canadian troops left their Stens behind. They took U.S. .45 Thompson submachine-guns (the 'Tommy gun' of movie fame),[23] M2s, and even Bren guns, which at 10.10 kg were quite a load to carry any distance in the dark. The Bren had been the standard British and Canadian section light machine-gun since almost the start of the Second World War. It was capable of 500 rounds a minute on full automatic and had an effective range of about 500 m. The Bren could be fired from the hip, but it was heavy and somewhat cumbersome used this way and was best employed with the bipod attached to its muzzle or a tripod set up to fire on fixed lines. The Bren was a habitual favourite and compared well with its U.S. equivalent, the Browning Automatic Rifle, or BAR. It was 3 kg heavier than the BAR, but its barrel could be changed in the event of damage from overuse or too prolonged fire.[24] It also held more ammunition and had greater penetrating power. The soldiers also thought highly of the Browning 9 mm pistol, which was standard Canadian army issue, as opposed to the U.S. .45 Colt. The heavier support weapons used in the field, including the 60 and 81 mm mortars, 4.2-inch mortars, and the Vickers and Browning machine-guns (of both .30 and .50 calibre), all withstood the test of combat well.[25]

0740: Breakfast

Once the weapons were cleaned and oiled and the ammunition was inspected, the men grabbed a few moments to clean up and shave before breakfast. A steady supply of nourishing and appealing food is a basic factor for the maintenance of good morale; after the static war began in the late autumn of 1951 the men usually had little to complain about when it came to their food. If the front was quiet, the men grabbed their mess tins and proceeded down the rear slope for a good helping of hot food and coffee brought forward from field kitchens just behind the lines. If the front was not quiet, they had to endure days, even weeks of C-ration meals.

Fresh, hot food had been a luxury in the Second World War, when advancing units and mobile field kitchens met only occasionally. That was not true for most of the war in Korea. The soldiers were stationed on a semi-permanent line, and so field kitchens could be set up not far behind the front and as close to actual company positions as possible. The field kitchens were well supplied with fresh produce, usually from Australia, while the meat generally came from the United States. Overall, the cooks were well-trained, and their equipment was first rate.[26]

Although the hot food sometimes cooled off as it was carried up to the company positions by Korean porters, there were few complaints. After all, the Canadians could have been eating British rations, a fate many thought worse than death. One aspiring poet among them composed the following rhyme after a short period in reserve eating British fare:

I pine for my pancakes and treacle,
I haven't seen jam for a week,
I haven't a clue about bully beef stew
And the rib-sides, they just make me weep
I sigh for my bars made by Hershey,
I yearn for my beer by Labatts;
The dried eggs are chronic, the bread gives me colic,
The biscuits aren't fit for the rats. ...
So roll me right back into action:
No messing about in reserve,
Big helpings of steak, that's what it takes,
To put back my weight and my nerve.
When you're chewing your issue tobacco,
and asking for 'seconds' all round;
Spare a thought, so you ought, for those fellows –
Where rations are tied to the pound!![27]

What was true for the fresh, American-style food went double for the hard rations that the men ate when it was not possible to arrange hot meals. The U.S. C-rations were far superior in quality and variety to the British compo-pack rations that had fed the Canadians in the Second World War. C-rations came in cartons of six boxes. Each box held a day's rations and included meal 'units' such as ground meat and spaghetti, ham and lima beans, or chicken stew. It had jam and crackers, cheese, fruit salad, cigarettes, coffee and sugar, and other necessities, such as matches, toilet paper, powdered milk, and a disposable can opener. The rations could be eaten cold or heated.[28] The construction of mini field 'stoves' made out of everything from large tins to shell casings was a cottage industry.

Soldiers have complained about their food since soldiering began, but the Canadians in Korea ate well, all things considered, as Paul Gauci, a communications instructor with the artillery would later remember: 'I was really surprised by the quality of food which was rationed out to us. Some guys constantly bitched about the food rations, but I found them to be pretty good considering the conditions we were living in. There were certainly more important things to complain about.'[29]

0800: Clean and stow kit other than weapons

Care and maintenance of the weapons came first, and checking and cleaning of other kit was done after breakfast. Almost no one bothered about their helmets. These First World War–era 'tin hat' battle helmets were one of the most useless pieces of kit supplied to the Canadian troops in Korea. Until mid-1952 virtually none of the troops of the Commonwealth Division wore it. It was heavy, uncomfortable, and virtually useless under Korean conditions. After mid-1952, the decision to wear or not to wear the helmet was made by the unit commander, although troops usually grabbed them when under heavy shell or mortar fire.[30] As one Canadian officer later put it: 'The less said about the present helmet the better. The need is for a battle-shaped helmet with a harness that is comfortable to wear.'[31] The British army's operational research team tried to compare head-wound rates between Commonwealth Division troops, who rarely wore helmets, and American troops, who always did. The attempt was not a success because the two armies classified and counted casualties differently and classified wounds differently.[32]

The Canadians were also sorely deficient in armoured vests. American troops began to receive these early in the Korean War; virtually none were available to Canadian and other Commonwealth Division infantrymen until late in 1952 and even then not in adequate numbers. The Commonwealth Division sought 1,900 vests in the autumn of 1952 but received only 860 by the end of November. When Commonwealth Division troops wore the vests into battle, the results were conclusive, as a divisional report noted: 'There is complete agreement about this. The vest has already saved the lives of some men and has prevented numerous others from being wounded. It is very good protection against splinters and ricochets, and sometimes even against S[mall] A[rms] A[mmunition].'[33]

One forty-nine-man raiding party from 1R22eR found that out on the night of 23–4 June 1952 in a night action against the Sami-Ch'on feature. The men went into action wearing armoured vests supplied by the 1st U.S. Marine Division. Three of their number were killed, taken prisoner, or missing after a clash with Chinese troops, and five were wounded, but none of the casualties were wounded through their armoured vests.[34] Although the vest weighed 3.6 kg (8 lb.) (a far cry from the Kevlar vests available today) and created a number of minor difficulties to the wearer, there could be no doubt that it ought to have become a regular part of a Canadian infantryman's kit. Yet Canadian troops, by and large, did without them until early 1953.

It was important to try to clean jackets, parkas, coveralls, or other combat-issue clothing of grease, which broke down cloth and fibre and undermined their insulating capabilities. On the line it was almost impossible to get an item of clothing replaced, and men did repairs using needle and thread. For one thing, the Korean porters were needed to carry food and ammunition to the hilltop positions. For another, there were repeated shortages of Canadian-issue clothing in Korea. When the clothing was available, it did not, with the exception of the boots, measure up to the standard-issue uniforms of the Americans or the British.[35]

Canadian winter clothing was designed for the dry northern climate of Canada where it had proven more than adequate in pre–Korean War exercises. Under the conditions of the Jamestown

Line, however, it failed to measure up, as Robert Peacock later remembered: 'It was not suitable for the rapidly changing temperatures in Korea – from frozen mud to muck in a few hours then back again. In winter, for patrols, we took off the outer shell of the parka and used the liner because the outer shell made so much noise. Brigadier [M.P.] Bogert was beside himself over this and issued orders that this was not to be done, but the practise continued.' The nylon parkas made a swishing or crackling sound when the wearer moved in very cold weather, adding an unnecessary element to the dangers of night patrol. And they had other faults. They were not wind-proof or water-resistant. The jacket shell had a low flashpoint and was easily holed by burning cigarette ash, bonfire cinders, or other sparks.[36] One Korean veteran even remembers that the static electricity building up on the nylon gave off periodic sparks.[37] In the words of Lt.-Col. K.L. Campbell: 'It seems unbelievable that Canada is far behind the United States and UK in the design of winter clothing.'[38]

Certainly Gen. G.G. Simonds was aware of this by early 1952. In a visit to the front in January of that year he wore the winter clothing and noticed both how noisy it was and that it melted easily. He brought the matter to the attention of the Canadian Army Operational Research team in Korea and the quartermaster general on his return to Ottawa. At that point, new winter combat clothing was in the pipeline, but it too was largely nylon. A large order of the new kit was cancelled, and work started on more suitable clothes. That was commendable and certainly to Simonds's credit. Simonds bitterly resented a newspaper article by war correspondent Bill Boss about the inadequacies of the winter gear and the apparent 'do nothing' attitude of the top brass.[39] The fact remains, however, that the problem was not even close to resolution a year after Simonds had pointed it out. Something might have been done far quicker if there had been pressure from battalion and brigade commanders, but there was little. In fact, 1 PPCLI's CO, Wilson-Smith, reported in January 1952 that the winter-issue clothing was 'excellent,'[40] which was patently absurd.

Pte Tom Bowell, 2PPCLI, with explosives

Personnel of 1R22eR examining complimentary cases of Labatt's Anniversary Ale, Korea, 5 Dec. 1952; left to right: Ptes Roch Boisvert, Jean Boily, and M.L. Wilson

Young Korean, exhausted by weight of carton of C-6 rations he is carrying to Canadian front-line troops and by early-morning start, 16 April 1951

'C' Company, 2PPCLI, packing U.S.-issue C rations

Tpr Andy Parenteau asleep on back of tank of 'C' Squadron, Lord Strathcona Horse (RCR), hidden under tree and camouflage net, guarding a likely Communist fording spot on the Imjin, 7 Sept. 1951

Ptes Monte Montag, John Oupis, and Bob Neeham, 3PPCLI, cleaning weapons in front of bunker, 16 Dec. 1952

Two men from 2PPCLI on 'R & R' in Japan

Soldiers of 2PPCLI washing

Hockey championship match between 1PPCLI and 2R22eR, Imjin Gardens,
11 March 1952

Imjin near Pintail bridge; Americans and British working on ferry and bridge,
22 Feb. 1952

Personnel of 2PPCLI crossing Imjin in assault boat, with two American soldiers at bow, 6 June 1951

Personnel of 2PPCLI passing through village during patrol, 11 March 1951. Note that they are *not* wearing their Second World War–style helmets.

12 Platoon, 2PPCLI, moving north through the Korean mud in May 1951

A section of 12 Platoon, 'D' Company, 2PPCLI, on foot patrol, May 1951

Pte Jon Hoskins, 2PPCLI, during advance on Hill 419, 24 Feb. 1951

RCR hilltop positions established in former Chinese defences, Oct. 1951; in the distance: two Sherman tanks of 'C' Squadron, Lord Strathcona Horse

12 Platoon, 2PPCLI, after crossing an 1,800-m-high mountain, mid-May 1951

Trucks ploughing through deep-rutted roads, 21 March 1952

Half track of the 2PPCLI mortar platoon, with a .50 machine-gun mounted on it, taken near Toksio-Ri, May 1951. Vehicles like this one helped stop the Chinese at Kap'yong.

12 Platoon, 'D' Company, 2PPCLI, mounted on M-48 Patton tanks of 'A' Company, 72nd Heavy Tank Battalion, U.S. Army

Ambulance jeep arriving at Regimental Aid Post, 1PPCLI, 21 April 1952

Ptes Bob Campbell (front) and Bob Bastien (behind) carrying wounded comrade from front line to regimental first aid post, 1951

Padre Capt. M. Lebel (right) with wounded soldier, Pte D. Grandin, and Pte N.P. Richard, R22eR, Oct. 1951

Captured Chinese casualty wrapped in blankets to keep warm, with Pte Johnny Decarie of St Catharines, Ont., tending to him, 2 Nov. 1951

Chinese soldier who penetrated first barbed-wire defence around RCR outpost, 3 Nov. 1951

Feet of dead Canadian soldiers abandoned by Chinese troops, Hill 419, 2 March 1951

Wounded soldier of 2RCR evacuated in USAF Sikorsky S-51 helicopter to No. 8055 MASH, U.S. Army, 22 June 1952

L/Cpl Robert Sobol, PPCLI, kneeling at grave of Pte Lloyd K. Whylie, United Nations Cemetery, Pusan, 25 April 1951

Dead soldier of PPCLI, 3 Nov. 1951

0900: Sleep, or prepare for leave

Most of the men went to sleep immediately after finishing their morning chores. They had been up all night, or had managed only two to four hours of sleep. They slept soundly until noon. A lucky few, whose companies were not too far under strength, hurriedly packed some personal items, descended the rear slope to the road-head, and were trucked off to 'A' Echelon to begin leave. Men gained leave by spending time in the line. After 100 hours at the front, a man could stay at 'A' Echelon for twenty-four hours. There he could clean up, eat, drink a few beers, rest, watch a movie or two, and sleep the night away in a real bed with sheets and blankets.

The best known of these rear-area rest camps was 'Pete's Paradise,' technically 'A' Echelon of the RCR, but it welcomed soldiers from any of the Canadian units. A collection of tents and huts, it provided those comforts soldiers could never have in the line – a shave, a haircut, a hot shower, good hot food, cold beer, movies, and a canteen where they could buy cigarettes, candy bars, writing paper, and other small comforts. A stay at Pete's lasted only a day, but it was a day of luxury compared to the Jamestown Line.[41]

A little longer in the line earned a man a seventy-two-hour pass, which he could spend at the divisional rest centre at Inchon or in Seoul. Neither choice was especially attractive. Inchon was a bombed-out, shelled-out, almost totally destroyed city that offered little in the way of recreation except hootch houses selling rot-gut liquor and whorehouses employing infected prostitutes. As for Seoul, one Canadian officer reported: 'it takes at least three hours driving over ghastly 'roads' to get there. Once there, the soldier finds himself in a half-gutted city with only other brassed-off soldiers as companions and no entertainment if one excepts the simian types, alleged to be human and female, that invest the off-limits area. Result – the man returns to his unit dirtier and more brassed-off than when he left and not infrequently with a permanent "souvenir." '[42] That 'souvenir' was venereal disease (VD).

VD was a serious problem for most of the Commonwealth Division for the entire period of the Korean War and was even a matter of concern to the War Office in London.[43] The Canadians, however, outstripped the other Commonwealth contingents in reported incidences of the condition. Part of the problem was that Canadian medical officers counted cases of non-specific urethritis (NSU) as VD, whereas other formations did not. Canadian war correspondent Bill Boss angered Brig. Bogert with his reports on VD in the Canadian brigade because he made no distinction between NSU and VD. At one point Boss was quietly and unofficially banned from the front lines because of these reports. Despite the apparent inaccuracies in reported incidences of VD among the Canadian soldiers, Commonwealth Division medical officers considered the Canadian situation 'alarming'[44] at four times the rate for troops in the U.S. army and the rest of the Commonwealth Division.[45] The high incidence of VD was not restricted to the first contingent, or Special Force soldiers. In the six months from June to November 1952, for example, when the first battalions or regular army units were in the line, Canadians continued to top the list of new cases reported in the division each month.[46]

Most of the men contracted their VD in Japan.[47] Canadian soldiers were eligible for five days of leave in Tokyo after three months' service in Korea, with up to eighty men allowed to go at any one time. They were flown from Kimpo to Tokyo aboard U.S. transports and lodged in the Australian-run Ebisu Leave Centre on the outskirts of the Japanese capital. Canadians felt like strangers at the centre; many hated the Australian rations, especially the mutton.[48] When they left the centre they could sightsee or they could carouse and drink, which many did to considerable excess. Prostitutes could be hired for the whole leave period for just a few dollars, and the Japanese beer, sake, and whiskey were dirt cheap. The result ought to have been predictable: 'Troops who have had this leave to date have not enhanced the reputation of the Canadian Army. There have been numerous cases of extreme drunkenness, theft and sale of Australian barrack stores, and, in general, very poor discipline and deportment.'[49]

For much of the Korean War, the Canadian army was not ready to take care of its men's morale or their overall physical or spiritual well-being behind the front. It failed its soldiers in not providing for their welfare, just as it let them down by providing them with some outmoded and ineffective weapons. When a team of three officers was dispatched from army HQ to Korea to examine soldiers' welfare in the summer of 1951, it concluded that the Canadian brigade was 'suffering from a complete disregard of [problems] fundamental to discipline (other than battle discipline), health, welfare and morale all of which contribute to conservation of manpower.'[50] Gen. Simonds eventually initiated measures to improve rest and recreational facilities for Canadians in Kure and Tokyo. Late in the war a 'Maple Leaf Club' opened to meet Canadian demands for Canadian food, cigarettes, beer, and entertainment, and Canadian Red Cross women were sent to Japan to help staff these centres.[51]

Rear-area rest and recreation facilities were one solution to the constant discomforts on the line, and a regular diet of competitive sports was another. One report from the front noted that 'competition under these conditions is the breath of life to a unit.' Though the battalions organized the usual panoply of sports activities, the Canadians loved hockey. Two large hockey rinks were built – a main rink and one for practice – on a frozen pond next to the Imjin, with spectator stands and huts serving coffee, hot dogs, and hamburgers. The facility was dubbed the Imjin Gardens and hosted the best hockey in Southeast Asia. The games were occasionally interrupted by the happenstances of war, however, as when a game between teams from 1PPCLI and 2R22eR had to be played on the poorer ice of the practice rink when a half-track broke through the ice of the main rink, flooding one end.[52]

In Korea, problems caused by the ready availability of liquor and prostitutes were compounded by the Canadian army's failure to make a serious effort to introduce Canadian soldiers to the people and culture of the country. Canadian soldiers received about an hour a week of indoctrination on Korea, the war, the UN, and other relevant topics and were provided with a variety of pamphlets and other written material on Korea.[53] But as one soldier later remembered, 'we were not trained on how to deal with the civilians.'[54] It remains therefore an open question how the indoctrination that did go on could offset the rampantly racist views of some officers, such as the one quoted above regarding the prostitutes of Seoul.

Canadian troops in general seem to have had ambiguous views about Koreans. First impressions formed at dockside and the trip to the front were rarely positive. The smell of human excrement, the strange customs and dress, the apparent passivity of Koreans about their surroundings, and their alleged disregard for human life probably strengthened traditional Canadian attitudes of the day towards Asia and Asians. Once in-country, especially at the front, the Canadian soldier began to come into contact with the Korean Service Corps (KSC), which provided most of the manpower to evacuate wounded, bring up supplies and ammunition, and build front-line fortifications and rear-area facilities. The Canadian soldiers referred to these Koreans as 'rice-burners,' some out of scorn, others out of endearment.[55] Time and propinquity usually strengthened the bonds between the KSC and the Canadians, but the ties were based on need, not underlying respect for a different culture.

Back of the front lines, booze, boredom, and the close proximity of hundreds of rear-area brothels sometimes combined with a ready availability of vehicles to create an explosive mixture that led to violent crime. No one has yet compared incidences of criminal behaviour by Canadian soldiers in Korea with those of comparatively sized Canadian units over a similar time span in the Second World War. Until that is done, no one can conclude that Canadian soldiers in Korea were more, or less, inclined to break laws, military or civil, than their Second World War predecessors.

The two offences committed most frequently by Canadian soldiers in Korea were being on leave too long (AWL) and conduct prejudicial to military discipline – a catch-all charge. Aside from serious crimes of violence, the longest sentences were served for theft of army property and being asleep or drunk at a post. In the period from May to November 1952, 261 Canadian soldiers were convicted for a variety of offences; three were sent back to Canada for imprisonment, the rest served sentences averaging twenty-eight days. The average number of men in detention in Korea or Japan at any one time was thirty-four – about the size of a rifle platoon. The 258 men served a total of a bit more than 7,300 days in detention, serious enough in time lost at the front, but a mere fraction of the more than 53,000 days lost through hospitalization of non-battle casualties.[56] Crimes tended to occur more frequently when a unit was in reserve,[57] which was natural because there were more opportunities to get illicit booze.

The Canadian justice system treated crimes of violence by Canadian soldiers against Koreans, soldiers or civilians, much differently than it treated those against fellow Canadian soldiers. In the course of the Korean War, Canadian soldiers were tried and convicted for thirteen crimes of violence: four of rape or attempted rape, two of shooting (but not killing) Koreans civilians, three of killing Korean civilians by a variety of means, three of killing ROK soldiers, and one of the shooting death of a Canadian soldier.

In all these situations, there were no efforts to sweep crimes under the rug. Investigations by the military police were swift and thorough, trials were equally swift, and sentences were, in most instances, appropriate to the crime, ranging from ten years' imprisonment to the death penalty. The story does not end there, however. In every case but that of the murder of Canadian Pte Harold Harrison – shot by a very drunken Signalman Robert Macdonald in a Korean brothel in late January 1952 – justice was not served in the end. In the words of historian Chris Madsen: 'Most soldiers found guilty of the murder or rape of Korean civilians were released within a year or two after their cases were reviewed in Ottawa by a panel of legal experts and civilian judges. The Canadian military justice system thus showed astounding leniency towards these men's criminal actions.' Harrison's killer's sentence was commuted from death to life in prison, but he, unlike the others, served his time.[58]

1300: Reception of reinforcements

At noon the soldiers emerged from their bunkers and rifle pits, ate lunch, and prepared for the afternoon's activities. Most of the soldiers spent afternoons digging, laying wire, or improving fighting and living positions. Some helped to receive and integrate into their units the day's allotment of reinforcements. The Canadian army uses the term 'reinforcements' to designate soldiers assigned to replace those permanently removed from a battalion by reason of death, evacuation caused by serious wound or injury, or serious illness. The reinforcements were supposed to have received four levels of training before leaving Canada: basic training at regimental battle schools, Corps training (as in Royal Canadian Infantry Corps) including section training for infantry, trades or specialist training, and sub-unit training – platoon, company, or equivalent.[59] In Japan, they ought to have been put through more advanced training at the Commonwealth Divisional Battle School at Hara Mura.[60] Training, housing, and other arrangements in Japan were the responsibility of the Canadian Reinforcement Group, which operated under authority of the Canadian Military Mission, Far East (CMMFE). The Reinforcement Group's primary mandate was to regulate the flow of reinforcements from Canada to Japan in such a way that there were no shortages of manpower at the front, but not too many troops languishing in Japan.[61]

Whatever the formal training requirements were for Canadian reinforcements, the reality was that many men sent to Japan were virtually green. In late summer of 1952 Brig. R.E.A. Morton, commander, Canadian Military Mission Far East, met a draft on arrival at Yokahama. He later reported: 'The great majority ... were youngsters who appear to have had only from 3 to 6 months or so service. Their bearing and turn out was fair, but the majority of them looked callow and appeared ignorant in military manners. I suppose this is to be expected with soldiers of so comparatively short training. They seemed unaware of such elementary points as standing to attention when addressing an officer and using the simple title "Sir."'[62]

This lack of training prior to leaving Canada could not possibly be made up for in Japan, and as a result many reinforcements who arrived at the front were 'not ... up to the required standard.'[63] The problem affected reinforcements sent to the regular-force units as much as it did the Special Force 2nd battalions. One measure of this lack of training was the high incidence of accidental wounds. From October 1951 to June 1952, almost 100 Canadian soldiers suffered non-battle wounds, six fatal. Some 70 per cent of these were accidents, and 70 per cent of these were caused by accidental discharge of weapons. One report noted: 'Special Force soldiers were no more and no less prone to negligence than Active Force soldiers.'[64]

People at higher levels sometimes asked how many of the accidents were truly accidental and how many were deliberately self-inflicted as a means of escaping further duty on the line. In virtually all cases it was impossible to tell. In the spring of 1952 Lt.-Col. Wilson-Smith warned the men of 1PPCLI that he had issued specific instructions to medical personnel to report immediately 'any case in which the Medical Officer has the slightest suspicion that a wound may be self-inflicted.'[65]

The inadequate training of many reinforcements related directly to another predicament – the periodic shortages of manpower at the front, especially in the R22eR. At one point the Royal 22nd was forced to reduce its front-line rifle strength to three companies, drawing on a company from the RCR to maintain strength in the line.[66] The two linked problems resulted from constant failure by army HQ to forecast reinforcement requirements for front-line units[67] and from pressure to keep the holdings in the Canadian Reinforcement Group as low as possible so as not to detain soldiers in the Far East who might be better deployed in Canada or NATO.

The latter problem was essentially political, rooted in the deep cuts made to the Canadian military up to 1947 and the maintenance of an army at well below establishment strength. By the autumn of 1951 Simonds and everyone else in the high command were struggling to meet an army commitment that had expanded more than three-fold in a bare eighteen months. Given the shortage of trained and even of undertrained personnel in the army, it was incumbent on Simonds to pare as much manpower away from Japan as possible without hindering the front-line unit's ability to maintain its manpower at establishment strength.[68] Clearly sometimes too much paring took place. At one point in April 1952, Rockingham described the number of reinforcements available in Japan as 'dangerously low' and certainly inadequate in the event that full-scale fighting resumed along the front line.[69] His successor, Brig. M.P. Bogert, wrote Simonds in the summer of 1952 that 'all the major units of the Brigade are at present well below full strength' and pointed to a tendency at army HQ to underestimate manpower requirements.[70]

Given what Simonds had to work with in late 1951 and throughout 1952, the difficulties plaguing the Canadian Reinforcement Group were unavoidable. That was not true of the army's almost constant need to cut training short in Canada or Japan to rush reinforcements through the system and out to the front lines. That need arose because of continued underestimation of the wastage or attrition rate of units undergoing training. As Major W.H. Pope noted in a June 1953 study, it was inevitable that men would drop out of such units for a variety of reasons and that younger, newer recruits were more likely to do so than more experienced men. When wastage rates were underestimated, fewer men than forecast reached front-line units, which then required yet more reinforcements. That call could be answered only by cutting training short in Canada, or Japan, so as to achieve the necessary draft to bring the front-line units up to strength.[71]

1300: Improvement of defences

Company areas in Korea were perched on hilltops so small that fighting and living positions were virtually the same. Under those circumstances, the soldiers' physical safety and physical comfort were directly related. No soldier in history could ever have been satisfied with daily life on a front line – it is a dangerous place, where sleep is virtually impossible, dirt and grime are everywhere, and civilian standards of sanitation and cleanliness are either distant memories or the stuff of dreams. The Korean front line was not unique, then, but it did pose special challenges to a soldier's safety and comfort.

Aside from the enemy, the foremost of those challenges came from the weather. In summer the troops baked in scorching heat, were attacked by swarms of flies, endured constant dirt and dust, or were soaked in blinding downpours and moved about in the thick gumbo produced by the heavy rain. In summer there was discomfort, but in winter there was danger from roads and paths made slick by freezing rain, by heavy snowfalls choking off supply roads and trails, or by the deep and bitter cold, especially at night.

As a Commonwealth Division publication entitled 'Conquer the Korean Winter; Simple Rules for All' put it: 'The Korean winter can be one of the most unpleasant in the world.' It warned officers that 'CONTEMPT of the WINTER means a CERTAIN CASUALTY.' Even the Canadians, some of whom had endured arctic exercises, had to be taught how to survive and fight for weeks in below-freezing weather, with high wind-chill factors and swirling snows that made night vision almost impossible, stopped road movement, and grounded fighter-bombers. Men were warned to keep dry, to wear layers of clothing, to leave room in their clothes for air to circulate, and to eat frequently to replenish calories that burned up quickly in the cold weather. They were taught how to avoid or to recognize frostbite and how to deal with it, how to keep weapons from seizing up, how to start frozen truck engines, and how to move tanks to prevent the treads from freezing to the ground.[72]

That stretch of the Jamestown Line occupied by the Commonwealth Division was in an area not unlike Quebec's Laurentian Mountains or Gatineau Hills, except with fewer trees. The peaks were usually no higher than 250 m above the valley floors, which were rocky and covered with scrub. Some of the hills had only recently been planted with young pine trees. Many of the valleys had been farmed for centuries, with diked paddies on the valley floor and terraced plots climbing up the hillsides. In more peaceful times those plots yielded beans, cotton, corn, and sorghum. Now, most of the small farmhouses were abandoned or destroyed.

From the beginning of the static war to the end of the conflict, units rotating into front-line positions always attempted to improve those positions to some extent. But a sort of 'capital investment' mentality grew up over time. It undermined initiatives to alter radically or greatly improve the defences. It discouraged inventiveness. It led to a slovenly attitude towards defence in general. As Canadian Capt. J.R. Madden observed following a visit to the

Jamestown positions: 'Company after company occupied the same hills, lived in the same bunkers and fought from the same trenches. A company commander was called upon to display little initiative. As long as he insisted upon the observance of certain fundamental principles he was safe.'[73]

These defences were wholly inadequate to repel a truly deter-mined enemy – the defensive lines to the rear such as the 'Wyo-ming' Line were better fortified and supported. But what was the alternative? As Madden pointed out: 'That even semi-permanent defences were not properly prepared was due to the lack of direc-tion from above; the uncertainty produced by the truce talks; the maintenance required during the rainy season to keep even the most primitive entrenchments usable; and the initial weakness of the enemy. It was only when the Chinese had more guns, more ammunition and learned to concentrate their fire that the weak-ness of our field works became painfully obvious.'[74] The lack of Chinese air power contributed to the sloth, as did the virtually per-manent status of the line. Over time the men saw little point in try-ing to conceal their positions from the enemy, who certainly knew where every rifle pit and crawl trench was – as the Canadians in fact knew of the Chinese positions.[75]

If the soldiers were somewhat blasé about hiding their positions from prying enemy eyes, they were anything but complacent about keeping warm and dry, not to mention safe. Since the army failed to provide effective heating units in winter, standard kit was supple-mented by all sorts of strange heating devices, many of which posed fire and carbon-monoxide hazards.[76] The bunkers them-selves were dug as deeply as possible, of course, and usually cov-ered by steel pickets, used to anchor strands of barbed wire, laid side by side. On top of this layer of steel, the men piled stone and sand-filled ammunition boxes and sandbags. In monsoon season, when the soil became waterlogged and could not support a heavy roof, bunkers collapsed in large numbers.[77]

Weather and constant use continually eroded the dirt walls of the firing pits and the trenches. The only solution was constant, daily maintenance. Throughout the afternoon the men dug,

repaired barbed wire, laid more barbed wire, shored up their positions with sheets of corrugated iron, and tried to waterproof their
positions. They were expert at scrounging anything that might
help heat a pill-box or protect a bunker roof. Anyone going to the
rear kept an eye peeled for what could be 'liberated' to make life
safer and easier. The constant battle for comfort, warmth, and
safety was even more unrelenting than the war with the enemy.

1500: A daylight raid

Every now and then one side or the other would attack the other
side in platoon or company strength during the day. Daylight
assaults larger than that were rare while the armistice talks were
going on, even when those talks seemed to be leading nowhere.
Daylight attacks, like those mounted at night, were aimed at gaining information, capturing an enemy soldier for interrogation,
keeping the enemy on its toes, or killing and destroying as much as
possible in a limited attack that lasted only a few hours. When the
Canadians attacked, they invariably did so after a thorough air and
artillery pounding of their intended objective, and they were
always supported by mortars and by direct fire provided by heavy
machine-guns, tanks, bazookas, and recoilless rifles.

In Korea the UN allies had complete control of the skies over
the front, and the U.S. military operated a joint tri-service system
to allocate tactical air resources. It based the system on three
elements – a tactical air control party (TACP), a joint operations
centre (JOC), and the tactical air formations. The TACP, consisting of an air-force pilot and an army observer, flew over the front
in a 'mosquito,' actually a single-engine AT-6 trainer (Harvard)
equipped with smoke rockets and radios. It marked the target with
smoke rockets, then guided incoming fighter-bombers onto it.

In Korea, it was almost never possible for a ground unit in trouble to get quick, effective air sppport. An air strike was either pre-
planned, usually the day before, when a brigade wanted a particular position softened up prior to attack, or it was ordered through
the JOC. The TACP was in radio contact with the JOC and with
division and brigade headquarters on the ground. If a patrol, pla-

toon, company, or battalion was in immediate trouble and needed a rapid air response, it had first to pass its request by radio or telephone up the line to brigade HQ. Brigade HQ would contact the TACP with the request. The TACP pilot would then scout out the situation, and he and his observer would decide if an air strike was really appropriate. If they decided that it was, they contacted the JOC to see if any fighter-bombers were available. If there was an unallocated inbound 'package' of napalm-laden fighter-bombers, the TACP would mark the target and guide the planes in. If such a package was not available, and the situation on the ground was especially dangerous, aircraft might be scrambled from Kimpo, near Seoul, or an allocated package might be diverted, but that was rare.[78] This procedure was quite different from what the Canadians had practised in training at Fort Lewis. There they had learned to work with a TACP that observed the ground ahead from forwardmost infantry positions, not unlike a forward observation officer (FOO). Naturally, it took some time before the Canadians were proficient in calling for air strikes.[79]

When there were raids, there were casualties. If a Canadian soldier was wounded in Korea, he was cared for by an army medical system that was vastly better than it had been in the Second World War.[80] This was the war of the mobile army surgical hospital (MASH) pioneered by the U.S. army but quickly replicated by the other UN allies. Until a Canadian field surgical team (equivalent to a MASH) was set up in 1953, wounded Canadians were almost always evacuated to a Norwegian MASH unit that served the Commonwealth Division sector. The units consisted of prefabricated surgical wards and related facilities set up as near to the front lines as possible. Although casualties were transported to MASH units by foot, truck, and jeep, the facilities will for ever be associated with helicopter evacuation of casualties. This was the first war in history wherein seriously wounded soldiers were flown almost from the battlefield to a surgical facility, sometimes within an hour of being hit. It was 'an inspiring ... life saving method,' according to one Canadian report on casualty evacuation. 'There is no finer sight than that of a helicopter coming up a Korean valley to evacuate a seriously wounded or injured soldier.'[81]

It was a marvellous innovation indeed, and it helped keep the ratio of wounds to deaths lower than in the Second World War, but its use was limited by the number of helicopters available and their carrying capacity. Korean War–era helicopters flown by the U.S. army could carry only up to two wounded men at a time ensuring that helicopter evacuation was reserved only for those soldiers 'seriously wounded or injured where the time factor [was] important.' This category included head wounds, penetrating chest wounds, penetrating abdominal wounds, fractured femurs, and serious burns. A request for a helicopter evacuation could be made by the medical officer at a regimental aid post (RAP), a casualty-collection point (CCP), sometimes set up close to the RAP, or an advanced dressing station (ADS), generally located about 10 km to the rear of the RAP. The request had to be approved by battalion HQ. This requirement was somewhat time-consuming but was imposed because RAPs were almost always located very close to the front and the call for a helicopter evacuation always had to be made within the context of the minute-by-minute tactical situation.

Evacuations by helicopter could take place only in daylight, under good weather conditions, and from flat forward areas protected from enemy fire. In large-scale actions, with many wounded, the total number of helicopter evacuees was always 'limited when compared to those occurring.'[82] When badly hurt Canadian soldiers reached a MASH unit, the surgeons repaired the worst of the casualties, who were then evacuated, by road and air, to Seoul and thence to the Commonwealth General Hospital in Tokyo. The most seriously wounded were then evacuated from Japan, usually by USAF medical evacuation aircraft.

When the 25th CIB was being formed, the 25th Canadian Field Ambulance was set up with it. It consisted of doctors and nursing sisters who were to serve with the Commonwealth Division until the end of the war. Although the U.S. army's helicopter evacuation and MASH system worked extremely well, it was thought necessary, as one report noted, for Canada's army 'to provide Canadian medical attention for Canadian casualties at all levels where such attention is necessitated.'[83] It was important for the morale of the wounded to be taken care of by someone who was not a total stranger. For this reason, Canada formed its own field surgical team – a MASH – before the end of the fighting.

Helicopter evacuation, MASH units, more effective infection-fighting drugs, and procedures and drugs that allowed doctors to overcome the worst effects of shock and blood loss meant better care, as did improved triage and handling of the wounded. In the summer of 1952 a Forward Regimental Air Post (FRAP) was established on the 25th CIB front. It was designed to operate even closer to the fighting front than the RAP and to be set up quickly 'at any given point in forward positions where moderately heavy or heavy casualties [were] anticipated.'[84] For every thousand Canadian men wounded in Korea, only 34 died from wounds, compared with 66 out of a thousand in the Second World War and 114 per thousand in the First.[85] What did not change very much was the way in which wounds were inflicted.

In the period from June through November 1952, a typical six-month stretch on the Jamestown Line, more than half the wounds to Canadian soldiers were the result of mortar and shell fire. This reflected the extravagant Chinese use of heavy mortars and artillery in both harassing mode and to cover infantry assaults. Only a little less than 16 per cent of wounds resulted from gunfire, with close to 13 per cent from grenades, which both sides used heavily in both attack and defence. Very few casualties – 3.1 per cent – were classified as battle exhaustion. For all the dangers from enemy action, however, the Korean War followed the age-old pattern wherein soldiers were laid low far more often by non–battle-related causes than by enemy fire. In these six months there were 294 Canadian battle casualties, but 1,635 admissions to medical facilities for disease and accidents. The most common afflictions were injuries not caused by enemy action (18.6 per cent), respiratory infection (11.5 per cent) and skin diseases. VD accounted for some 2.3 per cent of the total.[86]

Korea was a swamp of infectious diseases. Haemorrhagic fever, caused by a virus carried by a chigger mite, could kill – up to 7 per cent of all UN soldiers contracting it died. Malaria was more easily avoided through preventive medicines. Canadian and other Commonwealth soldiers treated at the Commonwealth Hospital in

Tokyo were more subject to jaundice than Americans in U.S. hospitals because of the employment of reusable intravenous equipment; the Americans had disposable plastic devices. After the war two Canadian army doctors studied the lessons that the UN armies had learned in Korea. They concluded: 'The Korean conflict may have been a localized war but it was a dirty, difficult one. It served as a training and testing ground and, [as] in the case of all wars, medical knowledge was advanced.'[87]

1730: Stand to and prepare for nightfall

If it had been a good day, with no enemy shelling, no raids, no one wounded or killed, the men might enjoy the beauty of a setting sun. But if they did, they knew that their real test lay ahead, in the hours of darkness.

Once again it was time for a 100 per cent stand-to, now with the sun in the men's faces and an enemy always able to inflict mayhem after nightfall. Eyes squinted at the enemy-held hills a few hundred metres away, fingers tightened on triggers, hands grasped grenades, and barely a sound was heard, but for the clink of metal, against metal, the rasp of a cigarette lighter, or the clunk of a machine-gun bolt pulled back. Binoculars scanned clumps of trees and outcrops of rock. The Chinese were masters at putting snipers far forward, almost up to the Canadian wire, crawling a metre or two at a time, all day, well camouflaged, from cover to cover, until they were in position to put a bullet through an eyesocket and snuff out another Canadian life. All along the line, the men waited. In winter, they pulled back their parka hoods to hear better. In summer they wiped the sweat from their brows to keep their eyes clear. They stayed at stand-to for ninety minutes, then stood down to grab some rations and go into their night defensive routine.

During the evening stand-to, Sgt Urquhart would make his final inspection of his platoon's position before dark.[88] Were the men dressed for the cold? Were the weapons clean and well-oiled? Was there ample spare ammunition in the rifle pits and the bunkers, or were open crates of grenades easily to hand? In the extreme stress of a fire fight in the dark, men sometimes found it very difficult to do the easiest things, such as open a crate of grenades. Once a frustrated non-com simply smashed the wooden grenade crate on a rock; the grenades spilled on the ground, forcing the men to hunt about in the dark, on their knees, as Chinese fire cut the night above their heads.

1900: Stand down, the night war resumes

After stand-down, one-third of the men in each company stayed in their defensive positions, watching, listening, waiting for any sound of the enemy. The valley in front of them had been pre-sited by the mortars, tanks, and field artillery. If there were no Canadian patrols out, the merest sound of enemy movement brought a torrent of fire on to pre-selected positions as powerful searchlights mounted at intervals along the line lit up the forward slopes. But when the Chinese were serious about attacking a Canadian position, they were rarely so clumsy as to announce their approach by clinking metal against metal, or by talking too loudly, or by letting cigarettes glow in the dark.

'B' Company, 1RCR, was in defensive positions along the Jamestown Line some 250 m southeast of and below Hill 227 on the night of 23 October 1952, when Chinese shell fire began to explode in and around the company positions. The bombardment intensified, and the men protected themselves as best they could. Suddenly the shelling stopped, and at least two companies of Chinese infantry, later reinforced by a third, rushed over and through the Canadian wire and into the Canadian trenches. How had the Chinese got so close so soon after nightfall? One post-battle analysis concluded that the feat 'could have been accomplished only if the [Chinese] approach had been made from lay-up posns immediately ahead of the FDL, occ during daylt hrs of 23 Oct or during darkness of the previous night.'[89] And no one in the Canadian positions had heard or seen anything!

The fighting was immediately close and in small groups. There were burp guns, Tommy guns, carbines, rifles, and lots of grenades right in the Canadian crawl trenches, rifle pits, and bunkers, in the dark, with the only light provided by burning timbers, explosions, or the flash of gunfire. With their artillery laying down walls of exploding steel between 'B' and adjoining companies, the Chinese pushed the Canadians out of the 'B' Company area by 2000. Then the firing ceased. Over the next half-hour the men in the nearest Canadian position heard movement, voices, and noises indicating that the Chinese were digging in to await the inevitable counterattack.

In fact, the Chinese were not doing that. They left an ambush party on the rear slope of the 'B' Company position, then pulled back. 'B' Company soon reoccupied the position after mounting a two-platoon probe which engaged and pushed off the Chinese ambush party without suffering casualties. The Chinese left behind lots of Bangalore torpedoes and satchel charges but carried away all the clothes, weapons, and personal kit that they could find. They had made no effort to prepare the position for a prolonged defence. No one could figure out why they had attacked as they had, and then left so suddenly.[90] It hardly mattered to the eighteen Canadian dead whom they left behind.

While each night one-third of the company stayed in defensive positions, two-thirds were assigned to work parties or patrols. Those not on patrol would switch places about every four hours, so that the men might grab two to four hours of sleep. Those assigned to patrol duty would begin to prepare themselves physically and mentally to head off into the dark and confront the enemy near its own defences. As Urquhart later remembered: 'The trick was to keep the men motivated and keep them alert during patrols and not too anxious if they knew someone who got hit the night before.'[91]

In one form or another, patrolling – soldiers going forward of a main body to find the enemy – has been part of warfare since time immemorial. Patrols serve two basic purposes; to make actual physical contact with the enemy in order to know where he is and to find out his disposition. It is an axiom of warfare that the enemy whose whereabouts is unknown is the most dangerous of all, because he can strike from virtually anywhere without warning. And although aerial reconnaissance, which began in the First World War, was and is certainly a major aid in finding the enemy

and knowing his position, there is still – to this day – no more certain way of doing that than through ground reconnaissance.

In Korea, as on the Western Front in the First World War, the
enemy's main disposition was well known. In the earlier war
he was quite obviously in that trench line 100 m across open
ground. In Korea, the enemy was in that string of hillside strongpoints across the valley. Why then the need to patrol? The answer
was the same in both wars – to deny the enemy freedom of movement, particularly at night. Such freedom would enable him to
approach your own defensive positions to spy or to attack across
the barbed wire on the heels of an artillery barrage. The successful Chinese assault on the 1RCR positions on the night of
23 October 1952 was glaring evidence of that battalion's failure
to patrol diligently in the twenty-four hours or so prior to the
attack, even though the RCR, according to the official historian,
staged the most raids against the enemy of the three battalions
during this period.[92]

Canadian patrolling doctrine in Korea was directly linked to
patrolling tactics first developed in the First World War and then
repeated on different fronts in the Second. There were five basic
types of patrols: raids or fighting patrols, ambushes, standing
patrols, lie-up or reconnaissance patrols, and 'jitter' patrols. Raids
were just that – attacks of up to a company in strength on a previously pinpointed Chinese position. If the raid aimed primarily at
taking a prisoner for intelligence purposes, it was dubbed a
'snatch' patrol. These raids were almost always carried out in two
or more stages, with 'firm bases' or fire bases – defensive positions
manned by at least one Bren gunner and several riflemen – set up
along the line of approach so as to provide support in the attack
and cover during withdrawal.

An ambush was similarly simple – to send out a group of men to
lie in wait across a well-known Chinese patrol route and attack the
enemy as he approached. A standing patrol was essentially a small
forward outpost of three to five men linked by telephone or wireless to the main company position. A lie-up patrol was conducted
to gain intelligence about the enemy. Under cover of night, a few
men, sometimes only two, made their way very close to the enemy,

camouflaged themselves, and observed his comings and goings for a day before returning the next night. In a 'jitter' patrol, ten to fifteen men moved into position near enemy lines, then suddenly made as much fuss as possible with whistles, shouts, or gunfire, and engaged the enemy with small arms.[93]

The mix of patrols and the number mounted by front-line units were established by divisional patrol policy, which was heavily influenced, if not dictated, by corps HQ. At the corps level, the Americans tended to favour vigorous and frequent patrolling – to increase their 'body count,' to keep their men sharp, and to wear down the enemy. At division level, British commanders tended to see active and vigorous patrolling as both unnecessary and wasteful of lives. There was as a consequence an almost constant push–pull effect on patrol policy at 25 CIB HQ. Whenever the British carried the argument, patrolling activity slackened off; whenever the Americans did, it picked up.[94]

A patrol was born at least twenty-four hours before the men walked out through the wire and the minefield and made their way into the valley below. Patrol leaders and their men studied the ground over which they would go, using maps and aerial photographs. It was seldom possible to study the ground at first hand because to do so involved enormous risks to personnel and the possibility of tipping off the enemy. Each unit had its own unique way of mounting a patrol – 3RCR, for example, mounted raids in three stages. On the first night the patrol leader would lead a reconnaissance party down the forward slope to about the centre of the valley, then return. On the second night, the raiding party would stay in company lines. On the third night, the entire raiding party would move to the same centre-valley position and set up a firm base, and from there the actual raiders would move right up to the Chinese positions for a look-see. Then the entire party returned. On the fourth night, the party again stayed in the company position. Only on the fifth would it finally attack.[95]

Whatever the preparation, it was important in the days immediately preceding the patrol for the supporting arms, particular the mortars, tanks, and artillery, to zero in on the position to be raided, on the approaches to it, and on particular spots in no

man's land chosen by the patrol leader to cover the raiding party
on withdrawal. The idea was that a single word spoken into a telephone or radio would bring the barrage down on a pre-selected
target. The only way to arrange this was to register those target
areas beforehand through fire and observation. The enemy also
used this technique. Such fire and observation, however, might
well tip off the enemy about an impending raid. Thus the registering fire was almost always masked by a larger barrage.

The patrol wore rubber-soled boots and dark clothes. They
blackened their faces. They strapped down rifle slings and grenades to prevent rattling. Then they moved out. Stealth was essential, but sometimes men threw caution to the wind and bravado
ruled. In early September 1952, for example, the intelligence
officer of 1PPCLI wrote of raiding parties: 'The majority of them
have been carried out with despatch and deliberation, however
there have been a few, if through ignorance or contempt, which
broke all rules of good patrolling. Members of a fighting patrol
were seen to go out wearing trousers which due to regular scrub-
bing and washing, were bleached almost white. Ambush members
were seen to light cigarettes ... Another night members of [a]
patrol were boisterous and jocular whilst proceeding to a position
at the foot of a suspected enemy position.'[96]

The simple truth is that Canadian soldiers had been trained
for almost everything but a war of constant patrolling. 'I felt that
when they were training us, they were still thinking about World
War Two,' 2PPCLI's William Powell later remembered. 'When I
got to Korea and started going on regular patrols, I realized we
were fighting a whole different war and I found that frustrat-
ing.'[97] That was not true of the Canadians alone. Cassels noted at
one point: 'Generally speaking we are extremely bad shots at
night. I am sure this is because it is seldom, if ever, practised.'[98]
What the Canadians and others did not appear to realize was that
night reconnaissance was a very specialized task that required specific training and that could not simply be assigned willy-nilly to
one platoon or another. As one recent study of Canadian patrolling in Korea concludes: 'Canadian commanders were guilty of
using inappropriate patrol tactics, of generally allowing patrols to

become routine and meaningless, and primarily, of inadequate reconnaissance. All these failings can be linked to the absence of an effective patrol doctrine.' That study also notes that 'a general lack of training contributed to the lackluster performance of Canadian patrols.'[99]

The cost in lives was sometimes appalling. In raids mounted by 1PPCLI on the night of 20–21 June 1952, 1RCR the following night, and 1R22eR two nights later (23–24 June), the brigade suffered fifty-five casualties – eight killed, forty-five wounded, one taken prisoner, and one missing.[100] Although specialized patrol training began at the battalion level, it was not until the late spring of 1953 that the 25 Canadian Infantry Brigade Patrol School was established under the command of Major W.H. Pope.[101]

Such was a soldier's day on the line in Korea. Few of those days on the Jamestown Line ever produced an item of news that made the front pages back home. There were no sweeping movements of troops and tanks, no capital cities under siege or about to fall, no last stands along beleaguered perimeters. Men died only in threes or fours. If the Chinese attacked some recognizable and oft-fought-over feature such as Old Baldy, or Pork Chop Hill, or The Hook, or Little Gibraltar, the evening radio newscast might contain a few words. Otherwise the story was always the same: 'The Korean front is "quiet"'; 'Our troops exchanged shell fire yesterday, but casualties were light'; 'Little progress was reported at the armistice talks at Panmunjom.' The veterans of that war tell a story of the time one Canadian newspaper ran the same Bill Boss dispatch from the front several days in a row and none of its readers noticed, or cared. If that did not really happen, it might as well have; Korea was not much of a war anymore, and everyone knew that it was going to end, sooner or later, just about where it started.

It was not long before cynicism began to pervade the ranks of men along the front line. The professional soldiers were there for the experience, for the future of their careers, because they were professional soldiers doing the work for which they were paid and had prepared. But why were the others there? For what were they fighting? Was any of it worth the lives of any of them? One U.S. soldier epitomized the feelings of many of the troops who manned the front line when he told a *Time* magazine correspondent: 'The days it's my turn to go out on patrol and some jerk over there cuts down at me with a burp gun or whatever – why, then its a hell of a big war for me that day. And the days I get to just lay around the bunker – with maybe only ten or 15 rounds incoming all day ... well, those days it's not much of a war at all, I guess.'[102] Or, as Canadian veteran Robert Molesworth of 2RCR later put it: 'When I hear people say today that Korea was not a war, but a "conflict," it really pisses me off ... It was a war, and people died. It's that simple.'[103]

EIGHT

Blood on the Hills

19 March 1952. Spring came all at once to central Korea. The upper air flow over Korea suddenly reversed itself, and instead of cold dry air arriving from Siberia, the jet stream pumped moist warm air from the East China Sea over the peninsula. The flow brought steady downpours, while rising temperatures thawed out the frozen paddies and the roads recently packed hard with snow or slick with ice. On the line, the rain leaked into bunkers and poured into trenches. It mixed with the thawed-out earth to make a thick gumbo that lay everywhere. Men walked about huddled under their ponchos as the mud collected on the bottoms of their boots. They slept in the wet. Their food was cold. They worked constantly to keep their weapons cleaned and oiled. But at least the Chinese were nowhere to be seen.[1]

The supply roads were suddenly impassable, even to half-tracks and 6x6 trucks. The lateral road along the south bank of the Imjin River connecting Rockingham's HQ and division HQ was closed until further notice. All vehicle traffic in the division was restricted to the absolute minimum; trucks and jeeps were allowed to leave only with the specific permission on the CO. One of the three bridges across the Imjin was restricted to jeeps only. Over in Panmunjon, the searchlight that marked the site of the truce talks still shone nightly. Rain or shine, hot or cold, the negotiators sat stone-faced across a large table and made the same points day after day. There was no progress. The war at the front continued. It was a war of attrition that the Canadians did not have resources to fight.

In December 1951, Minister of National Defence Brooke Claxton had visited Korea. He had not been impressed with the way he thought the Americans were running the war. He had been uneasy about 'the use of large bombers and heavy artillery against defenceless villages.' He did not like what he thought of as overly aggressive and belligerent language used by the U.S. military to describe its operations.[2] He thought Gen. James Van Fleet's staff officers 'far too old for their jobs' and too much 'in the habit of receiving and lying to Congressmen.' The Americans put on their patented lectures with charts, pointers, and tables of statistics showing how well the war was going, but Claxton simply refused to believe much of what he heard. On New Year's Day 1952, he had been treated to an artillery shoot at supposed Chinese positions in hills about 1000 m away. He had thought that 'about as useful as trying to dig a well with a lawnmower.' He was especially distressed to learn that Rockingham was constantly being told by his superiors to increase his estimates of enemy casualties.[3]

When Claxton returned from Korea, he was more pessimistic than ever about an early end to the fighting.[4] He thought that the cease-fire talks and the current lull in major ground operations had 'helped the Chinese build up their military strength.' He concluded that the Chinese had 'everything to gain by keeping things just about where they are.'[5] He told newspaper reporter Bruce Hutchison off the record that the main objective of the Communists was to pin down vast numbers of Western troops and bleed the Western economies dry.[6]

Claxton was convinced that Korea was becoming a bottomless pit into which Canada and the Western world would pour precious resources, sapping their ability to resist the Soviets. His fears were not groundless. When Charles Foulkes visited Washington in the second half of February, 1952, Bradley told him in no uncertain terms that Korea was to become a war of attrition: 'It is the aim of the Unified Command to demonstrate to the Communists that they are fighting a losing battle and that their superiority in numbers is of no avail against determined troops with first class equipment.'[7] Such words struck fear into Claxton's heart.

Unlike Claxton, Lester Pearson had been an enthusiastic supporter of Canadian participation in the Korean War from almost the very start. He had believed strongly that Korea was the test for NATO and that the Western powers had to meet it. But though a strong supporter of military intervention, Pearson had believed that that intervention should be essentially a UN enterprise, even though realism dictated that the United States would provide the bulk of the troops and call most of the shots both militarily and politically. Pearson's main objective was to try to subject U.S. Korea policy to the scrutiny of its UN allies and military junior partners wherever possible. In that he failed more often than he succeeded. His very efforts irritated American policy-makers, especially Secretary of State Dean Acheson. Thus, by the spring of 1952, he too was more than disenchanted with U.S. political leadership of the war.[8]

In mid-January 1952 the Canadian brigade had been taken out of the line for the first time since September and assigned to divisional reserve on the Wyoming Line for six weeks. Most of that six weeks was devoted to training, and much of that to trying to absorb and apply the lessons learned from the U.S. army and marines, or the other Commonwealth contingents, about how to fight and win in Korea.[9] The Canadian army was also supported by 1 Canadian Army Operational Research Team (1CAORT), which worked on its own but usually under the direction of the quartermaster general, to study a variety of problems. The team was small, however; its studies were statistical and concerned matters such as types of wounds, disease rates, and causes of burns and fires.[10]

When the Canadians returned to the Jamestown Line on 10 March 1952, they traded places with the 29th British Infantry Brigade astride the Sami-Ch'on, about 10,000 m southwest of the previous Canadian locations in the shadow of Hill 355 – Little Gibraltar. It did not take the Chinese long to welcome the Canadians back. At 0130 on 26 March 2RCR's 'C' and 'B' Companies suffered a two-hour barrage of Chinese mortar and shell fire; thirty minutes after the shells began to fall, a company of Chinese infantry slammed into 1PPCLI, concentrating on 'C' Company, while surrounding 7 Platoon of 2RCR. The attack was sudden and violent, and a 'C' Company outpost was ordered back. A desperate fire fight ensued, with Canadian 81 mm and 4.2-inch mortars firing close to 2,000 rounds trying to stop the Chinese from overrunning the Canadian positions. By 0430 the Chinese had pulled back, leaving four Patricias and four RCRs dead, four wounded, and three men evacuated because of battle exhaustion.[11] That was the way the war went in the last week of March: two men killed in action on the 22nd; one on the 24th; one killed, one dying of his wounds on the 25th; eight killed on the 26th; one killed on the last day of the month.[12]

For 1PPCLI, there was only more of the same to look forward to, but for 2RCR and the other formations that had arrived in Korea in April 1951 it was time to go home. This time the rotating units moved through Inchon, much closer to the front than Pusan. It took almost two months to rotate all the troops, including administrative and support units, but 1RCR and 1R22eR were in their front-line positions before the end of April. In the midst of the rotation, the division moved to the right to occupy once more the section of the line that it had held after Operation Commando the previous autumn.

For the most part the rotations went well, but all the battalions had problems integrating a number of the 2nd-battalion men who had not yet served their full year in Korea and were held over for some months to augment 1st-battalion strength.[13] Rockingham too was going home, to be replaced by Brig. M.P. Bogert, a Second World War veteran with a solid reputation for leadership and command. Cassels had nothing but praise for the departing Canadian unit commanders. He thought Rockingham 'a tower of strength' and the three 2nd-battalion commanders – Keane, Stone, and Dextraze – 'all excellent.'[14]

Born in Toronto, Bogert was a graduate of RMC. He had joined the RCR as a lieutenant prior to the outbreak of the Second World War, rising through the ranks to command the West Nova Scotia Regiment in Sicily and Italy. Leading a task force known as 'Boforce,' which combined his battalion with additional striking power from artillery, anti-tank guns, and other support units, he had played a key role in the battle for Potenza in September 1943. By the end of the war he had been promoted to brigadier in com-

mand of the 2nd Canadian Infantry Brigade and awarded the DSO.
He had stayed in the army, becoming director general of military
training in Ottawa before being given command of 25 Brigade.

The handover of brigade command took place at a brief ceremony on 28 April 1952; Bogert got to work immediately to put his
own stamp on the brigade. Over the course of his year in command, he diligently applied his own training experience to keep
his soldiers ready for war. With the exception of 1RCHA, which was
not fully trained on taking over from 2RCHA,[15] the permanent-
force units under Bogert's command were far better prepared to
fight than had been Rockingham's men when they had arrived in
Korea. Bogert was determined to make sure that they stayed that
way through intensive training every time units were pulled back
into reserve. His training aimed at removing weaknesses revealed
by action in the line, particularly in patrolling, night fighting, and
marksmanship, and ensuring that his men did not forget how
to fight a mobile war – advance to contact, contact, and withdrawal – in the event that the strategic situation in Korea suddenly
changed.[16]

The railway station at Tokchong, 23 May 1952, 1100. The men of
'B' Company, 1RCR, under the command of Major E.L. Cohen,
climbed aboard the train taking their personal kit with them. Their
weapons, company stores, and communications equipment were
placed in a separate car while a few jeeps and light trucks were
covered with tarpaulins and lashed to a flat car behind the engine.
Then, belching black smoke, the engine strained out of the station
and headed slowly south, down the uneven tracks, towards the
port of Pusan. They were heading for the prison compounds on
Koje-do (Koje Island), off the south coast of South Korea, to share
the burden of guarding those compounds with American, ROK,
and other UN troops. They were to form half of a two-company
contingent from 1st Commonwealth Division; a British company
formed the other half.[17]

By the end of May 1952, Koje-do had become notorious to anyone following the Korean War in the newspapers, newsreels, or
radio. A massive prisoner-of-war (POW) compound on the island

held some 70,000 North Korean and Chinese POWs in large barbed-wire compounds, which were only minimally patrolled by U.S. or ROK troops. The POWs ran the camp inside the wire compounds. Led by Communist political officers captured with the Chinese or North Korean troops, the prisoners had revolted in early May. They had enticed the camp commandant into one of the compounds, captured him, and forced him to sign a 'confession' about poor conditions and political oppression. The revolt had then been bloodily suppressed.

The Koje revolt stemmed from the Communists' determination in the peace talks to have their way on the issue of what was to be done with POWs once an armistice was signed. In fact that one issue – repatriation of prisoners – had become the major sticking point at the Panmunjom negotiations by the spring of 1952. The UN Command insisted that all prisoners be free to select where they would be released in the north or the south, while the Communists were determined that all prisoners be returned to their countries of origin. The Koje revolt was designed to show the world that the Communist prisoners there were 'still' committed Marxists and were suffering grievous conditions because of their political views.

The decision to add Canadian and British troops to the contingent guarding Koje-do was made at the very top by U.S. Gen. Mark W. Clark, who had just replaced Gen. Matthew B. Ridgway as commander-in-chief, United Nations Command, Korea. Initially Clark discussed the possibility of sending Commonwealth troops to Koje-do with Lt.-Gen. William Bridgeford, commander-in-chief, British Commonwealth Forces, Korea.[18] Like his predecessor, Lt.-Gen. Sir Horace Robertson, Bridgeford was also Australian and responsible for the overall administration of the Commonwealth Division. Clark was at the top of the operational chain of command, but Bridgeford was answerable directly to the chiefs of the general staffs of the countries contributing to the Commonwealth Division through their military representatives in Tokyo. In Canada's case, that was Brig. A.B. Connelly, commander, Canadian Military Mission, Far East (CMMFE).[19]

Without first consulting CMMFE, Bridgeford instructed Cassels to provide the necessary detachments if requested by U.S. Eighth Army headquarters. Cassels received the warning order from Eighth Army on 22 May and immediately instructed Bogert to ready one company for movement to Koje-do. Bogert told the OC of 1RCR, Lt.-Col. P.R. Bingham, to select one of his companies for the Koje-do duty and contacted Simonds to tell him what was happening.[20] Simonds was furious when he read the dispatch. He gathered his files and messages and rushed to take the news to Foulkes. This was the opening move in a crisis caused almost entirely by Ottawa's unhappiness with how the United States was conducting both the war and the peace negotiations.

It is still not clear from the record exactly why Clark wanted to send non-American units to Koje-do to augment the US and ROK troops already there. The Canadian ambassador to the United States, Hume Wrong, thought that Clark wanted to demonstrate 'that there was a common front among the Allies ... to clean up the situation [in Koje] as soon as possible.'[21] Given the political importance of the prisoner question and the riots on Koje-do, that was a reasonable assumption. If it is correct, there can be little doubt that Clark acted with the prior knowledge and approval 'at the highest level' of officials in the U.S. State Department.[22]

On the day Cassells received his orders from the Eighth Army, a liaison officer from Clark's headquarters summoned Brig. Connelly to tell him what Clark planned and to see if he had any objections. Connelly apparently thought about contacting Simonds, but when he was told by Clark's messenger that 'the U.N. Command hoped it would not be necessary to consult governments,' he decided not to. In his view, Canada's forces in Korea were 'at the disposal of the Unified Command ... [to] go wherever they were sent.'[23] He did not refer the matter to Ottawa until 28 May, five days after Major Cohen's men had left the front for Koje-do.[24]

Bogert's message to Simonds was understood one way by Foulkes, but another way by the cabinet. Foulkes was not happy that Canadian troops had been taken from the line and sent to the Koje hell-hole, but he did not think that much could be done about it from a military perspective. Instead, he suggested that the government take the matter up with the Americans.[25] Claxton and

Louis St Laurent, by contrast, were very upset. They immediately telephoned Hume Wrong in Washington with instructions to get the order countermanded.[26] Wrong was to tell the Americans that Clark's manoeuvre would undermine support for the Korean War in Canada and might lead Canadians to think twice before sending yet more troops to Korea.[27]

Whatever his personal misgivings at this overreaction, Wrong did as he was told and touched off a minor diplomatic crisis that lasted for several weeks. Ottawa insisted that the Canadians be pulled out of Koje:[28] the Americans insisted – correctly – that to countermand Clark's legitimate military order because a member government of the UN coalition was upset with it would establish a horrendous precedent.[29] The Canadians persisted, even firing off a public note of diplomatic protest,[30] much to the surprise – and the chagrin – of a large part of the Canadian public (those who cared about the issue), the parliamentary opposition, and much of the press. The *Ottawa Journal* probably put it best: 'So far as the ordinary American or Canadian citizen knows, the only contribution we have made to the prison camp situation at Koje is to proclaim publicly and before the Kremlin our maidenly modesty at having to go there at all or on such short notice.'[31]

The Canadian troops stayed their full tour at Koje-do and started back to the front on 14 July 1952. One month later, Connelly was quietly brought back to Ottawa and pensioned off. Simonds's decision to fire him was made with Claxton's active support. Claxton told one reporter, off the record, that Connelly had been 'incompetent for some time and that his failure to advise the government on the Canadians going to Koje was the last straw.'[32] When Connelly later sought employment with Canadian National Railways, its president, Donald Gordon, sought Simonds's opinion. Simonds wrote: 'I am of the opinion that Connelly is sadly lacking in energy and drive, and seems incapable of grasping the real essentials of a job and carrying them through.'[33] If that was true, Simonds had had no business assigning him to Tokyo in the first place.

The strange behaviour of the Canadian government over Koje-do can be explained only by Ottawa's growing unhappiness and frustration over the course that the Korean War was taking by the spring of 1952. St Laurent, Pearson, and Claxton ought surely to have known that whether or not Clark had been legally entitled to issue his order sending Canadian troops to Koje, there was no way that Washington was going to withdraw his order once the troops had actually left for the island. If the government felt compelled to protest at all, it ought to have done so through very quiet diplomacy. The incident accomplished nothing more than to make the Canadian government look foolish to its allies and to undermine its credibility.[34]

20 June 1952, 2330. Their faces blackened, weapons slings tied down, grenades, ammunition magazines or clips, and webbing secure against their bodies, one NCO, twelve men, and a stretcher-bearer from 'B' Company, 1PPCLI, moved silently through the minefield and wire gaps in front of 'D' Company and crept down the forward slope to the valley below. At the same time, a similarly sized party left the 'C' Company positions and moved ahead into the dark to set up a second firm base. The Patricias were about to mount the first major night raid in several weeks against the Chinese.

April and May had been relatively quiet along the front. After the Canadians reoccupied their old positions near Hill 355, the usual patrol activity resumed. No Canadians had been killed in action in April; twelve had died along the line from the beginning of May until mid-June. Now there occurred, in the words of the official historian, 'a brief, unexplained revival of the raiding policy.'[35] Bogert selected the Patricias to break the ice; thirty-five men from 'B' company got the short straw.

Under cover of a pre-arranged artillery barrage, the fifteen-man main body of the patrol crept forward ahead of the two firm bases until they were some 35 m below the Chinese crawl trenches. At about 0115 the patrol leader began to prepare for the assault and radioed back for Bofors 20 mm fire on two preselected positions inside the Chinese targets. The Boforses opened up, and the men saw the tracers hitting home. It was time to move. Suddenly, three muffled explosions tore the Canadian patrol apart. Confused radio reports came in to company HQ one after the other. There were

wounded. There were many wounded. The patrol leader was
down. All was bedlam. Mysteriously, the Chinese held their fire,
but the Canadians were in serious trouble anyway. The walking
wounded would make it back, but the rest had to be carried
through the night by their comrades, by stretcher-bearers, by anyone willing to come forward to help. The evacuation was almost
complete by 0410 when the Chinese opened up with a machine-
gun from across the valley. They hit no one and were answered by
the 25-pounders. The wounded were all recovered, but the short
night was already giving way to dawn, and some of the dead had to
be left out until the next night. The toll: seven dead and seventeen
wounded, with nothing to show for the effort.[36] Although correspondent Bill Boss reported that the Patricias had suffered a
'fluke' mortar hit,[37] the consensus among the men was that there
had been 'no whine of shells or swish of mortars,' strongly suggest-
ing a series of command-detonated mines.[38] The bad luck continued over the next three nights, as the RCR and the R22eR tried
their hand at mounting fighting patrols. Together they suffered
four killed and twenty-six wounded. Large raids were suspended
for the time being; at the beginning of July the brigade was pulled
out of the line.

After a month of intensive training, the Canadians returned to
the Jamestown Line on 10 August. They found the Chinese patrolling more actively than ever in an obvious effort to seize the initiative in, and thus dominate, no man's land by night. Well supplied
by the Russians, the Chinese had also built up massive stores of
artillery and heavy mortar shells and rockets despite the untiring
efforts of the USAF to interdict their supply lines. The forward UN
troops now found themselves subject to even larger and longer
bombardments than they had known previously. Each time the
Chinese shells rumbled in, there was a danger that Chinese infantry would follow in quick order.

In mid-August, the monsoon brought sheets of heavy rain
sweeping through central Korea. The rain and high winds flooded
trenches and weapons pits and collapsed most of the bunkers and
much of the trench line along the Canadian front. Most of the fortifications had to be laboriously rebuilt. The rain that caused so
much extra work for the Canadians kept the Chinese for the most

part hunkered down in their own caves and tunnels for about a week. Still, the increased enemy bombardments and raids raised the tempo of action and the casualties on the front. In August 1952, eighteen Canadians were killed in action or died of their wounds on the Jamestown Line.

The Chinese resumed aggressive patrolling and active shelling after August; the Commonwealth Division increased its own raiding activity in response. This time the RCR was assigned to occupy Hill 355 and the saddle between it and Hill 227, still held by the Chinese. This was by far the most exposed position on the Canadian part of the line, and as a result that battalion was more involved in the fighting in September and October than were the other two. It was almost as if the RCR and the Chinese were playing a game of tit for tat.

On the night of 24 September an RCR patrol captured a Chinese soldier and killed three would-be Chinese rescuers as they returned towards their lines. Several nights later the RCR was subject to heavy and prolonged shelling. Several nights after that, an RCR patrol attacked the Chinese on Hill 227 while the Patricias took on the Chinese at Hill 217, several kilometres to the east.[39] Then, on 17 October, the Chinese began a four-day bombardment of the RCR positions on the saddle and Hill 355. On the 21st alone they pumped in 1,600 shells. They flattened the barbed wire, buried the reserve ammunition, destroyed the telephone lines, blew up the minefields in front of the RCR positions, blasted apart the bunkers, collapsed the firing pits and crawl trenches, and killed five RCR soldiers.[40]

The Chinese still wanted Hill 355. Shortly after nightfall on 23 October, they came to take it. 'B' Company, 1RCR, was commanded by Major E.L. Cohen. He and his men had done the tour of duty at Koje-do the previous spring. Now they anchored the left flank of the battalion position, strung in a north–south line some 600 m due east of the Chinese positions atop Hill 227. Hour by hour they endured the shelling as it collapsed their positions around them; they even managed to drive off a Chinese patrol, killing three men, when it approached the Canadian wire in the early morning hours of 23 October.[41]

Chinese shells rained down through the day; the men took

whatever shelter they could and tried to keep their sanity as their position was methodically blasted to pieces. Nothing could live above ground. Out there, beyond the disintegrating wire, beyond the churned-up minefields, in caves and bunkers close to the Canadian positions, the Chinese infantry hunkered down. Its men had infiltrated into their hiding places the previous night as its gunners kept the Canadians from putting out patrols. Now they waited to rush into the Canadian trenches as soon as the barrage lifted.[42]

Just after sunset the exploding shells climaxed in a cataclysm of fire. More than a thousand rounds fell into what was left of the 'B' Company position in the space of ten minutes. Then the Chinese gunners shifted their fire to the left and right of 'B' Company, putting a curtain of exploding shells between Cohen's men and 'E' Company to the south and 'A' Company to the east. Then the barrage stopped; the blood-curdling sound of whistles and bugles rent the night, and Chinese infantrymen came shouting and shooting into the 'B' Company position.[43] Some of Cohen's men stayed put in their collapsed fire pits and the ruins of their bunkers and fired into the swarm of Chinese who were all around them. On both sides, men were shot down at close range, clubbed, grenaded. The screams of the wounded and dying mixed with the shouts of those killing amid the explosions of grenades and the bursts of automatic weapons. But while some of the Canadians stuck fast, others – bewildered, dazed, weaponless, wounded, or just plain scared – struggled into the 'A' and 'E' Company positions.

It was a moment for survival or death; many awards for valour were earned in the next few hours. Sgt Gerald Enright of 5 Platoon made his way under heavy fire to the 'A' Company position, reported the situation on the saddle to the company commander, Acting Major George Taylor, then grabbed a radio and as much ammunition as he could carry and headed back into the cauldron to help beat off the attack. He was awarded the Military Medal.[44] Acting Major Taylor won the Military Cross by moving from fire pit to fire pit along the 'A' Company line, encouraging his men to keep control, then organizing the 'B' Company survivors into an effective fighting group to retake their position.[45] Lieut. John

Clark threw grenades and emptied every weapon that he could find at the attackers, firing away with a rifle, a Sten gun, and a Bren gun until everything ran dry. Then he led the remainder of his platoon to safety, carrying one of his wounded on his back. He too was awarded a Military Cross.[46] Pte Charles Morrison clung to his weapon, firing into the mass of advancing Chinese, to give his platoon mates a few moments to reach safety. His body was found after the attack. He was posthumously given the 'Award of Mention-in-Despatches.'[47]

Others did well just to stay alive. Platoon commander Lieut. Russell Gardner was shot three times. He collapsed over the barbed wire and feigned death as the Chinese moved past him. Cpl Ellery M. Faulkner did the same thing. 'A group of twelve Chinese passed within five feet of me but did not look twice,' he later told a reporter. Sgt D. Rennie peered out from his shell hole and watched the Chinese carry a flag into one of the Canadian positions: 'One of them was going to plant it in the ground. The lads behind me cut them all down with a Bren gun.'[48]

While divisional artillery pounded Chinese approach routes from Hill 227 to the saddle, acting battalion CO Major F. Klenavic struggled to get a clear picture of the situation in the 'B' Company area. Although Chinese shell fire had cut the telephone lines from battalion to company, it is not clear whether or not Klenavic also lost radio contact with 'B' Company for part of the night.[49] He waited as long as he could for his men to get clear, or under cover, then ordered tank and field artillery fire to saturate the beleaguered position. At the same time he began to organize a counterattack that went in from 'D' Company at 0110. The advancing RCR infantry exchanged small-arms and automatic-weapons fire with some dug-in Chinese infantry, but most of the Chinese had pulled back. By 0330 the RCR was once again in control of the 'B' Company area. There it found Gardner and a few others still alive, with five Chinese bodies nearby.

The attack on Hill 355 was unusually heavy. After it was over, brigade and division headquarters speculated on what the Chinese had been trying to achieve. Was it a rehearsal to test methods of 'preparing and launching a battalion-sized raid or attack,' as divi-

sion thought?[50] Had the enemy been prepared to occupy the position permanently, as it had Hill 227 a year ago? Or was it just
another, larger hit-and-run attack?[51] There was no way to tell. What
was painfully obvious was the cost. From the beginning of the
heavy shelling on 22 October to the reoccupation of the 'B' Company position in the early morning hours of 24 October, the RCR
and other Canadian units suffered eighteen killed and thirty-five
wounded and had fourteen of their number captured and made
prisoners of war. The toll of Canadians killed, wounded, and missing or taken prisoner since the brigade's return to the line in early
August was now 283; 191 from the RCR, seventy-four from the
R22eR, and eighteen from the PPCLI.

In the weeks following the late October fighting, the divisional
boundaries of the Commonwealth Division were shifted westward,
and 1PPCLI was rotated back to Canada and replaced by 3PPCLI.
The Canadian brigade was assigned to the 'the Hook' – a fortified
crestline some 3 km long in the shape of an angle-iron. The position was about 12 km southwest of Hill 355. It was the easternmost
point of a line of hills that ended at the Sami-Ch'on, which at that
location cut from northwest to southeast across the UN front lines.
The Hook was the key to the Jamestown Line in this sector, a con-
tinual target of Chinese probes and artillery and rocket fire. Simonds thought it 'virtually untenable' as a defensive position.[52]

The Hook had been fought over for months by the Chinese and
British when the Canadians arrived, and its three main defended
localities were honeycombed with deep firing bunkers connected
by tunnels and sandbagged, lined crawl trenches.[53] They were
ringed with barbed wire. The men slept in four- to six-man bunkers
built on the reverse slopes. The floors of these bunkers could be as
much as 4 m below the surface, with 2 m of cover over top. But
Bogert was somewhat hamstrung in manning the Hook's defences
because 1R22eR was well below establishment strength. In the last
four months of 1952 the battalion was on average some 235 men
short.[54] Bogert could not use the full battalion on the front line in
such depleted condition[55] and was forced to rotate 3PPCLI and
1RCR.

On the night of 18–19 November, 3PPCLI was blooded on this steep and craggy feature. The battalion had only recently entered the line and was assigned as reserve for the 1st Battalion, Black Watch – a British unit. Fortunately it had rehearsed for this role five days before. The Chinese shelling began at 1700, and the infantry assault four hours later. The Scots beat off the Chinese as long as possible and then withdrew to prepare for a counterattack. Two Patricia companies, 'B' and 'C,' under Black Watch command, were ordered forward, one to relieve a Black Watch position, the other to buttress the line. In the long night that followed and into the next day, the two Patricia companies helped retake the position and ferret out Chinese stragglers. In the course of the fighting, four Patricias were killed in action.[56]

Towards the end of November, the new GOC 1st Commonwealth Division, Maj. Gen. Michael West, ordered all three of his brigades into the line. Henceforth, instead of two brigades in the line and one in reserve, each brigade would hold its own sector and rotate its three battalions, with two in the line and one in reserve. Australian historian Jeffery Grey claims that West did this partly because the British and Australians hated taking over unkempt and badly maintained Canadian defensive positions. West explained the change to Simonds this way: 'Each Brigadier has a complete and compact sector to study and develop, and we shall get proper continuity ... It might appear that this new lay-out will deprive me of my reserve brigade, but in fact I never really had one as each Battalion of the Reserve Brigade was ear-marked for certain counter-attacks and it would have been very difficult to use the Brigade as such.'[57] Of course, if one brigade received constant pounding, or boredom set in, West could shift the brigades around.

As part of this realignment the Patricias occupied the Hook on 29 November. Bogert assigned R22eR to a quieter section of the line, across the Sami-Ch'on. The Patricias alternated with 1RCR until the end of January 1953, when the entire Commonwealth Division, except for the divisional artillery, went into reserve until early April.

'This is a wearing, wearying war,' Canadian war correspondent Bill

Boss broadcast on the CBC Radio network on the night of 10 February 1953. 'It's harder on the nerves to sit and take it than to be up and at them. There's no change of scenery or even of conversation.'[58] The drawn-out armistice negotiations gave rise to complacency on the line – a dangerous state of mind when an army is on the defensive. The battalion commanders, however, saw what they wanted to see, and presumably acted accordingly.

Lt.-Col. Herbert Fairlie Wood was CO 3PPCLI – the first of the new battalion commanders to rotate into Korea in late autumn 1952. West thought him 'very keen' but worried whether he had 'the personality to drive his men if required.'[59] West was prophetic; Wood was removed from command before his rotation was due. When Wood arrived in-theatre, he was greatly impressed by the 'orderly discipline' that he saw at and near the front. Everyone saluted smartly. Officers and NCOs wore boots 'polished until they shone' and metal rank badges that were 'gleaming in the sun.' He was delighted with the atmosphere of 'terrific form and high morale' on the line.[60]

Lt.-Col. J.G. Poulin, CO 3R22eR, saw the front quite differently. Interviewed by a historical officer at the end of May 1953, he declared: 'Our tactics have a stereotyped quality that deprives us of initiative and forewarns the enemy. We rarely try to trick the Chinaman. We do not use deception and have lost our aggressive spirit. Commanders and men are dug-out minded. The fear of receiving casualties deadens our reactions and lessons our effort. We are thoroughly defensive minded and yet not thorough in our defence.'[61] Brig. Jean Victor Allard, who took command of the brigade on 21 April 1953, ensured that Poulin's views would not be reflected by the official history,[62] even though other officers had expressed similar opinions earlier in the war. Similar short shrift was given Major C.E.C. MacNeill's assessment of the men in his battalion. Interviewed in the field while acting CO 3PPCLI, he declared: 'Allowing for numerous exceptions, the young soldiers in the ranks have not a highly developed sense of duty, not even to each other.'[63]

The third Canadian rotation of the war had been completed while the brigade was in reserve; the 3rd battalions, formed largely out of original Special Force volunteers, regulars, and subsequent recruits, were now in the line. On 8 April the division returned to the front, and on 21 April Bogert handed command of the brigade to Allard. Born in Nicolet, Quebec, Allard had received a *collège classique* education and had been a militia officer at the outbreak of the Second World War. In December 1943, while temporarily in command of the Royal 22e Regiment, he had been awarded the DSO for his part in the Battle of the Arielly River. Though wounded shortly afterward, he had been given command of the R22eR in January 1944. In March 1945 he had been promoted to command the 6th Canadian Infantry Brigade. By the end of the war he had received two bars to his DS0. He had remained in the army after the war, serving in a variety of roles before assuming command of the Canadian brigade in Korea.

In his memoirs, Allard noted the special difficulties that he and his troops faced at this juncture of the Korean War: 'our orders were to wage a strictly defensive war ... A brigade commander could not, on his own initiative, mount an offensive that would involve more than a platoon ... I was unable to test either the defensive capability of my opponents or the offensive capability of my own troops ... If our enemy happened to dominate our positions, we had to let him snipe at us, with the ensuing loss of life that might have been avoided by capturing certain peaks from our adversary.'[64] Korea had long since become the epitome of the Clausewitzian war.

The three 3rd battalions of infantry that formed the bulk of Allard's command by the end of April 1953 may have been the least prepared of the nine Canadian infantry battalions that saw combat in Korea. The experience of 3RCR was no doubt typical of 3PPCLI and 3R22eR, given the overall state of the army's manpower crisis, its deficiencies in training, and its failure to build a workable reinforcement system.

Interviewed in late June 1953, while his battalion was in reserve, 3RCR's CO, Lt.-Col. K.L. Campbell, listed the many obstacles that had had to be overcome before his formation had entered the front lines. The training in Canada had been badly hampered when most of the unit's trained soldiers, NCOs, and officers were

stripped away in March 1951 and sent to the 25 Canadian Reinforcement Group in Japan. Despite this depletion of first-class
manpower, 3RCR continued to supply reinforcements to 2 and
1RCR until the autumn of 1952. It did not receive its full complement of officers until very late, and, Campbell pointed out, 'not
one of the company commanders who took a company overseas'
had been assigned to 3RCR as early as the summer of 1952. One
arrived in January 1953.

This problem of rapidly rotating company commanders was
compounded, in Campbell's view, by the assignment to company
command of older, Second World War, retreaded majors. Many
had had to be replaced before they went to Korea. They were not
young enough, not physically fit enough for Korea, not energetic,
and not ambitious. Campbell thought that his younger officers
were 'pretty damn good' but could have been 'better disciplined'
and were 'inclined to take the easy way out.' They were 'not fully
acquainted with the technical side of their profession.' In particular, 'patrolling skills [had] been neglected.'[65]

When the Canadian brigade returned to the Jamestown Line, it
was assigned to the central sector of the Commonwealth Division
front, holding several hilltops near a prominent feature known as
Hill 187. The brigade position was roughly half-way between the
Hook and Little Gibraltar. Atop Hill 187, Campbell placed his four
rifle companies at the corners of a rough square. The position closest to the Chinese was held by 'C' Company; its three platoons – 7,
8, and 9 – ran east–west along a ridge line.

The RCR-defended locality was in poor shape. Recently held by
the Americans, it had been occupied by 1R22eR before the RCR
took it over on 19 April 1953. Campbell reported that the position
was 'badly run down. The wiring was insufficient. The trenches
were not deep enough. There were gaps in the communication
trenches. The fire bays were of a poor design and had no adequate
overhead cover. The bunkers were too high, too lightly timbered
and had too little overhead cover. They were also too far removed
from the fighting positions.'[66] In the key 7 Platoon position, the
defensive plan called for the emplacement of one Browning and
six Bren guns. The platoon had the guns, but only two of the Brens

had been positioned. There were supposed to be ten solidly built bunkers, but as of the night of 2–3 May only two had been constructed. None of the roughly 150 m of trench within the platoon area or leading to the next platoon had been properly covered with barbed wire.[67]

After the Canadians moved back into the line, Chinese patrols, usually covered by shell fire, probed unceasingly forward towards the Canadian positions. The Chinese learned much about their opposition – its patrol patterns, its patrol routes, its defences, its rawness. No doubt they also knew that the brigade was under new command, given the increased patrol activity, and most of their shell fire seemed to concentrate on 'C' Company's position. Campbell and a British counter-battery officer seconded to Allard's staff were both certain that the Chinese were not simply harassing the Canadians but were also registering targets in the 'C' Company area.[68] The signs of impending attack grew by the day. Finally, on the last day of April, Major P.A. Mayer, GSO 2 (Intelligence) on the divisional staff, passed a warning to Allard's HQ 'in so many words' that 'certain intelligence sources revealed the enemy's plan to attack shortly.'[69] There is no indication that divisional intelligence knew the exact timing of the impending Chinese attack or its intended objective.

Late on the afternoon of 2 May, Allard flew to Seoul to accept an invitation to dinner and an overnight stay with U.S. Gen. Maxwell Taylor.[70] He should not have. He arrived at Taylor's HQ just in time for cocktails and settled in for an evening with the brass. The Chinese had other plans. Allard later told a newspaper reporter: 'I got hot feet about 10:30 [p.m.]. I had an uneasy feeling and cut the evening short.' Taylor had tried to reassure him that the Chinese rarely attacked these days, but Allard left anyway and was driven back to the front. On the way he heard radio reports that the sporadic pattern of shell fire that the Chinese had thrown at Hill 123 for many days had suddenly changed. Allard feared that the storm was about to break.

On 26 April 1953, armistice talks had resumed at Panmunjom. Negotiations had been suspended indefinitely on 8 October 1952, after repeated failure to make any headway on the prisoner-exchange issue. In New York the UN General Assembly grappled with the question that, it was now clear, was the last major stumbling block in the way of a cease-fire. In early December the General Assembly overrode Soviet-bloc objections and adopted an Indian-sponsored resolution that a commission of neutral nations be formed to which all prisoners be turned over after a cease-fire. The prisoners would then indicate to the commission where they wished to go. The Communists rejected this idea until the end of February 1953, when they unexpectedly accepted an invitation from Mark Clark to begin discussions that might lead to an exchange of sick and wounded prisoners. By the end of March the Communists had agreed to the exchange, dubbed Operation Little Switch.

What had happened? According to David Rees, Moscow and Beijing had decided sometime in March to 'write off the war.' He believes that three factors were behind this reversal: the ruination of the Chinese economy by the continued fighting; the election of Dwight David Eisenhower as U.S. president the previous November; and Stalin's death on 5 March. Eisenhower's election brought to the White House an experienced soldier, who was determined to end the war by using nuclear weapons against the Chinese mainland if necessary. Stalin's death removed the Chinese and North Koreans' chief benefactor.[71]

In mid-April, no doubt in anticipation of the looming armistice, the Chinese began to increase the pressure along the front lines. They renewed efforts initiated in November 1952 to capture the Pork Chop Hill/Old Baldy complex held by the Americans at the eastern base of the Iron Triangle. In one intense battle between 16 and 18 April, the Americans eventually beat the Chinese back, but not before expending close to 78,000 artillery rounds. After their failure to take Pork Chop and Old Baldy, the Communists turned to Hill 123.

2 May 1953, 2220. In the valley between the Canadians and the Chinese, a sixteen-man fighting patrol from 'A' Company, 3RCR, lay prone, watching and listening. They had moved out of their

lines hours earlier to set up an ambush. Now they waited anxiously along the low wall of a rice paddy as a group of some sixty Chinese infantrymen moved cautiously towards the Canadian positions just clear of the north minefield gap. Lieut. J.G. Maynell waited until he thought the Chinese were past, then whispered into his radio to ask for a flare. As the flare popped into brilliance, the Canadians poked their heads and weapons above the low paddy wall and opened fire, throwing grenades. The Chinese dove for cover and returned fire. Maynell was shot in the head.

Cpl Joseph McNeill, second in command, radioed for help, then began to move the remainder of the 'A' Company patrol back towards the Canadian lines. The wounded were dragged and carried; those still capable of shooting or throwing grenades formed a rear guard.[72] McNeill's men broke contact as they approached their own minefield but were ambushed by a second group of Chinese. The surprise of the ambush and the intensity of fire broke up the little group of Canadians, who now made their way individually back to the 'A' Company positions.

2250. As they approached the top of the hill, the survivors of the 'A' Company patrol met a patrol led by Lieut. Doug Banton, commander of 8 Platoon, 'C' Company, sent to help Maynell's beleaguered men. Hushed greetings were exchanged, then the second group of men disappeared down the hill. Within moments, McNeill and his men heard a heavy volley of small-arms fire. Pte W. Hummer was Banton's patrol: 'Banton dropped off Boyce and myself, I had the Bren gun, to cover the section when it withdrew. Shortly after I saw the flash of weapons as Banton's party and the Chinks opened fire on each other.' Banton was hit by a grenade or mortar. One of his men hefted him onto his back and tried to carry him back, but another grenade blew Banton off. He was dead. The Chinese fire was too intense for anyone to recover his body.[73]

2400. The men in the valley were struggling to survive when the Chinese barrage on 'C' Company intensified. Then Chinese heavy machine-guns opened up on the 7 Platoon position, and 'B' Company reported that it too was under heavy shell and mortar fire. The fire on 'C' Company suddenly lifted to the rear of the RCR positions, and the Chinese infantry swarmed over what was left of the wire into the 7 Platoon positions. Moments later, they hit neighbouring 8 Platoon. Despite a growing volume of Canadian defensive fire on the position, the Chinese surged forward, throwing concussion grenades as they moved along the trenches. They pulled out dazed Canadian soldiers to take as prisoners. Hummer and his comrades fought back: 'We fired at them and they fired at us ... We saw six Chinks walking along the top of the crawl trench where we were crouched. Greenaway got three of them with his Sten gun but the others crawled around behind us and dropped grenades into our crawl trench.' Hummer and the others were wounded.[74]

Lieut. Laurie Cote was not far away. He later described the scene to correspondent Bill Boss:

> In the communications trench between two Bren-gun pits we saw them. There were Chinese in the trench with me and more on the parapet. There were more up top and in the centre of the position throwing grenades into the trenches while a party worked towards me throwing grenades into the weapons pits.
>
> Then the bombardment started and forced me to lie in the trench ... The Chinese also took shelter though some crawled along the parapet. ...
>
> One was killed and fell on top of me, affording that much more cover.

The shell fire that killed the Chinese infantryman was Canadian. It was directed by Lieut. Edgar H. Hollyer, hunkered down in his bunker while the Chinese poured over the wire. Hollyer was in direct contact with the newly arrived 81st Field Artillery Regiment, which Allard had put directly under battalion control as soon as he arrived back from Seoul. Allard and the CO of the 81st, Lt.-Col. H.W. Stearne, then worked with the balance of the divisional artillery and the corps's heavy guns to isolate the fighting and prevent Chinese reinforcement.[75]

Out on the hill, Hollyer tried to get above ground to size up the situation; one time he was attacked, and the other he was blown back into his hiding place. He tried to defend his bunker with grenades. It was hopeless. Miraculously, the radio was still working. Hollyer got on the air to call for proximity fire on his own position. Within minutes the field gunners were slamming breeches shut and pulling lanyards; some 4,000 shells rumbled towards the hilltop or towards the approach routes that Chinese reinforcements might use. Scores of Chinese standing in the open on the hill were blown to pieces. Hollyer and signals officer Lieut. J.G. Cote radioed company HQ for permission to withdraw to the 8 Platoon locality, about two hundred metres to the east. When this was given, the 7 Platoon survivors moved out.

0145. Back at battalion HQ, Allard refused to allow Campbell to stage a company-sized counterattack because Campbell had no reserve. Allard and Campbell then agreed to order up a company of 3R22eR, which could fill in for 3RCR's 'D' Company if Campbell sent it forward to recapture the lost ground.[76] Just at this point, however, Hollyer reached his company command post and told the CO over the radio that he thought that the main body of the Chinese was pulling back and that a patrol might be enough to reoccupy the lost position. Campbell then sent one group of ten men under Hollyer to take back the position and another group of ten to recover casualties. Supported by tank fire, Hollyer led this group back into the 7 Platoon position, but when it clambered into what was left of it, it came under concentrated Chinese mortar fire. It was pinned down until first light, when it discovered that the Chinese had pulled out.

0400. The R22eR company arrived to relieve 'D' Company, 3RCR, which then moved out towards 'C' Company's positions. As the men moved cautiously towards the sound of firing, Chinese smoke shells began to blossom around the 'C' Company area as mortar fire intensified on the 7 and 8 Platoon positions. The Chinese appeared to be breaking contact, using the smoke and mortar barrages to cover the pull-back.

0642. The sound of helicopter blades cutting the air resounded through the early morning as one chopper after another weaved its way around the peaks and up the valleys, landed, and carried away the wounded. No one was really sure what the Chinese had meant to accomplish, although speculation centred on their seizing prisoners and providing deception for an even larger attack on British positions on the nearby Hill 159.[77] The short, sharp battle proved to be Canada's costliest single encounter of the war: twenty-six Canadians were dead, twenty-seven had been wounded, and eight had been taken prisoner. Korean soldiers attached to the Canadian units for training purposes ('Katcoms') were also casualties – four killed, fourteen wounded, and four missing.

One of the Canadian prisoners, Pte John Junkins of Ottawa, was released shortly after the battle. A member of Maynell's first patrol, he had been left behind after the initial fire fight, when McNeill led the survivors back towards the RCR positions. Junkins then took refuge in an unoccupied bunker: 'I lost the main party. Shells and mortars were bursting all around and I was pinned down. I crawled into a bunker and after a time I heard Chinese voices outside. I ... flattened myself against the wall. ... Someone suddenly ripped away the poncho waterproof cape covering the doorway and sprayed the back of the bunker with a burp gun. I lay there for 15 minutes. Two Chinese eventually came into the bunker, pulled me out and told me I was a prisoner.'

After searching him, the Chinese brought up three more prisoners and then began to move them off towards their lines. For some unexplained reason they left Junkins behind. A Chinese medical orderly gave him a drink of water, stuffed some papers into his uniform – probably propaganda leaflets – and departed with the rest of the Chinese patrol. Junkins crawled back into the bunker and waited for the Canadians to reoccupy the position.[78]

Allard studied this fight closely. In his opinion, the Chinese had scored a clear victory, inflicting heavy casualties on the Canadians and destroying most of what was left of the Hill 123 fortifications. There were lessons to be learned here, and Allard – apparently the only one of the three brigade commanders truly concerned to benefit from the Korean experience – closely analysed his troops' performance. He found three major weaknesses in doctrine and practice: ineffective patrolling; too great a dependence on rigid artillery-fire plans; and poor positioning and preparation of the defences. He ordered 3RCR out of the line for refresher training, saw to improvements in defences, opened a brigade patrolling school under Major W.H. Pope, and organized a more flexible system of artillery spotting from far-forward positions.

Allard's most innovative move, however, was intended to weaken the enemy's grip on its own forward slopes, whence it easily observed the Canadian positions. Allard procured a very powerful telescope for the brigade observation post and had his intelligence men spot and mark every Chinese slit trench and observation post they could see. He then moved tanks from their sandbagged positions near the hilltops to the valley floor and provided the tank commanders with oblique aerial reconnaissance photographs of their intended targets. Then, one morning after first light, the tanks opened fire. They wreaked havoc on the Chinese observation network. This set the pattern for daily fire tasks carried out by tanks, mortars, and heavy machine-guns against all conceivable Chinese positions. The tactic, combined with vigorous and aggressive patrolling, kept the Chinese at bay.[79]

The battle for Hill 123 was the last major engagement between Canadian troops and their Chinese adversaries, although eighteen other Canadians would die at the front between 3 May and the armistice. On 26 April, Operation Little Switch began, as sick and wounded prisoners were transferred across the front lines. There were two Canadians among them. The limited prisoner exchange paved the way for a cease-fire. On 7 June agreement was reached at Panmunjom for the rest of the POWs to be treated along the lines laid out by the UN General Assembly the previous December. India was selected as the 'neutral' country to decide the final disposition of the prisoners. On 27 July, the armistice agreement was finally signed. It provided for a complete cease-fire twelve hours later, followed by withdrawal of all troops from the newly designated demilitarized zone within seventy-two hours. The armistice would be supervised by a Military Armistice Commission, composed of five representatives from each side.

On the night of 27 July 1953, the active phase of the Korean War ended. Canada had sent 21,940 of its soldiers to what U.S. President Harry S. Truman had once called a 'police action.' *Strange Battleground: The Official History of the Canadian Army in the Korean War* lists 1,543 army casualties – 309 killed in action, dead of wounds, or missing and officially presumed dead; 1,202 wounded; 32 prisoners of war; and 93 soldiers and sailors dead from non-battle causes.

Although many of the Canadians who fought in Korea were veterans of the Second World War, they were nevertheless the first of a new generation of post-war soldiers. They fought a far-away war for a principle and a concept, not because the fate of their nation was at stake. The principle was that Communist states must not be allowed to swallow up non-Communist neighbours; Communist aggression would not be tolerated as Nazi aggression had been sanctioned by the appeasement policies of the 1930s. Those Canadians and the many more soldiers from the United States, the Republic of Korea, the rest of the Commonwealth, indeed the entire UN Command were the thin red line of their day; and they held.

Home from the Hills

Home is the sailor, home from the sea,
And the hunter home from the hill
– Robert Louis Stevenson

Canada was reluctant to commit ground forces to a war in Asia in the summer of 1950; Ottawa began making preparations to withdraw the 25th Brigade even before the armistice. London floated the idea of a continued joint Commonwealth military presence, in Malaya perhaps, or Hong Kong, but that idea was as welcome to the Canadian government as haemorrhagic fever. Korea had been Canada's second military experience in Asia, but Canada was, first and last, a North Atlantic nation, and NATO would be Canada's number-one military priority for the next forty years.

In October 1953, 3PPCLI left Korea; within the next eight weeks 25 Brigade's operational status was suspended, and brigade HQ was closed. In the spring of 1954 3RCR and 3R22eR went home, and although a battalion of the Black Watch (Royal Highland Regiment of Canada) was sent to replace them, the numbers of Canadians in Korea diminished rapidly. By the end of May 1955, there were 500 Canadian soldiers left in Korea serving in various roles; there were 33 by February 1957, and in June 1957 the last Canadian combat soldier left.

By the end of September 1953, 75,000 North Korean and Chinese prisoners returned to the Communist side; almost 13,000 UN prisoners, including 32 Canadians, were released from Chinese-controlled prison camps along the Yalu River. A handful of UN prisoners, including Canadian fighter-pilot A.R. Mackenzie, were held for some period after the war on one trumped-up pretence or another. Mackenzie was finally released on 5 December 1954. There are still close to 40,000 U.S. troops in the Republic of Korea; the demarcation line between the Communist north and the non-Communist south is now the most heavily guarded border in the world.

The Canadian way of war is not to be ready when armed conflict begins; the Canadian effort in Korea was no exception to the rule, despite claims to the contrary by those who wrote the authorized version of the Canadian effort there. The initial variation of the official line was promulgated in *Canada's Army in Korea: A Short Official Account*, published in 1956. After summarizing the UN and Canadian ground campaign in Korea, the pamphlet concluded: 'As for Canada, thanks to her possessing forces and weapons suitable for intervention in Korea, she was able to make a contribution to the defence of the West.'[1]

Lt.-Col. Herbert Fairlie Wood was more honest in his evaluation of both the preparedness and the performance of the Canadian army in Korea when he wrote the official history – *Strange Battleground* – which appeared in 1966. However, his work did suffer from many of the shortcomings that so often mar official histories. Wood tended to lionize the British way of war. He glossed over some of the major Canadian failures in both offensive and defensive operations, and he claimed that, for the most part, the army had set things right by the summer of 1952. As a result of its experiences in Korea, Wood maintained, the post-Korea Canadian military was 'in a position to meet [Canada's] international commitments. The lesson, for the time being at any rate, had been learned.'[2]

That assertion was simply untrue. The 3rd battalions that rotated into Korea in the autumn of 1952 and spring of 1953 were less ready for combat than their predecessors. Their soldiers were not short on courage, tenacity, or dedication. But they went to Korea unprepared in doctrine, untrained in tactics, and woefully ill-equipped to fight a defensive war. If the formations that Canada sent to NATO beginning in 1952 were comparable, it is a good thing indeed that the USSR did not attempt to seize western Europe in the early 1950s.

Just prior to relinquishing command of the Canadian brigade in Korea, Jean Victor Allard, summarized his views on the performance of his soldiers in Korea. He had actually led them in combat for only a bit more than three months – the battle for Hill 123 was his only major engagement – but his evaluation of the formation's state of preparedness in its third year of war ought to have stunned his superiors.

Allard did not believe that all lessons learned in the Korean War would be useful in the years ahead. Special factors 'made the Korean War somewhat unreal,' he pointed out, so that it was difficult to judge how much the Canadian army might learn.[3] The political constraints imposed by the UN Command prevented 'a true testing both of the enemy defensive strength, and of ours in the offensive,' he wrote. Front-line commanders such as Allard essentially had to be content to sit and take it; they could not press the Chinese with any consistency or apply sufficient force at any one time to make the enemy adopt a defensive posture. The other factors that made Korea so very different from the type of all-out war against the USSR that Allard thought Canada might one day fight were the UN's complete air supremacy, the static nature of the war after the autumn of 1951, and the massive and uninterrupted flow of UN Command supplies.

Allard believed that part of the Canadian failure to mount more effective, less costly defence in Korea was the result of a failure at higher command. Specifically, field defences along the Jamestown Line were inadequate largely because divisional HQ did not take sufficient interest in imposing a master plan on the formations under its command. This could not have been done at the army or corps level, Allard pointed out, 'because of the different-sized companies among the ROKs, US Marines, US Army and ourselves.' Nor could it have been done at brigade or battalion levels, because both brigades and battalions were shifted too often. The fault, in other words, lay at the door of the British divisional commanders and their Commonwealth staffs.

Allard's criticism of the divisional command was circumspect. In

style as well as substance, it very much reflected observations made
by Major W.H. Pope, who operated the brigade's first and only
patrol school at Allard's direction. Given the intense Anglophilia
that pervaded Canadian army ranks in the decade (and more)
after the Second World War, Allard's tone was not surprising. Simply put, to most Canadian army officers of the day, the British
could do no wrong and the Americans could do no right.

Barbara Tuchman once claimed that 'no nation has ever produced a military history of such verbal nobility as the British.
Retreat or advance, win or lose, blunder or bravery, murderous
folly or unyielding resolution, all emerges alike clothed in dignity
and touched with glory.'[4] Having been rooted in that tradition,
Canadian army officers of the 1940s and 1950s shared it fully. With
the notable exception of Allard (and Pope), they were incapable of
examining the performance of their British superiors with a critical eye. Allard was one of the few officers of high rank to see the
faults in British command procedures. Later, before he became
chief of the defence staff in 1966, he was actually to command a
British division in Europe – a singular achievement for a Canadian.

Although Allard placed part of the responsibility for the poor
state of the defences along the Jamestown Line on divisional HQ,
his evaluation of the preparedness of his soldiers was scathing. The
ordinary soldiers were 'generally good and willing but their standard of knowledge in the handling of weapons was poor.' They did
not know how to patrol. The NCOs were 'generally good but their
knowledge of minor tactics and employment of weapons was very
limited ... though they reacted very well to battle conditions, were
brave in front of the enemy and were resourceful in difficult situations.' The junior officers were 'all potentially good, but were very
deficient in professional knowledge.' Allard was in fact 'astonished
at their lack of appreciation of their problems.' They appeared to
have no battle plans for their platoons, depended entirely too
much on artillery, and were mystified as to how best to defend
their terrain.

Allard reserved his most telling criticism for his company commanders. They were 'all brave and loyal' but lacked knowledge of
the defensive battle: 'The co-ordination of fire was not existent ...

There were some exceptions, but I would say that the majority did not know how to build a defensive fire plan.' Their most serious weakness, in his view, was 'their apparent ignorance of infantry weapons, and particularly of their tactical handling.'

The problem lay not with the calibre of the men, but with their inadequate training and preparation. The soldiers were brave, they fought furiously, the NCOs and officers held their ground and rallied their men under fire, the company commanders kept their heads about them under the most intense Chinese assaults, and there were many deserved commendations for valour awarded Canadians in Korea. But large numbers of those same soldiers did not have the proper skills or the professional know-how to do a better job with what they had. When they were specially trained in patrolling, or in designing a fire plan, or in preparing and siting automatic weapons for defence against night assault, they learned quickly and well.

From the late summer of 1950, the Canadian military played 'catch-up' to the expanding political commitments of the Canadian government. Having cut the military budget to the bone, indeed almost to the marrow, in the twenty-four months after VE day, the government turned about almost overnight to accept commitment after commitment. Before the end of 1953 it agreed to raise a brigade for Korea, a brigade for NATO, and an air division for Europe. It also committed itself to a massive air-defence program for North America and to an Atlantic fleet equipped with the best in anti-submarine-warfare (ASW) technology and the newest and best ASW vessels. There were never enough soldiers, sailors, or airmen during the Korean War era to do these jobs properly.

The Special Force's 2nd battalions sent to Korea were slapped together and equipped basically with whatever lay around or the Americans could spare. Sometimes, as at Kap'yong, they performed miracles. Sometimes, as at Chail-li, they did the opposite. They were meant as a 'hold-the-line' expedient, and they did much better than might have been expected of them. Their reputation has undeservedly suffered because of allegations that there was an inordinate number of misfits among them.

The 1st battalions that followed were probably the best-trained ground force that Canada has ever put directly onto a field of battle. They were professional soldiers in every respect. When called on to use the skills that they had acquired, they did so with determination and courage. And yet they sustained the same rate of accidents in the field (one measure of training) as their 2nd-battalion predecessors. Nor did they possess the specialized knowledge that they needed to fight continuous night actions against the Chinese, to patrol effectively, or to lay out their defences in the unique Korean terrain. By the time they arrived, the army, to its credit, was distributing 'lessons learned,' commissioning operational research reports, and trying to train its troops for the special conditions of the war in Korea. Once they were on the line, however, inertia, fatigue, complacency, and resignation seemed to defeat every effort to take a fresh look at tactics and do whatever was necessary to hold down casualties.

The real measure of how prepared the Canadian army was for war was in the performance of the 3rd battalions. These units had been raised, equipped, and trained for eighteen months, especially for Korea. They ought to have performed the best of all in that theatre. Though not tested in the line for long, they did not distinguish themselves as formations. Perhaps they would have done much better over time, particularly after Allard's reforms took hold, but that can never be known for certain. And even if they had, their unpreparedness for combat in Korea in the autumn of 1952 and spring of 1953 reflects poorly on the Canadian army of the day, and on the Canadian government.

The Canadian army learned some important generic lessons from the Korean experience. As Robert Peacock later remembered: 'The legacy for many of us was training, training, and more training in fundamentals. Promotion exams and Staff College entrance examinations helped weed out those who would not or could not adapt to change. The result was a succession of highly trained brigade groups in NATO which were the pride of NATO.'[5] And yet there was a decided reluctance in some army circles to admit that anything specific had been amiss during Canadian operations in Korea or that there were key tactical lessons to be learned from the experience. When Major Pope attempted to publish articles in the *Canadian Army Journal* on lessons to be learned from Korea on defence and patrolling, the editor asked him to revise the articles so as to be 'less critical of our operations in Korea.' Pope revised an article, but to no avail. In the end, the editorial board rejected his pieces.[6]

No doubt the failure of the Canadian army to recognize the importance of Korea stemmed from the rapid shifting of focus of the Canadian military to Europe and the problems presented by the possibility of Soviet and Warsaw Pact attack. That emphasis was certainly understandable at first, given Canada's historic ties of culture and trade with northern Europe and its lack of interest (until recently) in Asia's affairs. But it is hard to justify the army's single-mindedness after the U.S. experience in Vietnam showed conclusively what sort of war was most likely to be fought under the nuclear umbrella.

Things have changed, however, as a result both of the end of the Cold War and of Asia's rising importance to Canada. It is all too obvious now that Korea was the first post–Second World War interstate conflict of any significance. It set the pattern for virtually all the wars that have followed in that it was fought within defined political limits, and there were in fact many lessons that the Canadian government and military ought to have learned from such a limited war and can learn still.

Korea should have taught Canadians that the outbreak of war is almost never predictable; that a slow build-up to war, as in the 1930s, is the exception in history, not the rule. Korea ought to have taught Canada that it does not matter if Canadian interests are actually involved in an armed conflict. If our most important allies have decided that Canadian participation is not, for reasons symbolic or otherwise, open to debate, Canada has very limited options. Korea ought to have taught the Canadian military that each specific war must be fought on the basis of doctrine that is specifically adapted to that conflict and to Canadian resources and experience. Korea ought to have taught Canadian governments to maintain armed forces ready to fight, because an effective, well-trained, well-equipped military cannot be plucked from a tree like a piece of fruit.

In his recent book *The New World Strategy*, noted U.S. military historian Col. Harry Summers classified the war options that face the U.S. armed forces at the end of the twentieth century. These are the same ones that face the Canadian military, which of course would participate in war only as part of a larger coalition. Summers's list contains only four possibilities: general conventional war, general nuclear war, limited conventional war, and low-intensity conflict.[7]

Summers believes that general conventional war of the Second World War variety is extremely unlikely. It is arguable that there have only been two wars in history when the antagonists (or coalitions of antagonists) sought the complete annihilation of each other – the Second Punic War and the Second World War. Even the First World War, with all its destructiveness, was 'limited,' in that its objective was not 'unconditional surrender.' General nuclear war simply cannot be prepared for in any accepted sense; such a war can be initiated, of course, but it cannot be 'fought.'

Virtually all wars, in one sense or another, have been 'limited conventional wars,' with limited political aims, no matter how intense or bloody the fighting. The Korean War was such a conflict; however, the fact that it seemed to resemble the First World War in so many ways blinded the militaries of virtually all the non-Communist participants to its actual lack of similarity. One illustration of the vital differences will suffice. The Western Front stalemate of 1914–18 was the result of a balance of force and the Allies' inability to re-establish a war of manoeuvre in the face of massive German defensive fire-power. The stalemate in Korea was the result of a political decision by the UN Command, once the armistice talks began in earnest, to fight a defensive battle for the duration. That political decision made a world of difference on the Korean front line. It determined that Canadian and other UN soldiers would essentially be live targets until the other side – which bore no responsibility to its citizens for its actions – decided that its political interests were best served by ending the killing.

Brooke Claxton was right in the end. Korea was a quagmire made largely by the indecision and fear that dominated Washington's policy-makers from the late autumn of 1951 to the end of the war. Their policy – to hold the line while talking to the Communists – was a recipe for high and probably unnecessary casualties. No one will ever know whether, if Ridgway's push north in the spring and summer of 1951 had continued, it might have caused the Communists to quit sooner than they did, thus saving UN forces' lives. But what is indisputable is that far more Canadian soldiers – indeed far more UN soldiers overall – were killed in action after the start of the armistice talks at Panmunjom than were killed in the initial war of movement.

A half-century after the end of the Korean War the Republic of Korea's newly developed democracy is guarded by a curtain of firepower, steel, and armed soldiers. It took decades for that democracy to develop, and the process is not over yet. However long it took, however, it would not have happened at all if North Korea, China, and the Soviet Union had had their way. For this apparently meagre result some 370,000 U.S., ROK, Commonwealth, and other UN soldiers paid with their lives. In fact, the result was not meagre; Korea constituted the first effort by a Communist state to take control of a non-Communist neighbour, against the will of its people, by force of arms. The UN stopped that effort cold and held the line. Korea never became the Munich of the Cold War. In a very real sense, the first real victory of the West in the Cold War was won in the bloody hills of central Korea, and 516 Canadians paid the ultimate price for that victory.

Notes

Introduction: The Forgotten War

1 *Globe and Mail*, 23 Nov. 1951.
2 *Halifax Chronicle-Herald*, 26 Nov. 1951.
3 *Vancouver Sun*, 23 Nov. 1951.
4 For a general overview of the war up to this point, and the part played by the Canadian army, see Wood, *Strange Battleground*.
5 Public Record Office (PRO), London, England, WO308/28, 1 Commonwealth Division Periodic Report, 15 Oct. 1951–15 Feb. 1952.
6 Rees, *Korea*, 256–7.
7 *Calgary Herald*, 24 Nov. 1951.
8 Stone and Castonguay, *Korea*, 330–1; PRO, WO281/53, '1 COMWEL DIV 00 NO 5,' order issued 21 Nov. 1951.
9 *Calgary Herald*, 23 Nov. 1951.
10 PRO, WO281/53, War Diary of 'G' branch, 1 Commonwealth Division, 23 Nov. 1951.
11 Stone and Castonguay, *Korea*, 33.
12 WD 2R22eR, 23 Nov. 1951.
13 Directorate of History (DHist), Department of National Defence (DND), file 410b25.013 (D89), 'Principal Engagements of Canadian Troops in Korea,' 25 Aug. 1954, 2.

Chapter One: Canada's Post-War Army

1 James Eayrs covers the planning in his *In Defence of Canada*, vol. III, *Peacemaking and Deterrence* (Toronto: University of Toronto Press, 1972), 77–9.
2 J.W. Pickersgill, ed., *The Mackenzie King Record*, vol. IV (Toronto: University of Toronto Press, 1970), 6.

3 National Archives of Canada (NA), Ottawa, RG 2, 16 (Privy Council Office, Cabinet Conclusions), vol. 7, meeting of 7 Nov. 1946.

4 NA, King Diary (microfiche), 3 Jan. 1947.

5 NA, King Papers, series J1, vol. 422, Claxton to King, 7 Jan., 1947. Claxton further refined his thinking on these subjects in mid-February 1947. See NA, Arnold Heeney Papers, vol. 1, file 'Clerk of the Privy Council, 1947–49,' Claxton to Heeney, plus attachments, Feb. 17, 1947.

6 P.C. Paterson 'The Defence Administration of Brooke Claxton,' MA essay, Royal Military College, Kingston, Ont., 1975, 126.

7 Ibid. (emphasis added).

8 Ibid., 127.

9 NA, King Papers, series J4, vol. 421, file 'PCO Defence Committee, Jan/47–Apr/48,' meeting of Cabinet Defence Committee, 14 Jan. 1947.

10 DHist, file 81/609, Defence Council Minutes, meeting of 23 Dec. 1948.

11 The post-1946 establishment situation is outlined in DHist, file 112.3M2 (565), Cabinet Defence Committee Papers, Appendix B of 'Memorandum for Cabinet Defence Committee,' 18 July 1950.

12 Eayrs, *Peacemaking*, 105–7.

13 King Papers, series J4, vol. 421, file 'PCO Defence Committee, Jan/47–Apr/48,' meeting of 28 Oct. 1947.

14 DHist, file 81/609, Minutes of the Defence Council, meeting of 13 May 1948.

15 Paterson, 'Defence,' 127; Bercuson, *True Patriot*, 206.

16 *Industrial Canada* (Oct. 1949), 68–9.

17 Wood, *Strange Battleground*, 18–19; DHist, file 112.3M2 (565), Cabinet Defence Committee papers, Appendix B of 'Memorandum for Cabinet Defence Committee,' 18 July 1950.

18 King Papers, series J4, vol. 421, file 'PCO Defence Committee Jan/47–April 48,' Cabinet Defence Committee minutes for 1 April 1947.

19 Ibid.

20 For details on the reopening of RMC, and so on, see Richard A. Preston, *To Serve Canada: A History of the Royal Military College since the Second World War* (Ottawa: University of Ottawa Press, 1991), 24–8. See also Eayrs, *Peacemaking*, 67ff.

21 DHist, file 112.009 (D58), memo to the Secretary of the Cabinet Defence Committee, 3 Aug. 1949.

22 King Papers, series J4, vol. 249, file 2579, minutes of the Cabinet Defence Committee, 2 June 1948.

23 William Johnston and Stephen J. Harris, 'The Post-War Army and the War in Korea,' in John Marteinson et al., *We Stand on Guard: An Illustrated History of the Canadian Army* (Montreal: Ovale Publications, 1992), 333ff.

24 This is the central theme of Tamara A. Sherwin, 'From Total War to Total Force: Civil–Military Relations and the Canadian Army Reserve (Militia), 1945–1995,' MA thesis, University of New Brunswick, 1997.

25 *Canadian Army Journal* 1 no. 2 (May 1947), 25–7.

26 Ibid. 1 no. 6 (Nov. 1947), 22–5.

27 NA, RG 2, Privy Council Office (PCO) Records, vol. 73, file D-19-1, 1947–48, 'A Situation Report on Standardization ...,' 6 Aug. 1947.

28 R.D. Cuff and J.L. Granatstein, *American Dollars, Canadian Prosperity* (Toronto: Hakkert, 1978), 170ff.

29 NA, RG 2, PCO Records, vol. 60, file C-10-9-M, 1948–49, minutes of the Cabinet Defence Committee, 28 Oct. 1948.

30 Sean M. Maloney, 'The Mobile Striking Force and Continental Defence, 1948–1955,' in *Canadian Military History* 2 no. 2 (autumn 1993), 75–88.

31 Stevens, *Princess Patricia's*, 262ff.

32 NA, R9 2, PCO Records, 18, vol. 74, file D-19-2.

33 *Canadian Aviation* (Sept. 1949).

34 Ibid.

35 *Edmonton Journal,* 8 Aug. 1949.

36 Maloney, 'The Mobile Striking Force.'

37 Vladislav Zubok and Constantine Pleshakov, *Inside the Kremlin's Cold War: From Stalin to Khrushchev* (Cambridge, Mass: Harvard University Press, 1996), 64.

38 One of the best summaries of the events surrounding the outbreak of the Korean War is still Rees, *Korea,* 3–35.

39 *Canada and the Korean Crisis* (Ottawa: King's Printer, 1950), 18.

40 Rees, *Korea,* 23.

41 *Canada and the Korean Crisis,* 21.

42 Grey, *The Commonwealth Armies,* 23–4; Joseph C. Goulden, *Korea: The Untold Story of the War* (New York: Times Books, 1982), 64, 87–8.

43 Denis Stairs, 'Canada and the Korean War: The Boundaries of Diplomacy,' *International Perspectives,* (Nov.–Dec. 1972), 27.

44 NA, Claxton Papers, vol. 215, file 'Claxton, David,' Claxton to David Claxton, 27 June 1950.

45 NA, St Laurent Papers, vol. 224, file E 3–47 Korean War, Arnold Heeney memorandum of 30 June 1950.

46 Wood, *Strange Battleground,* 13; Stairs, *The Diplomacy of Constraint,* 59.

47 NA, RG 1, PCO Records, Cabinet Conclusions, 5 July 1950.

48 Walter Isaacson and Evan Thomas, *The Wise Men: Six Friends and the World They Made* (New York, 1986), 507.

49 Claxton Papers, vol. 67, file 'Tarr, Edgar J.,' Tarr to Claxton, 31 July 1950.

50 *Canada and the Korean Crisis,* 27.

51 Ibid., 28.

52 Blair Fraser, 'Uncle Sam Thinks We Let Him Down,' *Maclean's Magazine,* 1 Sept. 1950.

53 Wood, *Strange Battleground,* 23.

54 DHist, file 112.3M2 (565), Memorandum for Cabinet Defence Committee, 18 July 1950; Wood, *Strange Battleground,* 20.

55 *Canada and the Korean Crisis,* 29.

56 Fraser, 'Uncle Sam Thinks.'

57 Claxton Papers, vol. 67, file 'Tarr, Edgar J.,' Claxton to Tarr, 4 Aug. 1950 (letter not sent).

58 DHist, file 112.3M2 (565), Minutes of the Cabinet Defence Committee, 19 July 1950.

59 Ibid., 'CGS Brief for the 65th Meeting of the Cabinet Defence Committee – 19 July 50.'

60 Fraser, 'Uncle Sam Thinks.'

61 Grey, *Commonwealth Armies*, 35.

62 Cabinet Conclusions, 27 July 1950.

63 NA, Pearson Papers, vol. 35, file 'Korea–Cdn Policy 1950–51,' Pearson to St Laurent, 3 Aug. 1950.

64 Ibid.

65 Cabinet Conclusions, 2, 3, and 7 Aug. 1950.

66 *Canada and the Korean Crisis*, 31–4.

Chapter Two: The Special Force

1 The meeting and telephone call are recreated from NAc, MG 31, G 12, 'Recollections of Korea,' by Maj. Gen. John M. Rockingham, CB, CBE, DSO, ED, CD, LLD, Aug. 1975, 3–6 (henceforth Rockingham memoir), and DHist, file 112.3H1.001 (D13), 'Notes prepared after an interview with Major-General Rockingham,' March 1960.

2 Fehrenbach, *This Kind of War*, DC: 120–1.

3 *Vancouver Sun*, 9 Aug. 1950.

4 Stacey, *The Victory Campaign*, 193.

5 Alexander McKee, *Caen: Anvil of Victory* (London: White Lion Publishers, 1976), 318.

6 Rockingham memoir, 4–5.

7 *Vancouver Sun*, 9 Aug. 1950.

8 Claxton Papers, vol. 124, file 'Organization of the Special Force,' Macklin to CGS, 5 Jan. 1951.

9 Cabinet Conclusions, 8 Nov. 1950.

10 Wood, *Strange Battleground*, 27.

11 PRO, WO 281/53, Commonwealth Division HQ to Brigades, 17 Nov. 1951.

12 Claxton Memoirs, vol. 7, 146.

13 Wood, *Strange Battleground*, 27–8; Claxton Memoirs, vol. 6, 1146–8; DHist, file 112.3H1.001 (D9), Confidential narrative, n.d.

14 Claxton Papers, vol. 83, file 'Political Comments,' Wallace to Claxton, 14 Aug. 1956.

15 Cabinet conclusions, 22 Aug. 1950.

16 War Diary (henceforth WD), 2nd Battalion, Royal 22e Regiment, 1 Sept.–

30 Sept. 1950, W.H. Pope to Adjutant, R22eR Training School, 11 Sept. 1950 (henceforth WD 2R22eR with appropriate date).

17 Claxton Papers, vol. 83, file 'Political Comments,' Wallace to Claxton, 14 Aug. 1956.

18 DHist, file 112.3H1.009 (D27), 'Absence without Leave in the C.A.S.F.' nd.

19 National Archives (USNA), Washington, DC, State Department Records (SDR), decimal file 1950–54, 742.55 12/10–1950, Brown to Department of State, 19 Oct. 1950.

20 NA, G 24, vol. 18,238, War Diary, 25 Canadian Infantry Brigade (CIB) HQ, Feb. and March 1951, Macklin to Department of National Defence, 15 Feb. 1951.

21 Wood, *Strange Battleground*, 29–32.

22 Claxton Memoirs, vol. 6, 1143.

23 Melady, *Korea*, 40.

24 Claxton Papers, vol. 83, file 'Political Comments,' Wallace to Claxton, 14 Aug. 1956.

25 WD, 25 CIB, Foulkes memo, 'Canadian Army Special Force Reinforcement System,' 11 Oct. 1950.

26 USNA, SDR, decimal file 742.55/12–1350, U.S. Embassy in Ottawa to State Department, 13 Dec. 1950.

27 Cabinet Conclusions, 8 Dec. 1950; Grey, *The Commonwealth Armies*, 94, 101. For the experience of 2PPCLI, see Watson, 'From Calgary to Kap'yong,' 23ff.

28 Bruce McIntyre interview with John K. Blampied, Calgary, Aug. 1996.

29 McIntyre interview with Harry Repay, Calgary, Aug. 1996.

30 McIntyre interview with Ross Wilkes, Calgary, Aug. 1996.

31 McIntyre interview with J. Robert Molesworth, Calgary, Aug. 1996.

32 Although it is not a statistically significant sample, very few of the seventy-two Korean War veterans interviewed at the Calgary reunion of the Korean War Veterans Association (KWVA) in August 1997, or who filled in questionnaires, claimed to have gone to Korea for idealistic or ideological reasons. The interviews and questionnaires are on deposit at the Museum of the Regiments in Calgary.

33 Peacock, *Kim-chi, Asahi and Rum*, 3.

34 Rockingham memoir, 6–7; Wood, *Strange Battleground*, 32–4.

35 DHist, file 112.3H1.1 (D13), 'Notes Prepared after an Interview with ... Rockingham ... March, 1960,' n.d.

36 Ibid.; Gardam, *Korea Volunteer*, 46–7.

37 Watson, 'From Calgary to Kap'yong,' 26.

38 DHist, file 145.2R13 (D11), 'Royal Canadian Regiment Commanding Officers, 1933–1961,' n.d.

39 Gardam, *Korea Volunteer*, 48.

40 Wood, *Strange Battleground*, 34.

41 Watson, 'From Calgary to Kap'yong,' 25.
42 WD, 25 CIB, Canadian Army Training Instruction (henceforth CATI) No. 7: Canadian Army Special Force (henceforth CASF), 30 Aug. 1950.
43 Wood, *Strange Battleground*, 41.
44 WD, 25 CIB, CATI No. 6: CASF, 14 Aug. 1950.
45 Watson, 'From Calgary to Kap'yong,' 23–6.
46 WD, 25 CIB, CATI No. 6: CASF, 14 Aug. 1950, Appendix A.
47 WD, 25 CIB, 'Summary – September [1950] War Diary.'
48 WD, 2R22eR, 1 and 10 Oct. 1950; Wood, *Strange Battleground*, 40.
49 DHist, file 112.3M2 (D437), 'Notes on Fighting in Korea – 25 August 1950,' issued 18 Sept. 1950.
50 WD, 25 CIB, CATI No. 7: CASF, 30 Aug. 1950.
51 Ibid; see also CATI No. 6. There is an especially good description of the training in 2PPCLI in Watson, 'From Calgary to Kap'yong,' 31–4. The complete syllabi for 2PPCLI are in DHist, file 327.039 (D5), 'Western Command Training Instruction No. 13: 2 Bn PPCLI – Individual Training Instruction,' which lists all training blocks and shows how many periods of each block were devoted to particular aspects of the course.
52 WD, 25 CIB, CATI No. 8: CASF Small Arms Weapon Training, 13 Sept. 1950. See also 'Daily Programme – Advanced Training Wing' in WD, 25 CIB.
53 WD 25 CIB, CATI No. 6: CASF, 14 Aug. 1950.
54 DHist, file 327.039 (D5), 'Safety Precautions – Use of Live Ammunition,' 21 Aug. 1950.
55 Watson, 'From Calgary to Kap'yong,' 33.
56 Cabinet Conclusions, 18 Aug. 1950.
57 DHist, file 406.019 (D2), Report of Canadian Army Transition Team, 29 March 1951.
58 USNA, files of the Permanent Joint Board on Defence, file 'PJBD General, 1948–1956,' memorandum of conversation re: Canadian requests for U.S. equipment, 25 Aug. 1950.
59 WD, 25 CIB, 2 Oct. 1950.
60 Wood, *Strange Battleground*, 35; DHist, file 112.3M2 (565), Cabinet Defence Committee (henceforth CDC) Papers, meeting of 5 Oct. 1950, memo of 7 Sept. 1950.
61 DHist, file 112.3M2 (565), CDC Papers, meeting of 5 Oct. 1950, memo of 7 Sept. 1950; WD, 25 CIB, 'Summary Sept. (1950) War Diary'; Wood, *Strange Battleground*, 34–5.
62 Peter Archambault and D.J. Bercuson, '"We Didn't Plan for This Type of War": The Canadian Army in Korea, 1950–1952,' A paper read to the 1995 meeting of the Organization for the Study of the National History of Canada, Ottawa, Nov. 1995.
63 Bercuson, *Claxton*, 219–21.

64 NA, RG 2, series 18, file c-10-9-m, 1950, CDC, meeting of 5 Oct. 1950.

65 Claxton Papers, vol. 123, file 'St. Laurent,' unsigned memo dated 24 Sept. 1950.

66 Wood, *Strange Battleground*, 43; Claxton Papers, vol. 123, file 'St. Laurent,' Pearson to St Laurent, 24 Oct. 1950; Cabinet Conclusions, 25 Oct. 1950 and 1 Nov. 1950; Claxton Papers, vol. 124, file 'Organization of the Special Force,' Foulkes to Ridgway, 26 Oct. 1950; USNA, Office of the Secretary of Defense (OSD), CD 092, Korea, folder no. 3, Acheson to Marshall, 20 Oct. 1950.

67 Wood, *Strange Battleground*, 45–6.

68 DHist, file 410B25.009 (D5), Rockingham to Nicholson, 1 July 1953.

Chapter Three: Preparing for Battle

1 See Watson, 'From Calgary to Kap'yong,' 39ff. for a good description; also Rees, *Korea*, 48ff.

2 *Canadian Army Journal* 5 no. 10 (Jan. 1952), 'The Patricias in Korea,' 4–18.

3 Museum of the Regiments, Calgary, KWVA questionnaires. Those filled out by Lorne Warner, Harry Repay, and Donald F. Hibbs were typical.

4 Wood, *Strange Battleground*, 53, 55.

5 DHist, file 145.2P7.013 (D6), Stone to Rockingham, 23 Dec. 1950.

6 Flint, Kozumplik, and Waraska, *The Arab–Israeli Wars*, 95.

7 Vladislav Zubok and Constantine Pleshakov, *Inside the Kremlin's Cold War: From Stalin to Khruschev* (Cambridge, Mass.: Howard University Press, 1996), 64–7.

8 Hastings, *The Korean War*, 134ff.

9 Summers, Jr, *Korean War Almanac*, 24.

10 Flint et al., *Arab–Israeli Wars*, 95.

11 DHist, file 81/229, 'Enclosure No. 2 to G-2 PIR No. 150,' typed, undated notes on Chinese tactics translated from Chinese, found on enemy dead in 1st ROK Division sector, 25 Nov. 1950.

12 For Chinese small-unit tactics, see Leckie, *Conflict*, 182ff; George, *The Chinese Communist Army*, 1–5; Rees, *Korea*, 138–9.

13 Flint et al. *Arab–Israeli Wars*, 99–100.

14 DHist, file 112.3M2 (FD318), Fleury to Secretary, Chiefs of Staff Committee, 22 Nov. 1950.

15 Rees, *Korea*, 155–61.

16 Kirkland, 'Soldiers and Marines,' 257–74.

17 Rees, *Korea*, 161–6.

18 DHist, file 145.2P7.013 (D6), Report of Lt.-Col. J.R. Stone, 23 Dec. 1950.

19 Wood, *Strange Battleground*, 53–5.

20 Ibid., 54.

21 Cabinet Conclusions, 8 Dec. 1950.

22 Wood, *Strange Battleground*, 54.

23 Ibid., 54–5.
24 Gardam, *Korea Volunteer*, 38.
25 .DHist, file 145.2P7.013 (D6), Report of Lt.-Col. J.R. Stone, 23 Dec. 1950.
26 WD, 2PPCLI, 20–21 Dec. 1950.
27 J.R. Stone, 'The Battle of Kapyong,' in Stone and Castonguay, *Korea 1951*, 14.
28 WD, 2PPCLI, 20–21 Dec. 1950.
29 Ibid., 6 Jan. 1951.
30 WD, 2PPCLI, 8 Jan. 1951.
31 DHist, file 81/229, Canadian Military Mission, Far East (Tokyo) to Army HQ, 14 Dec. 1950.
32 See Watson, 'From Calgary to Kap'yong,' 56–60, for an excellent overview of the equipment acquired by 2PPCLI upon arrival in Korea.
33 Cabinet conclusions, 8 Dec. 1950; Wood, *Strange Battleground*, 55.
34 Rees, *Korea*, 176–85.
35 DHist, file 81/229, 'Appendix "A" to Report Number 12. dated 30 Nov. 1950.'
36 See, for example, DHist, files 314.009 (D464) and 111.41 (D22).
37 DHist, file 111.41 (D22), 'Extract from Report by CO 2 PPCLI on Fighting in Korea, dated 23 Dec 50.'
38 These and other points are made in the reports contained in DHist, files 314.009 (D464) and 111.41 (D22).
39 WD, 2PPCLI, 6 Jan. 1951.
40 Ibid., 3 Jan. 1951.
41 DHist, file 145.2P7.013 (D6), Report of Lt.-Col. J.R. Stone, 23 Dec. 1950.
42 WD, 2PPCLI, 6 Jan. 1951.
43 Wood, *Strange Battleground*, 58–9.
44 Summers, *Korean War Almanac*, 24.
45 DHist 111.41 (D22); Wood, *Strange Battleground*, 59.
46 Wood, *Strange Battleground*, 67.
47 Watson, 'From Calgary to Kap'yong,' 91–7; Wood, *Strange Battleground*, p. 60.
48 Department of External Affairs files (DEAf), 50069–D-40, Reid to various missions, 11 Dec. 1950; Reid to Pearson, 20 Dec. 1950.
49 DHist, file 112.3M2 (565), Pearson and Claxton to the cabinet, 28 Dec. 28, 1950.
50 *Montreal Star*, 6 Jan. 1951.
51 Cabinet Conclusions, 24 Jan. 1951.
52 DHist, file 81/229, 'Extract from Minutes of CGS Conference,' 16 Nov. 1950.
53 CDC, Minutes, 20 Feb. 1951.
54 Cabinet conclusions, 21 and 22 Feb. 1951.
55 Rockingham Memoir, 9–10; WD, 2R22eR, 5 Dec. 1950; WD, 25 CIBG HQ, 1 Dec. 1950.
56 DHist, file 681.011 (D3), 'Report on Interview of Lt-Col GWL Nicholson with Brigadier JM Rockingham ... 17 Nov. 52.'

57 WD, 25 CIBG HQ, 25 Dec. 1950.

58 There is an excellent discussion of battle drill in John English, *The Canadian Army and the Normandy Campaign: A Study of Failure in High Command* (New York: Praeger, 1991), 107–23. See also David Bercuson, *Battalion of Heroes: The Calgary Highlanders in World War II* (Calgary: Calgary Highlanders Regimental Funds Foundation, 1994), 35–40.

59 WD, 25 CIBG HQ, 14 and 17 Feb. 1951.

60 Ibid., 20 Feb. 1951.

61 Ibid., 21 Feb. 1951.

62 DHist, file 112.3M2 (D318), Command Instructions, 14 Nov. 1950.

63 Rockingham memoir, 11–12.

64 Ibid., 13.

65 Ibid., 14.

66 Wood, *Strange Battleground*, 263.

Chapter Four: Kap'yong

1 Rees, *Korea*, 178–89.

2 Ibid., 186.

3 Simonds Papers (privately held), Claxton to Foulkes, 19 March 1951.

4 Ibid., Foulkes to Simonds, 20 March 1951.

5 Watson, 'From Calgary to Kap'yong,' 96–7.

6 Hastings, *The Korean War*, 102.

7 PRO, WO216/821 Harding to Coad, 12 Dec. 1950.

8 PRO, WO 216/836, 'Notes on Visit to British Units in KOREA,' by Lt.-Gen. Sir Robert Mansergh, 2 Feb. 1951.

9 Ibid., Lt.-Gen. Sir Robert Mansergh to HQ, British Forces, Hong Kong, 2 Feb. 1951.

10 Ibid., 'Comments by Brigadier B.A. Coad ...,' as reported by Lt.-Gen. Sir Robert Mansergh, 2 Feb. 1951.

11 Ibid., 'Notes on Visit,' by Mansergh.

12 Dhist, file 314.009 (D464), 'Notes on Fighting in Korea,' 23 April 1951.

13 Ibid., file 145.2P7011 (07), 'Transcript of Interview Held at AHQ, between Lt-Col G.W.L. Nicholson ... and Lt-Col Stone ... 5 Jun 51.'

14 Watson, 'From Calgary to Kap'yong,' 98, from WD, 2PPCLI, 19 Feb. 1951.

15 Melady, *Korea*, 66.

16 WD, 27 BCIB, 20 Feb. 1951.

17 Berton, 'Corporal Dunphy's War,' 7. The story is told in somewhat different form in G. McKeown, 'Kapyong Remembered.' Conditions during this advance to the 38th parallel are well described in DHist, file 145.2P7013 (D5), '2 PPCLI Action Kapyong Area ...,' 26 Nov. 1954.

18 WD, 2PPCLI, 22 Feb. 1951.

19 For a good discussion of the difficulties of mounting platoon or company attacks in these hills, see O'Neill, *Australia in the Korean War*, 116–20.

20 WD, 27 BCIB, 22 Feb. 1951.

21 Ibid., 23 and 26 Feb. 1951.

22 WD, 2 PPCLI, 23 Feb. 1951.

23 Ibid., 23 Feb. 1951.

24 Ibid.

25 *Calgary Herald*, 5 March 1951.

26 Ibid., 64; O'Neill, *Australia in the Korean War*, 118; WD, 27 BCIB, 24–25 Feb. 1951.

27 Wood, *Strange Battleground*, 64; WD, 27 BCIB, 28 Feb. 1951.

28 McIntrye interview with Cpl William Lee, on deposit at the Museum of the Regiments, Calgary, Alberta.

29 McIntrye interview with Sgt Don B. Urquhart, on deposit at the Museum of the Regiments, Calgary, Alberta.

30 Ibid., file 314.009 (D464), 'Notes on Fighting in Korea,' 23 April 1951.

31 Ibid. Also see 'Notes Prepared by Canadian Liaison Officers with OCAFF, US Army,' in the same package.

32 Berton, 'Corporal Dunphy's War,' 7.

33 Watson, 'From Calgary to Kap'yong,' 100.

34 Rees, *Korea*, 191.

35 The description of the fight for Hill 532 is from WD, 2PPCLI, 7 and 8 March 1951, and WD, 27 BCIB, 7 and 8 March 1951, unless specifically cited.

36 WD, 27 BCIB, 7 March 1951.

37 DHist, 'Transcript of Interview between Nicholson and Stone.'

38 DHist, file 681.011(D3), 'Notes on Talk given by Lt-Col J.R. Stone ... 5 Jun 51.'

39 WD, 27 BCIB, 8 March 1951.

40 Wood, *Strange Battleground*, 67.

41 Ibid.

42 WD, 2PPCLI, 20 and 21 March 1951.

43 WD, 2PPCLI, 20 March 1951; Watson, 'From Calgary to Kap'yong,' 106.

44 WO216/728, UK Military Attaché, Tokyo, to War Office, 12 March 1951.

45 DHist, 'Notes on Talk by Stone.'

46 Wood, *Strange Battleground*, 71.

47 WD, 27 BCIB, 11 April 1951.

48 Ibid., 14 April 1951; Wood, *Strange Battleground*, 71.

49 WD, 27 BCIB, 16 April 1951.

50 Rees, *Korea*, 245–6.

51 WD, 27 BCIB, 22 April 1951.

52 The full story of the battle for the Imjin is in Farrar-Hockley, *The British Part*, II, 111–37.

53 DHist, file 145.2P7013(D4), 'The Kapyong Battle.'

54 O'Neill, *Australia in the Korean War,* 134–7.

55 Speech by Col. J.R. Stone to Officers of 3PPCLI, 18 Dec. 1973. Gray, 'A Researched Report.'

56 Gray, 'A Researched Report,' p. 21 apps. 21 and 25.

57 Watson, 'From Calgary to Kap'yong,' 111–15; WD, 27 BCIB, 23 April 1951; WD, 2PPCLI, 23 April 1951.

58 The description of the fight for Hill 504 is from: O'Neil, *Australia in the Korean War,* 140ff.; WD, 27 BCIB, 24 April 1951; Lt.-Col. George B. Pickett, 'Tanks in Defence in Korea,' in *Canadian Army Journal* 5 no. 11 (Feb. 1952), 64–72; DHist, file 145.2P7013(D4), 'The Kapyong Battle'; DHist, file 497.013 (D3), 'Letter from Brigadier Burke ...,' n.d.

59 WD, 2PPCLI, 24 April 1951. The description of the fight for Hill 677 is from WD, 2PPCLI, 24 and 25 April 1951; WD, 27 BCIB, 24 and 25 April 1951; DHist, 'The Kapyong Battle'; DHist, file 145.2P7013(D5), '2 PPCLI Action Kapyong Area – 23–26 Apr 51 ... Account by Capt APP McKenzie (formerly IO, 2 PPCLI)' unless specifically cited.

60 Calgary Herald, 26 April 1951.

61 Melady, *Korea,* 76.

62 Ibid., 77.

63 J.R. Stone, 'The Battle of Kapyong,' in Stone and Castonguay, *Korea 1951,* 20–1.

64 WD, 2PPCLI, 25 April 1951.

65 Gray, 'A Researched Report,' app. 25.

66 WD, 27 BCIB 25 April 1951.

67 Blair, *The Forgotten War,* 838–9.

68 Rees, *Korea,* 249–51.

Chapter Five: The Brigade

1 Wood, *Strange Battleground,* 93–4.

2 WD, 25 CIB Public Relations Unit, 4 May 1951.

3 WD, 25 CIB HQ, 16 May 1951.

4 DHist, file 145.2R13011 (D4), 'Deployment for Battle – 1 Bn R.C.R.,' n.d.

5 Rockingham memoir, 17.

6 PRO, WO281/134, 'Notes from tactical discussion held 30 April, 1951,' from HQ 28 BCIB, 8 May 1951.

7 Rees, *Korea,* 251.

8 Rockingham memoir, 20.

9 PRO, WO281/137, '28 British Commonwealth Brigade in Korea,' memo by Lt. C.W. Crossland (n.d.).

10 Farrar-Hockley, *The British Part,* II, 157.

11 Rees, *Korea*, 251–5.
12 WD, 25 CIB HQ, 17 May 1951.
13 Rockingham memoir, 22.
14 p. 98.
15 Farrar-Hockley, *The British Part*, II.
16 WD, 25 CIB HQ, 17–19 May 1951.
17 '28 British Commonwealth Brigade in Korea,' memo by Crossland.
18 WD, 25 CIB HQ, 24 May 1951.
19 Wood, *Strange Battleground*, 97.
20 *Calgary Herald*, 28 May 1951.
21 WD, 25 CIB HQ, 25–26, 1951.
22 *Calgary Herald*, 28 May 1951.
23 DHist, file 145.2R13013 (D2), 'The Battle of Chail-Li.' This report was pre-pared by a historical officer, no doubt in consultation with Rockingham and Keane, in late 1951.
24 The attack plan and the battle that followed are based on ibid; WD, 25 CIB HQ, 30 May 1951; WD, 2RCR, 30 May 1951; WD, 'C' Squadron LdSH (RC); Wood, *Strange Battleground*, 101–5. Incidents and or events are specifically cited.
25 DHist, 'The Battle of Chail-Li.'
26 Rockingham memoir, 25.
27 DHist, 'The Battle of Chail-Li.'
28 Ridgway, 180–1.
29 Rees, *Korea*, 255–7.
30 Ridgway, 178–81.
31 Wood, *Strange Battleground*, 110.
32 WD, 25 CIB HQ, 24 June 1951.
33 Events leading to the cease-fire offer are detailed in Rees, *Korea*, 258–63.
34 WD, 25 CIB HQ, 30 June 1951.
35 Ridgway, 183.
36 WD, 25 CIB HQ, 2 July 1951.
37 DHist, file 410B25.013 (D3), 'The Imjin River Incident,' report by historical officer, 7 Oct. 1951.
38 PRO, WO281/46, Cassels to O'Daniel, 23 July 1951.
39 Farrar-Hockley, *The British Part*, II, 211.
40 Hastings, *The Korean War*, 261.
41 Stevens, *Princess Patricia's*, 334.
42 Wood, *Strange Battleground*, 119.
43 Ibid., 120.
44 Author's interview with Field Marshal (ret'd) A.J.H. Cassels, 2 Sept. 1994.
45 PRO, WO308/27, 1 Commonwealth Division Periodic Report, 2 May – 15 Oct. 1951.

46 Marshall Library, Lexington, Va., Van Fleet Papers, box 81, folder 9, Commanding General's Journal, 24 July 1951. I am grateful to Col. Jack English for this reference. See also Rockingham memoir, 38.

47 The best summary of these differences is found in Grey, *The Commonwealth Armies*, 133–149. See also Farrar-Hockley, *The British Part*, II, 213ff.

48 Farrar-Hockley makes this point well; see *The British Part*, II, 202–3.

49 DHist, file 314.009 (D464), Wrinch to CGS, 6 April 1951.

50 Simonds Papers, Simonds to Vokes, 14 Aug. 1951.

51 Canada, *Canada's Army in Korea*, 40; DHist, file 681.013 (D17), 'The Relief of 2 P.P.C.L.I. by 1 P.P.C.L.I. in Korea ...,' Account of an interview with Lt.-Col. N.G. Wilson-Smith, 19 June 1952.

52 DHist, file 410B25.033 (D1), 'Notes on Training ...,' 9 July 1951.

53 WD, 25 CIB HQ, Aug. 1951, folder 8, 'Minutes of GOC Conference ... 1 Aug 51.'

54 Farrar-Hockley, *The British Part*, II, 196–7. The Canadian government had been informed that such an eventuality was possible. See Cabinet Conclusions, 8 Aug. 1951.

55 DHist, file 112.3H1.009 (D113), '25 Canadian Infantry Brigade Operation Instruction No. 3,' 15 Aug. 1951.

56 DHist, file 112.#h1.009 (D113), '25 Canadian Infantry Brigade Operation Instruction No. 1,' 31 July 1951; '25 Canadian Infantry Brigade Operation Instruction No. 2,' 10 Aug. 1951.

57 DHist, file 410B25.016 (D8), Report on Operation Dirk, n.d.

58 WD, 25 CIB HQ, Aug. 1951, folder 8, 'Report on Operation Claymore,' n.d.

59 See, for example, Ridgway, 185ff; Rees, *Korea*, 289ff.; Farrar-Hockley, *The British Part*, II, 185–205.

60 Indeed, Farrar-Hockley *The British Part*, II, says that he initiated it. It is possible that the move across the Imjin was his idea, but highly unlikely that I Corps simply followed along, since the offensive involved much more than a single division.

61 Ibid., 216.

62 WD, 25 CIB HQ, 10–12 Sept. 1951.

63 Based on Wood, *Strange Battleground*, 127; WD, 25 CIB HQ, 12 Sept. 1951: Simonds Papers, Rockingham to Simonds, 17 Oct. 1951.

64 WD, 25 CIB HQ, 13 May 1951.

65 Ibid., 18 Sept. 1951.

66 Ibid.

67 PRO, WO281/51, 'Op Commando – Summary Ops 3 Oct,' n.d.

68 WD, 25 CIB HQ, 4 Oct. 1951.

69 Simonds Papers, Rockingham to Simonds, 17 Oct. 1951.

70 WD, 25 CIB HQ, 4 Oct. 1951.

71 PRO, 'Op Commando – Summary Ops 3 Oct.'

Chapter Six: The Saddle

1 This account is based on WD, 26 CIB, 9 and 10 Nov. 1951, and WD, 2R22eR, Nov. 1951, Appendix V9, 'Operation Toughy.'
2 WD, C Squadron, Lord Strathcona's Horse (Royal Canadians), 9 Nov. 1951.
3 WD, 2R22eR, 10 Nov. 1951.
4 Wood, *Strange Battleground*, 132.
5 Claxton Papers, vol. 106, file 'Far East Visit, 1951,' Menzies to Pearson, 7 Dec. 1951.
6 Hastings, *The Korean War*, 359–361.
7 Fehrenbach, *This Kind of War*, 348.
8 DHist, file 410B25.059 (D1), 'Preliminary Report on Battle Casualties of 25 Canadian Infantry Brigade,' 5 Dec. 1951.
9 DHist, file 681.011 (D1), 'Personal Recollections of the Field Works of the Jamestown, Wyoming and Kansas Lines,' by Capt. J.R. Madden, 10 Sept. 1954.
10 Claxton Papers, vol. 97, file '25th Canadian Infantry Brigade-27th Canadian Infantry Brigade (1),' Menzies to Pearson, 31 Oct. 1951.
11 Major W.H. Pope, 'Infantry Defences in Korea,' 19 Sept. 1953. Supplied to the author by Major Pope.
12 WD R22eR, 23 Nov. 1951, notes that the roads to the rear of the battalion had become impassable because of snow and mud. This was after twenty-four hours of Chinese shelling.
13 George G. Blackburn, *The Guns of Victory: A Soldier's Eye View, Belgium, Holland and Germany, 1944–45* (Toronto: McClelland and Stewart, 1996), xii.
14 WD, 2RCHA, 1–30 Nov. 1951.
15 Pope makes these points well; 'Infantry Defences.'
16 The account of the fighting on 2–6 November is based on WD, 25 CIB; WD, 2RCR; and WD, 1PPCLI, except for specific citations as noted.
17 WD, 2RCHA, 3 Nov. 1951.
18 PRO, WD, HQ Main, 1 Commonwealth Division.
19 WD, HQ 25 CIB, 5 Nov. 1951.
20 WD, 1PPCLI, 6 Nov. 1951.
21 Ibid.
22 Stevens, *Princess Patricia's*, 264–7.
23 WD, 1PPCLI, 6 Nov. 1951.
24 Pope, 'Infantry Defences.'
25 *Calgary Herald*, 23 Nov. 1951.
26 But see Pope, 'Infantry Defences.'
27 Robert Peacock to author, 14 Aug. 1998.
28 WD, 1 PPCLI, 26 Nov. 1951.
29 WD, 25 CIB, 17 Nov. 1951.
30 PRO, WO281/53, '1 COMWEL DIV OO NO 5,' order issued 21 Nov. 1951.

31 Stone and Castonguay, *Korea, 1951*, 330–1.

32 Claxton Papers, vol. 106, file 'Far East Visit, 1951,' Menzies to Pearson, 7 Dec. 1951.

33 Gardam, *Korea Volunteer*, 49.

34 WD, 2R22eR, Nov. 1951, Appendix 6, 'Commanding Officer's Conference,' 19 Nov. 1951.

35 This account of the positioning of the 2R22eR and the subsequent fighting for the saddle between Hills 227 and 355 is derived from Stone and Castonguay, *Korea, 1951*, 32–9; Gardam, *Korea Volunteer*, 59–60; PRO, WO281/53, '1 COM-WEL DIV INTREP NO 121,' 24 Nov. 1951; NA, RG 24, vol. 18357, WD, 2R22eR, 21–24 Nov. 1951. A significant action or development within the larger battle will be specifically cited.

36 DHist, file 4101325.013 (D12), 'Interview with Maj R. Liboiron, Lt R. MacDuff, Lt W. Nash, Lt T.R. Webb, 2 R22eR ... 1 Dec 51.'

37 PRO, WO281/53, WD, 'G' branch, 1 Commonwealth Division, 23 Nov. 1951.

38 WD, 2R22eR, 23 Nov. 1951.

39 WD, 25 CIB, 26 Nov. 1951.

40 WD, 2R22eR, Nov. 1951, Appendix VIII, casualty list for 23–27 Nov. 1951.

41 PRO, WO281/142, 'Statistical Summary of Enemy Ops ... 17/25 November, 51,' Appendix B to Intrep No. 134 of 7 Dec. 1951.

42 Stone and Castonguay, *Korea, 1951*, 40.

Chapter Seven: The Line

1 McIntyre interview with Don B. Urquhart, Aug. 1996.

2 PRO, WO281/142, Appendix 'A' to 28 BRITCOM Infantry Brigade. Intelligence Report, 23 Jan. 1952. W.H. Pope to author, 8 Sept. 1998.

3 Ibid., WO291/1892, Report of the Operational Research Section, March 1953.

4 Peacock, *Kim-chi, Asahi and Rum*, 20; DHist, file 111.41 (D22), vol. II, Memorandum dated 6 Feb. 1952; PRO, WO 281/62, 'Notes for battalions proceeding to Korea,' April 1952.

5 McIntyre interview with William Powell, Aug. 1996.

6 Lt.-Col. A. Wilson, Curator, Weapons Museum, Warminster Training Centre, to author, 12 July 1995.

7 DHist, file 145.2R13019 (D1), 'Sum of Experiences, Korean Campaign,' report of Lt.-Col. K.L. Campbell, n.d.

8 DHist, file 145.2R13019 (D1), 72/1223 series 1, file 422.

9 Ibid.

10 Marshall, *Battlefield Analysis*, 47.

11 McIntyre interview with Bill Nasby, Aug. 1996.

12 DHist, file 112.009 (D87), CGS Office file on 25 CIB, March–Sept. 1951, 'Brief Notes on Visit to Korean Theatre,' 23 Aug. 1951.

13 Marshall, *Battlefield Analysis*, 49ff.
14 McIntyre interview with Stanley Carmichael, Aug. 1996.
15 McIntyre interview with James W. Morrice, Aug. 1996.
16 Ibid.
17 McIntyre interview with David Cathcart, Aug. 1996.
18 McIntyre interview with Don Bateman, Aug. 1996.
19 McIntyre interview with Lorne E. Warner, Aug. 1996.
20 DHist, file 145.2R13013(D4), interview with Lt.-Col. Bingham, n.d.
21 Virtually every Korean war veteran interviewed by Bruce McIntyre at the Calgary reunion of the KVA in 1996 reflected that opinion. Most of their comments about the Sten are unprintable!
22 DHist, file 115.3A1 (D2), 'Report on a Visit to Korea,' n.d.
23 Peacock, for instance, armed himself with a 'Tommy gun' fed by a drum magazine, Chicago gangster–style. See Peacock, *Kim-chi*, 22.
24 See DHist, file 145.2R13019 (D1), 'Sum of Experiences, Korean Campaign,' report of Lt.-Col. K.L. Campbell, n.d., and file 410B25.013 (D52), 'Summary of Experience,' 4 Feb. 1954.
25 Peacock, *Kim-chi*.
26 Ibid.
27 WD, 25 CIB HQ, Aug. 1952, Appendix P.
28 Les Peate, 'Food for Thought,' *Esprit de Corps* 5, no. 9 (19XX), 16–17.
29 McIntyre interview with Paul Gauci, Aug. 1996.
30 PRO, WO291/1896, Operational Research Section, Memorandum No. 6/53, 'Comparison of the Proportion of Head Wounds Experienced by Commonwealth and American Troops in Korea,' n.d.
31 DHist, 'Sum of Experiences,' by Campbell.
32 Ibid.
33 PRO, WO281/75, Memo 'Armoured Vests,' 25 Nov. 1952.
34 DHist, file 410.B25.013 (D19), 'Account of Interview Given by Lt-Col LF. Trudeau, DSO GD (CO 1 R22er) ...,' 15 Aug. 1952.
35 DHist, 'Sum of Experiences,' by Campbell.
36 Robert Peacock to author, 14 Aug. 1998. DHist, file 112.3M2.1 (D4), 'Cold Weather Clothing,' n.d.
37 McIntyre interview with R. James Wilson, Aug. 1996.
38 DHist, 'Sum of Experiences,' by Campbell; Simonds Papers (privately held), Simonds to Bogert, 22 Jan. 1953, and Simonds to Claxton, 21 Jan. 1953.
39 Simonds Papers, Simonds to Bogert, 22 Jan. 1953.
40 WD, 1PPCLI, 8 Jan. 1952.
41 DHist, file 81/229, 'Canada's War in Korea,' Article No. 4, n.d.
42 DHist, file 112.009 (D87), 'Report by Lt-Col DSF Bult-Francis ...' 10 Aug. 1951.
43 See, for example, PRO, WO 216/515, for letters between Cassels and Field Marshal William Slim on the subject.

44 DHist, 'Report by Bult-Francis.' Re Boss: Robert Peacock to author, 14 Aug. 1998.
45 Claxton Papers, vol. 162, file 'Elections, 1953,' Hunter to JAG, 31 July 1953.
46 Statistics compiled from monthly medical returns.
47 PRO, WO 216/515, unaddressed memo signed by Cassels, 16 Nov. 1951.
48 DHist, file 81/229, 'Canada's War in Korea,' Article No. 4, n.d.
49 DHist, 'Report by Bult-Francis.'
50 Ibid.
51 Simonds Papers, Simonds to Claxton, 13 Aug. 1952.
52 WD, 25 CIB HQ, 1 and 4 Feb. 1952.
53 DHist, file 112.1 (D157), Pearson to Claxton, 4 Oct. 1951 and attachments.
54 McIntyre interview with L. McLean, Aug. 1995.
55 Les Peate, 'No Pay – No Uniforms – No Glory,' *Esprit de Corps* 5 no. 5 (1997), 28–9.
56 DHist, file 410B25.059 (D1), Canadian Operational Research Team, Preliminary Report on Crime Casualties, 17 Feb. 1952.
57 WD, 1PPCLI, 3 Feb. 1952.
58 Madsen, 'The Canadian Army.'
59 NA, RG 24, vol. 18,220, c3, file 1 Jan. 51–31 Dec. 51, WD, Vice Chief of the General Staff, CATI No. 25; DHist, file 111.41 (D22), vol. II, 'Infantry Replacements for 25 CIB,' 9 June 1951.
60 Simonds Papers, Simonds to Bogert, 31 May 1952.
61 Ibid., Simonds to Claxton, 9 Sept. 1952.
62 Ibid., Morton to Simonds, 4 Sept. 1952.
63 W.H. Pope, 'The Training and Provision of Reinforcements,' 1 Sept. 1953, in possession of the author.
64 WD, 25 CIB HQ, Sept. 1952, Appendix 18, 'Manpower Wastage Project,' 16 Sept. 1952.
65 WD, 1PPCLI, March 1952, 'Part I' orders for 31 March 1952.
66 Simonds Papers, West to Simonds, 30 Dec. 1952.
67 Pope, 'Training and Provision.'
68 Simonds Papers, Simonds to Claxton, 9 Sept. 1952.
69 DHist, file 410B25.059 (D1), Rockingham to CANARMY, 6 April 1952.
70 Simonds Papers, Bogert to Simonds, 26 July 1952.
71 Pope, 'Training and Provision.'
72 DHist, file 681.023 (D21), 'Conquer the Korean Winter; Simple Rules for All.'
73 DHist, file 681.011 (D1), 'Personal Recollection of the fd Works of Wyoming, Jamestown and Kansas Lines in Korea Prepared by Capt Madden, Sep 54.'
74 Ibid.
75 DHist, file 410B25.013 (D53), Lt-Col. J.G. Poulin, CO 3 RCR, 'Summary of Experience,' 4 Feb. 1954.
76 DHist, 'Sum of Experiences,' by Campbell.

77 Peacock, *Kim-chi*, 20–1.
78 DHist, file 681.013 (D81), 'Report on Air Ground Support in Korea,' n.d.
79 WD, 1PPCLI, 26 Nov. 1951.
80 DHist, file 112.3M2.1(D4), 'Commonwealth Medical Services in Korea,' a report by Col. J. S. McCannel, 30 Dec. 1953.
81 WD, 25 Canadian Field Dressing Station, Aug. 1952, Appendix 9.
82 Ibid.
83 DHist, file 147.013 (D4), 'The Royal Canadian Army Medical Corps in the Korean War.'
84 WD, 3RCR, March 1953, Appendix 12, 'The Advanced Regimental Aid Post in Static Warfare.'
85 DHist, 'The Royal Canadian Army Medical Corps.'
86 Figures compiled from monthly returns.
87 DHist, 'The Royal Canadian Army Medical Corps.'
88 McIntyre interview with Don B. Urquhart, Aug. 1996.
89 WD, 25 CIB HQ, Appendix A to Intelligence Summary 3-4-1, 25 Oct. 1952.
90 Ibid.
91 McIntyre interview with Don B. Urquhart, Aug. 1996.
92 Woods, *Strange Battleground*, 187.
93 Ibid., 189.
94 Ibid., 185–9; Doary, 'Miniature Set-Piece Battles' It is difficult to trace the permutations and combinations of patrol policy from Dec. 1951 to July 1953. The best guides are the various appendices dealing with patrol policy in the divisional and brigade war diaries.
95 DHist, file 145.2R13019 (D1), 'Summary of Experiences, 3 RCR,' March, 1954.
96 WD, 1PPCLI, 6 Sept. 1952.
97 McIntyre interview with William Powell, Aug. 1996.
98 PRO, WO281/62, GOC Personal Memorandum No. 1, 2 April 1952.
99 Doary, 'Miniature Set-piece,' 31.
100 Wood, *Strange Battleground*, 188.
101 Doary, 'Mianiature Set-piece,' 32; Major W.H. Pope, 'Infantry Patrolling in Korea,' 2 June 1953, copy provided to the author by Major Pope.
102 *Time*, 4 Feb. 1952, 24.
103 McIntyre interview with Peter Molesworth, Aug. 1996.

Chapter Eight: Blood on the Hills

1 WD, 25 CIB HQ, 19 March 1952.
2 DHist, file 193.002 (D1), Claxton to Foulkes, 19 March 1951.
3 Claxton Papers, vol. 31, file 'Ferguson, G.V.,' Claxton to Ferguson, 27 May 1953.
4 Claxton Papers, unpublished memoirs, vol. 6, 1178–85.

5 Claxton Papers, vol. 27, file 'TWL MacDermot,' Claxton to MacDermot, 12 Feb. 1952.

6 Dexter Papers, box 6, file 41, Hutchison to Dexter, 26 Jan. 1952.

7 Simonds Papers, Record of Discussions – Washington, 19 Feb. 1951.

8 Pearson's views and experiences have been set out in Pearson, Mike, vol. II; Stairs, *The Diplomacy of Constraint*, and John English, *The Worldly Years.*

9 NA, RG 24, vol. 18,220, c3, file 1 Jan. 51–31 Dec. 51, WD, Vice Chief of the General Staff, CATI No. 25.

10 DHist, file 112.3M2.1 (D4), 'Commonwealth Medical Services in Korea,' a report by Col. J.S. McCannel, 30 Dec. 1953.

11 WD, 2RCR, 26 March 1952.

12 DHist, file 79/704, Canadian Army, Fatal Casualties, Korean War.

13 DHist, file 410B25.013 (D33), '1st BN The Royal Canadian Regiment; May 1952–March 1953.'

14 Simonds Papers, Cassels to Simonds, 13 Oct. 1951.

15 PRO, WO281/65, WD, HQ 1 Commonwealth Division, Periodic Report, 15 Feb.–30 June 1952.

16 DHist, file 410B25.053 (D6), Interview of Major T.M. MacDonald, 21 Sept. 1953.

17 DHist, file 681.013 (D11), memo re 'Commonwealth Participation on Koje,' prepared by F.R. McGuire, n.d.

18 DEAF, file 50069–J-40, Wrong to Secretary of State for External Affairs (SSEA), 6 June 1952. This document contains a good summary of the events leading to, and following, the sending of the Canadian troops to Koje-do.

19 Grey, *The Commonwealth Armies*, 110.

20 EAF, file 50069–J-40, Wrong to SSEA, 6 June 1952.

21 Ibid.

22 USNA, Files of the Office of the Secretary of Defence (OSD), box 318, file CD092 (Korea), Matthews to Lovett and attachments, 24 May 1952.

23 EAF, file 50069–J-40, Menzies to Reid, 29 May 1952.

24 Ibid., Connelly to Canarmy, 28 May 1952.

25 DHist, file 112.009 (D92), 'Note to File' of 23 May 1952.

26 EAF, file 50069–J-40, Wrong to SSEA, 6 June 1952.

27 Ibid., file 50069–J-40, SSEA to Wrong, 22 May 1952.

28 Ibid., Reid memo for file, 23 May 1952.

29 EAF, file 50069–J-40, MacKay to Pearson, 24 May 1952.

30 Grey, *The Commonwealth Armies*, 155; EAF, file 50069–J-40, SSEA to Canadian Ambassador, Washington, 26 May 1952; EAF, file 50069–J-40, Reid to Pearson, 26 May 1952; Wrong to Bruce, 28 May 1952.

31 USNA, RG 84, Ottawa Post files, box 13, file 321.4, POW/310 Defense (Canadian Effort), 'Press Comments on Koje Island POW Question,' 16 June 1952; Rayner to Bliss, 5 June 1952.

32 Dexter Papers, box 6, file 42, Confidential memo from 'V.J.M.,' 8 Oct. 1952.

33 Simonds Papers, Simonds to Gordon, 4 Feb. 1953.

34 USNA, Rg 84, Ottawa Post files, box 13, file 321.4, POW – Koje, 'Press Comments on Koje Island POW Question,' 16 June 1952; Grey, *The Commonwealth Armies*, 155ff.

35 Wood, *Strange Battleground*, 188.

36 WD, 25 CIB HQ, June 1952, 'Report on Fighting Patrol ...,' n.d, and 'Patrol Report,' n.d.

37 *Calgary Herald*, 25 June 1952.

38 WD, 25 CIB HQ, June 1952, 'Report on Fighting Patrol ...,' n.d.

39 Wood, *Strange Battleground*, 203–5.

40 WD, 1RCR, Nov. 1952, Appendix 2, 'Report on 1 RCR Action Night 23/24 Oct. 52,' 25 Nov. 1952.

41 DHist, file 410B25.013 (D24), 'The Attack on "Little Gibraltar"' (pt 355), 23 Oct. 52,' n.d.

42 PRO, WO308/52, 'Attack on Point 355 – 23/24 Oct. 52,' n.d.

43 The account of the fighting is based on WD, 1RCR, Nov. 1952, Appendix 2, 'Report on 1 RCR Action Night 23/24 Oct. 52,' 25 Nov. 1952; DHist, 'The Attack on "Little Gibraltar"'; WD, 28 BCIB HQ, 23 Oct. 1952; WD, 1 RCR, 23 Oct. 1952; WD, 25 CIB HQ, Oct. 1952, Appendix 2/3 'Notes on Enemy Attack on B Coy 1 CR 23 Oct. 52,' 25 Oct. 1952, unless otherwise specifically cited.

44 DHist, Korea Valour Awards file, 'Award of the Military Medal to ... Sergeant Gerald Enright.'

45 Ibid., 'Award of the Military Cross to ... Captain (Acting Major) George Gray Taylor.'

46 Ibid., 'Award of the Military Cross to ... Lieutenant John Clark.'

47 Ibid., 'Award of Mention-In-Despatches (Posthumous) to ... Private Charles Joseph Morrison.'

48 The stories of Gardner, Faulkner, and Rennie are related in *Calgary Herald*, 28 Oct. 1952.

49 DHist, file 112.3H1.001 (D6), 'Interview with Lietenant-Colonel F. Klanevic ...,' n.d.

50 PRO, 'Attack on Point 355.'

51 WD, 25 CIB HQ, Oct. 1952, Appendix 2/3, 'Notes on Enemy Attack.'

52 Simonds Papers, Simonds to West, 15 June 1953.

53 See Barker, *Fortune Favours the Brave.*

54 See WD, 25 CIB HQ, Weekly strength returns for October through Nov. 1952.

55 *Ibid.*, West to Simonds, 30 Dec. 1952.

56 WD, 3PPCLI, 18 and 19 Nov 1952; DHist, file 410B25.013 (D28), 'First Action of 3 PPCLI, 19 Nov. 52.'

57 Simonds Papers, West to Simonds, 30 Dec. 1952.

58 NA, St Laurent Papers, vol. 222, file D-12, 'Broadcast by Bill Boss.'

59 Simonds Papers, West to Simonds, 30 Dec. 1952.

60 DHist, file 410B25.011 (D12), 'Chapter XI; In the Line.'

61 Ibid., file 410B25.013 (D53), 'Interview: Given by Lt-Col JG Poulin ... on 31 May 1953.'

62 Ibid., covering memo by J.R. Madden, 4 July 1953.

63 DHist, file 410B25.013 (D49), 'Interview: Given by Major CEC MacNeill ... 12 May 53.'

64 Allard, with Bernier, *Memoirs*, 173.

65 DHist, file 410B25.013 (D57), 'Interview: Given by Lt-Col KL Campbell Jun 53.'

66 Ibid.

67 DHist, file 410.B25.013 (D51). Madden to Stacey, 25 June 1953.

68 Allard, *Memoirs*, 175.

69 DHist, file 681.013 (D40), 'Interview given by ... Major PA Mayer ... 21 Jul 53.'

70 Allard, *Memoirs*, 175.

71 Rees, *Korea*, 406–7.

72 The account of the battle for Hill 187 is based on WD, 25 CIB HQ, 2–3 May 1953; WD, 3RCR, 2–3 May 1953; DHist, 'Interview by Campbell, and 'Report of Action,' 6 May 1953, attached to the interview; Allard, *Memoirs*, 174–6; *Calgary Herald*, 4 and 6 May 1953.

73 McIntyre interview with W. Hummer, Aug. 1995.

74 Ibid.

75 Dhist, file 112.3H1.001 (D7), 'Interview with Major-General J.V. Allard ... 17 Dec. 1963 by Lieutenant-Colonel Wood.'

76 Ibid.

77 DHist, 'Interview by Mayer.'

78 *Calgary Herald*, 4 May 1953.

79 Dhist, 'Interview with Allard.'

Epilogue: Home from the Hills

1 Canada, *Canada's Army in Korea*, 103.

2 Wood, *Strange Battleground*, 259.

3 DHist, file 410B25.013 (D100), Report of Brigadier J.V. Allard, 13 June 1954.

4 Barbara Tuchman, *Stilwell and the American Experience in China: 1911–1945* (New York: Macmillan Company, 1970), 436.

5 Robert Peacock to author, 14 Aug. 1998.

6 Pope to 'Commander' re 'request to Publish Writings,' 7 April 1959, in the possession of Major (ret'd) W.H. Pope.

Sources

Government Records

National Archives of Canada (NA), Ottawa
Records of the Department of National Defence
  War Diaries
  Files as listed in notes
Records of the Privy Council Office
  Cabinet Conclusions
  Files of the Privy Council Office
Records of the Department of Foreign Affairs and International Trade
  Files as listed in the footnotes

National Archives (USNA) Washington, DC
Files of the Office of the Secretary of Defense (OSD)
General Records of the Department of State (DSR)
Ottawa Post Files
Files of the Permanent Joint Board on Defence (PJBD)

Public Records Office (PRO), London
Records of the War Office (WO)
  War Diaries
  Files as listed in the notes

*Canada, Department of National Defence (DND), Directorate of History and Heritage
  (DHist)*
Kardex Files
Korea Valour Awards File
Cabinet Defence Committee files

Canada, Department of Foreign Affairs and International Trade
Files held in the department

Private Papers

National Archives
Brooke Claxton Papers
Louis Stephen St Laurent Papers
John M. Rockingham Papers

Queen's University Archives, Kingston
Grant Dexter Papers

Marshall Library, George C, Marshall Foundation Research Library and Museum, Lexington, Virginia
Van Fleet Papers

Privately held
G.G. Simonds Papers

Government Published Sources

Canada, Historical Section, General Staff, Army Headquarters. *Canada's Army in Korea: The United Nations Operations, 1950–53, and Their Aftermath.* Ottawa: Queen's Printer, 1956.
Canadian Army Journal 5 no. 10 (Jan. 1952), 'The Patricias in Korea,' 4–18.
Farrar-Hockley, Anthony. *The British Part in the Korean War,* vol. I, *A Distant Obligation.* London: Her Majesty's Stationery Office, 1990.
– *The British Part in the Korean War,* vol. II, *An Honourable Discharge.* London: Her Majesty's Stationery Office, 1995.
O'Neill, Robert. *Australia in the Korean War: 1950–53,* vol. II, *Combat Operations.* Canberra: Australian Government Publishing Service, 1985.
Pickett, Lt.-Col. George B. 'Tanks in Defence in Korea.' In *Canadian Army Journal* 5 no. 11 (Feb. 1952), 64–72.
Wood, Herbert Fairlie. *Strange Battleground: Official History of the Canadian Army in Korea.* Ottawa: Queen's Printer, 1966.

Newspapers and Magazines

Calgary Herald
Globe and Mail
Halifax Chronicle-Herald
Maclean's
Montreal Star

Time
Vancouver Sun

Interviews

Interviews conducted by Bruce McIntyre, August 1996. Those listed below are directly cited in notes. The entire collection of interviews, along with questionnaires filled in by other veterans, is on deposit at the Museum of the Regiments, Calgary, Alberta.

Don Bateman
John K. Blampied
Stanley Carmichael
David Cathcart
Paul Gauci
W. Hummer
William Lee
L. McLean
J. Robert Molesworth

Peter Molesworth
James W. Morrice
Bill Nasby
William Powell
Harry Repay
Don B. Urquhart
Lorne E. Warner
R. James Wilson
Ross Wilkes

Author's interview with A.J.H. Cassels, 2 Sept. 1994.

Books, Articles, and Theses

Allard, Jean V., with Serge Bernier. *The Memoirs of Jean V. Allard*. Vancouver: University of British Columbia Press, 1988.

Archambault, Peter, and Bercuson, D.J. '"We Didn't Plan for This Type of War": The Canadian Army in Korea, 1950–1952.' Paper read to the 1995 meeting of the Organization for the Study of the National History of Canada, Ottawa, Nov. 1995.

Barker, A.J. *Fortune Favours the Brave: The Hook, Korea, 1953*. London: Leo Cooper, 1974.

Bercuson, David. *True Patriot: The Life of Brooke Claxton, 1898–1960*. Toronto: University of Toronto Press, 1993.

– *Battalion of Heroes: The Calgary Highlanders in World War II*. Calgary: Calgary Highlanders Regimental Funds Foundation, 1994.

Berton, Pierre. 'Corporal Dunphy's War.' *Maclean's Magazine*, 1 June 1951.

Blackburn, George G. *The Guns of Victory: A Soldier's Eye View, Belgium, Holland and Germany, 1944–45*. Toronto: McClelland and Stewart, 1996.

Blair, Clay. *The Forgotten War: America in Korea, 1950–1953*. New York: Times Books, 1987.

Cuff, R.D., and Granatstein, J.L. *American Dollars and Canadian Prosperity*. Toronto: Samuel-Stevens, 1978.

Doary, Christopher. '"Miniature Set-Piece Battles": Infantry Patrolling Operations in Korea, May–June 1952.' *Canadian Military History* 6 no. 1 (spring 1997), 20–33.

English, John. *The Worldly Years: The Life of Lester Pearson, 1949–1972*. Toronto: Knopf Canada, 1992.

Fehrenbach, T.R. *This Kind of War*. Washington, DC: Brassey's, 1963.

Flint, Roy K., Kozumplik, Peter W. and Waraska, Thomas J. *The Arab–Israeli Wars, the Chinese Civil War, and the Korean War*. West Point, NY: United States Military Academy, 1987.

Gardam, John. *Korea Volunteer: An Oral History from Those Who Were There*. Burnstown, Ont.: General Store Publishing, 1994.

George, Alexander L. *The Chinese Communist Army in Action: The Korean War and Its Aftermath*. New York: Columbia University Press 1967.

Gray, H.A. 'A Researched Report on 2nd Bn Princess Patricia's Canadian Light Infantry at the Battle of Kapyong, Korea, as it Affected "D" Coy, April 23–25,' ms., Calgary, 1998.

Grey, Jeffrey. *The Commonwealth armies and the Korean War*. Manchester: Manchester University Press, 1988.

Hastings, Max. *The Korean War*. London: Michael Joseph, 1987.

Kirkland, Faris R. 'Soldiers and Marines at Chosin Reservoir: Criteria for Assignment to Combat Command.' *Armed Forces and Society* 22 no. 2 (winter 1995–6).

Leckie, Robert. *Conflict: The History of the Korean War*. New York: Da Capo Press, 1996.

McKee, Alexander. *Caen: Anvil of Victory*. London: White Lion Publishers, 1976.

McKeown, Michael G. 'Kapyong Remembered: Anecdotes from Korea.' Published by 2PPCLI for the 25th anniversary of the Korean War, PPCLI Archives, Museum of the Regiments, Calgary.

Madsen, Chris. 'The Canadian Army and the Maltreatment of Civilians: The Korean Example,' paper given at the Qualicum History Conference, Parksville, BC, 5 Feb. 1994.

Marshall, S.L.A. *Battlefield Analysis of Infantry Weapons (Korean War)*. Cornville, Ariz. 1984.

Melady, John. *Korea: Canada's Forgotten War*. Toronto: McClelland and Stewart, 1983.

Peacock, Robert S. *Kim-chi, Asahi and Rum: A Platoon Commander Remembers Korea* (n.p.: Lugus, 1994).

Pearson, Lester B. *Mike: The Memoirs of the Rt. Hon. Lester B. Pearson*, vol. II. Toronto: University of Toronto Press, 1973.

Peate, Les. 'No Pay – No Uniforms – No Glory.' *Esprit de Corps* 5 no. 5 (1997), 28–29.

– 'Food for Thought.' *Esprit de Corps* 5 no. 9 (1997), 16–17.

Rees, David. *Korea: The Limited War.* New York: St Martin's Press, 1964.

Stacey, C.P. *The Victory Campaign.* Ottawa: Queen's Printer, 1960.

Stairs, Denis. *The Diplomacy of Constraint: Canada, the Korean War, and the United States.* Toronto: University of Toronto Press, 1974.

Stevens, G.R. *Princess Patricia's Canadian Light Infantry: 1919–1957,* vol. III. Griesbach, Alta.: Historical Committee of the Regiment, n.d.

Stone, James R., and Castonguay, Jacques. *Korea: 1951: Two Canadian Battles.* Canadian Battle Series. Ottawa: Canadian War Museum, 1988.

Summers, Harry G. Jr. *Korean War Almanac.* New York: Facts on File, 1990.

– *The New World Strategy: A Military Policy for America's Future.* New York: Simon and Schuster, 1995.

Tuchman, Barbara. *Stilwell and the American Experience in China: 1911–1945.* New York: Macmillan Company, 1970.

Watson, Brent Byron. 'From Calgary to Kap'yong: The Second Battalion Princess Patricia's Canadian Light Infantry's Preparation for Battle in Korea, August 1950 to April 1951.' MA thesis, University of Victoria, 1993.

Illustration Credits

H.A. (Hub) Gray, 2PPCLI, Calgary, Alberta: 12 Platoon moving through mud; 12 Platoon on foot patrol; 12 Platoon after crossing mountain; 2PPCLI half track; 12 Platoon on tanks

National Archives of Canada: Dextraze, PA-128847; Claxton with Van Fleet and Rockingham, PA-140703; Allard with Canadian POW, PA-175913; Lebeau and Davignon at 'stand-to,' PA-134500; RCCS, PA-136788; Canadians wearing U.S. vests, PA-184797; Boshman and Cassidy, PA-128817; Howard in poncho, PA-188773; dug-out shelter, PA-171330; checking trenches, PA-174207; observation post, 25CIB, PA-176758; maintaining lookout, PA-184955; Lapointe and Ethier behind machine-gun, PA-134498; Gunners of 2RCR, PA-184254; Robertson et al. with 25-pounder, PA-133626; site of battery after heavy shelling, PA-188757; PPCLI steadying themselves, PA-179973; R22eR under fire, PA-128848; survivors of Chinese attack, PA-128839; soldiers with Labatt's ale, PA-108218; young Korean, PA-151518; Parenteau asleep, PA-143954; Montag, Oupis and Neeham, PA-170774; hockey match, PA-128859; Imjin near bridge, PA-170801; crossing Imjin, PA-132638; PPCLI personnel on patrol, PA-115564; Hoskins, PA-116785; hilltop positions, PA-193470; trucks ploughing through roads, PA-170807; ambulance jeep arriving, PA-140171; Lebel with wounded soldier, PA-128874; captured Chinese casualty, PA-183965; Chinese through first barbed-wire defence, PA-132060; feet of dead Canadian soldiers, PA-140410; evacuation by helicopter, PA-128851; Sobol at grave, PA-128813; dead soldier of PPCLI, PA-170790

Robert Peacock, Sidney, British Columbia: Lieut. Peacock

PPCLI Regimental Museum and Archives, Calgary, Alberta: Williams; Bradley presents citation; instruction on recoilless rifle; firing anti-tank rocket; Duroche, Smith, and Ouellette; PPCLI soldier with two rifles; Munro and Bouregon; Prince; controlling indirect mortar fire; Bowell with explosives; packing C rations; soldiers washing; on 'R&R'; Campbell and Bastien

MAPS

Key Porter Books Limited: Cartography, James Loates. In J.L. Granatstein and David J. Bercuson, *War and Peacekeeping: From South Africa to the Gulf – Canada's Limited Wars* (1991).

Index